I

MUST

SAY

I MUST SAY

MY LIFE AS A HUMBLE COMEDY LEGEND

MARTIN SHORT

WITH DAVID KAMP

HARPER

An Imprint of HarperCollinsPublishers

HarperCollins books may be purchased for educational, business, or sales promotional use. For information, please e-mail the Special Markets Department at SPsales@harpercollins.com.

FIRST EDITION

Designed by William Ruoto

Excerpts from "Jackie Rogers Jr.'s $100,000 Jackpot Wad" and "Men's Olympic Synchronized Swimming" © 1984 NBC Studios, LLC. Distributed by Broadway Video Enterprises. Courtesy of Broadway Video Enterprises and NBC Studios, LLC.

Library of Congress Cataloging-in-Publication Data

Short, Martin
  I must say : my life as a humble comedy legend / Martin Short ; with David Kamp.—First edition.
     pages cm
1. Short, Martin 2. Television actors and actresses—Canada—Biography. I. Kamp, David. II. Title.
  PN2308.S53A3 2014
  791.4502'8092—dc23
  [B]
                                                    2014028617

ISBN: 978-0-06-230952-5

ISBN: 978-0-06-236884-3 (HarperCanada)

ISBN: 978-0-06-236457-9 (Signed Edition)

ISBN: 978-0-06-236885-0 (HarperCanada Signed Edition)

14 15 16 17 18   OV/RRD   10 9 8 7 6 5 4 3 2 1

TO KATHERINE, OLIVER,
AND HENRY

CONTENTS

I
MUST
SAY

AN ED-UCATION

It's May 1977, and I am having an argument with the woman who will become my wife. We're not arguing about anything serious—Nancy and I rarely do. But I've been behaving rudely, or so Nancy thinks (though I think it's the other way around), and the tension is real.

"Why do you have to start suddenly screaming?" she asks.

"I'm not remotely screaming. You'll know when I start screaming," I respond.

"Oh, so you mean we need to bring out the Nixonesque recording devices to determine the truth around here?"

"Good, by all means, turn them on, 'cause I'll be proven right. And by the way, if I *did* raise my volume a decibel or two, why would that be my fault?"

"So you didn't raise your voice?"

"No, of course I did. But that's like complaining about a guy who's been pushed off a mountain and screams 'Ahhhhh!' on the way down. Sure, he's screaming. But doesn't the person who gave him a shove bear some of the responsibility?"

"Okay, you know what? I don't want to talk to you anymore," Nancy says. "I want to talk to Ed."

Ed is a character I've been developing over the last few months onstage at the Second City in Toronto. He does not yet have his last name, Grimley.

"Ed?" she says, looking impatiently over my shoulder, past me, as if he might trip through the doorway of our apartment on Roxborough Street in Toronto. "Ed, are you there?"

I assume Ed's posture: shoulders hunched, upper lip exposing the teeth. "I certainly am, Miss Nancy."

"Ed, what's Marty's problem?"

"Oh, who can possibly know? It's just so sad, Miss Nancy, 'cause like he's, like, he's just so mentally jealous of you, I must say."

"Jealous how, Ed?"

"Jealous of your beauty and wisdom and saddened by his own tragic limitations, and that's no lie."

"*Thank* you, Ed."

"Although his endowment has certainly been blessed by the lord."

"Okay, Ed, that's enough."

Argument defused.

In my brief time as the conduit through which Ed channels himself, I have discovered two remarkable things about him. One: that he seems to be amusing to audiences, which is a relief, because I'm still new at this improvisational comedy thing, having been more of a traditional theatrical performer up to this point in my career. Two: that Ed's sweetness has a disarming effect on Nancy. When trouble arises, she calls out for Ed to moderate, and when he appears, all things calm down.

Hmmm, I think, what other magic powers might Ed hold?

"Miss Nancy?"

"Yes, Ed?"

"My, you seem very fetching in that halter top, I must say. How I wish my fingers were scissors so I could snip those straps and release the hostages."

"Go away, Ed! We're done here."

Well, if nothing else, I have now discovered a third thing about Ed: Nancy has absolutely no interest in having sex with him.

I joined Second City in March 1977. The troupe was midway through its winter-spring show, *The Wizard of Ossington*, and I was replacing John Candy, who had just departed.

One of the sketches in *The Wizard of Ossington* was called "Sexist." The premise was simple: A male executive is interviewing two candidates for a job, a woman and a man. The woman is smart, competent, and qualified. The man is an idiot. Nevertheless, after questioning both candidates, the interviewer declares, "Your credentials are so darn equal that I don't know how to decide. I can't make up my mind!" The male candidate proposes that the matter be settled by arm wrestling. The interviewer agrees. Then the man pins down the woman's arm, thereby winning the job. SCENE.

Peter Aykroyd, Danny's little brother and a gifted comic performer in his own right, played the interviewer. Catherine O'Hara was the female candidate. John Candy had played my part, the male candidate, in a brilliantly John way: as a bashful, nervous, sweet-faced soul who was heartbreakingly aware of how out of his depth he was—in other words, as a guy who could be in that situation in real life. I knew I couldn't replicate that. Only a fool would try to replicate anything that John did. So I decided to go in a broader, more pop-art direction.

First, my character would talk funny. I took his unusual timbre from my sister Nora's husband, Ralph, who spoke in a kind of resigned, sleepy voice. Then I added a Canadian tic that's not unlike Valley Girl upspeak, wherein even declarative sentences end . . . like *questions*? In high school I'd had a geeky friend named Patrick who talked this way. He was an amateur photographer. I'd ask him, "Patrick, what'd you do this weekend?" He'd say, "I took a lot of *slides*?" I'd respond, "Really? Did you develop them?" And he'd say, "No, I didn't feel I have to *develop them*? 'Cause I, like *took them*? So I *know what they are*? In *my mind*?" You could almost chart out the notes of his speech musically, on staff paper. I couldn't help but make a mental note of Patrick's speech patterns. Hmmm, I thought, I must remember this, for someday I just might make millions off of it.

For the character's wardrobe, I unearthed an old shirt from my teen years with a dated rust-and-gray checked pattern. I buttoned it up to my neck and hitched my trousers high above my navel. Ed, as I'd decided to call my underqualified-idiot job candidate, was complete.

Well, maybe not quite. I decided to apply some grease to the front of my hair so it stuck up a little, to make Ed's physical appearance more awkward still.

The audience seemed to like Ed from the outset. Catherine, as prim job applicant Barbara O'Leary, confidently rattled off to the interviewer all the degrees that she held—a bachelor of mathematics from McGill, a masters in business administration from Columbia, and so on. As she did so, Ed, in full view of the audience, would register increasing panic, his smile turning into a grimace, his breaths deepening, his eyes cast downward, his whole body palpitating. This silent meltdown always got a big laugh, the biggest in the sketch, which was an utter revelation to me.

Part of my trepidation about improvisational comedy was that I thought I would have to come up with funny lines all the time, on the spot. What I discovered, through Ed, was that I simply needed to *commit*: to not worry about jokes. The reaction seemed to get the biggest laughs, not the action. I didn't need to be a stand-up comedian delivering punch lines. If I just sincerely devoted myself to Ed's panic with every fiber of my being, the audience would commit to him.

The deeper I got into my first season with Second City, the more confident I became about pushing Ed further. One day, backstage, Peter Aykroyd remarked, "Boy, Marty, that hair is standing taller every time you do that scene!" He was right—I was putting more and more grease into it. So, to make Peter laugh, I pushed my forelock straight up into a point, like a unicorn's horn, and left it that way. When we did "Sexist" that night, my entrance drew its biggest laugh yet. Well, I thought, isn't that what we're trying to achieve here? Thus, forevermore, did Ed have pointy hair.

Four years earlier, when Second City first set up shop in Toronto, I couldn't bring myself to audition. I was afraid to. The improvisational troupe and theater had been a going concern in Chicago since 1959, and its decision to open a branch in Canada was like an answered prayer to most of my friends. Many of them were castmates from the musical *Godspell*, whose Toronto production, mounted in 1972, included such then-unknowns as Eugene Levy, Andrea Martin, Dave Thomas, Victor Garber, Gilda Radner, and me. For all of us, along with the show's musical director, Paul Shaffer, *Godspell* was our big break, our first serious professional job in show business. We were a tight, rowdy little band of longhairs, and Gilda and I became romantically involved as well.

Gilda and Eugene, along with two other friends I'd made in Toronto, Danny Aykroyd and John Candy, enlisted in Second City as soon as they could. But me? I played it cool. "Marty, are you going to audition, too?" "Nah, I don't think so. I don't really care about Second City."

But of course I cared. I was just scared—of the anxiety I saw my friends going through as *they* auditioned, and of the concept of being funny on demand. From *Godspell*, I had developed confidence in my ability to command a stage, sell a song, fake-dance with frenetic energy, and work off a script. But improv? Terrifying. So I did other stuff, and took other jobs: in musicals, in straight plays, on television. "Oh, I've heard of you," said Bill Murray the first time I met him, when he came up to Toronto from Chicago in one of Second City's occasional talent swaps between the two branches. "I hear you're known," he said in that deadpan of his, "as Mr. Entertainment."

And I was. In 1974 I had a regular slot as the boy singer on *Everything Goes*, a variety program launched by Global Television, a then-small private Canadian network. It was hosted by Canadian personalities Mike Darrow and Catherine McKinnon, plus, for that crucial bit of American swagger, the comedian Norm Crosby. *Everything Goes* aired in primetime five nights a week, Monday through Friday. I would come out with my shoulder-length Andy Gibb hair and formfitting Ban-Lon turtleneck and do straight renditions of Jimmy Van Heusen's "Here's That Rainy Day" and "Corner of the Sky" from *Pippin*, things like that.

Eclectic as my young career was, though, it was hardly what you would call an unmitigated triumph. One night on *Everything Goes* was an outright disaster. Tony Bennett was the big scheduled guest. Right away, I was nervous, because Tony was one of my idols; it might have been 1974, the Year of Pink Floyd, but I

was a fan of the pre-rock guys—Tony, Frank Sinatra, Mel Tormé.
Intimidated as I was, the producers of *Everything Goes* assured me
that Tony was opening the show, which was a comfort. I, needless
to say, would not be going on until near the program's very end, by
which time the force of Tony's brilliance would have dissipated.

But Tony's plane into Toronto was delayed by a snowstorm.
For a while it was touch and go whether he would even make it.
He finally arrived with ten minutes remaining in the program, as
charmingly at ease as one would hope. They hustled him out onstage. Tony never broke his cool, and he was in perfect voice. As
he was killing it with one of his signature songs, "When Joanna
Loved Me," the stage manager tapped me on the shoulder and
said, "You're next."

"Wait!" I said. "You can't follow a singer with a singer!" The
stage manager tersely replied, "Watch."

I was beyond petrified. The number-one rule in show business
is: Never follow a singer with a singer. The number-two rule in
show business, incidentally, is: Never look Barbra Streisand in the
eye when she is walking onstage, or during foreplay.

Anyway: as Tony continued performing, I made my way to
my sad little stool downstage. Tony finished big, with Leslie Bricusse and Anthony Newley's "Once in a Lifetime"—"I'm gonna
doooo . . . greeeat . . . *thiiiiiiings!*"—and the crowd went insane.
The cameras cut over to Norm Crosby, who said, "Thanks, Tony.
And now here's a kid that sings really good . . . Marty Short." And
then the cameras cut to me, perched unsteadily on my stool in an
outfit that tragically combined a winter wool sweater with flared
clamdiggers.

"What a spot, following Tony Bennett!" I said. Crickets.

So I started singing: "Here we are, on earth together. . . . It's
you and me!" Already, I was wrong. The lyrics are "It's you and

I." That's because the song I was singing, by Stevie Wonder, is called . . . "You and I."

This little slip was enough to knock me completely out of orbit. I suddenly forgot the rest of the lyrics—and worse, for reasons I still cannot fathom, I started to *impersonate Tony Bennett while improvising new lyrics.* Perhaps my subconscious was telling me that the only way I could follow Tony was to *be* Tony, but what viewers of *Everything Goes* got was a spasmodic young man who was twenty-four years old but looked eighteen, and was inexplicably bullshitting new words to a Stevie Wonder song while doing a flop-sweat impression of Tony Bennett having a heart attack: "Our love was made, it was made in heaven, too. . . . Let's have . . . a great big bowl of stew!"

I somehow stabilized just enough to save the tiniest bit of face: I reverted to my own voice and hit Stevie's high notes at the end, a credible finish. But I was devastated. Mortified. I had totally screwed up.

Afterward I went into the bathroom to splash cold water on my face and steady my nerves. I heard the door open, and someone came in. It was Tony. I straightened up, expecting that my hero would have some pearl of wisdom for me, words to make me feel better. With his genial Tony Bennett face, he looked me square in the eye.

"You froze good, kid," he said.

That was all I got. "Well, good night," he said, and off he went.

I went out on a lot of auditions in those days, too: an endless string of humiliating cattle calls where it was essential to stand out, but not so much so as to appear needy or desperate. I learned about this distinction the hard way at an audition for Tang, the fruit-flavored drink mix favored by the astronaut John Glenn on his first Mercury flight. I walked into the waiting room where the audition was being held and saw twelve guys, all my age. We kind of looked the same, and we were dressed the same. As we sat there with our eight-by-ten head shots, going over our Tang-commercial copy, I was struck by a brainwave.

I went into the bathroom with my head shot and, with a Sharpie, drew a mustache and a goatee on my photographed face. Then, after the casting director came through the waiting room and collected our head shots in advance of calling us in to meet the client, I returned to the bathroom and, using the same Sharpie, drew a mustache and goatee on my actual face, to match the photo. When I was finally called in, the client—an unsmiling executive—looked at my head shot, which he held in his hand, looked back up at me, and, without remotely acknowledging my clever comedic choice, said, "So, have you had a chance to read the copy?" My hand hovering over my face in a futile attempt to obscure my hand-drawn facial hair, I quickly realized that no Tang-related windfall was headed my way.

E ager to stretch, I took a part in a minimalist gay-themed prison drama called *Fortune and Men's Eyes*. The show was originally mounted off-Broadway in New York in 1967, but it was its 1969 Los Angeles production, directed by the actor Sal Mineo, that put it on the map.

To say that I was miscast as Rocky, the toughest and most sexually predatory of the inmates, would be a massive understatement. I was required to do a lot of bullying and posturing in my best proto–Sylvester Stallone voice: "Hey, whaddya doin', wimpass!" The director was very Method oriented, locking us actors down for twelve hours a day in the theater so we could improvise in close quarters and really get the *feel*, man, of what it's like to share a cell with three other guys. On top of that the production was down in Hamilton, Ontario, which—though it was my beloved hometown, where I'd grown up—was an hour's commute each way.

Worst of all, as part of the immersive Method experience of doing the show, the director required us to be onstage in character for half an hour before the show began—pacing around the "cell" in our prison garb, which consisted solely of tight white underpants. No shirts for Rocky and his pals. And we had to do our pacing and brooding silently as the audience filed in, because if we engaged with its members verbally, they might think that the show was starting. It was humiliating, and again, not to mince words, I was really bad. One reviewer said that I was unconvincing not only as Rocky but also as a male.

One night Gilda Radner, Eugene Levy, and Paul Shaffer came to see the show. I would have preferred that my girlfriend and two closest friends stay away, sparing me the embarrassment. But on the bright side, we planned to go to dinner after the show at a really good high-end restaurant in Hamilton called Shakespeare's. Paul was especially excited about this, because I had told him that Shakespeare's had the best garlic bread in Canada. It was all Paul could talk about for days: "I'm so excited to try the garlic bread! Oh, and of course to see you in the role of Rocky in a fabulous production of *Fortune and Men's Eyes*!"

That night I took my usual position onstage for the preshow period, mutely pacing and brooding in my underwear. As I did so, I saw Paul coming down the aisle, toward the stage. I hated that he, Gilda, and Eugene were there in the first place. And now I was wondering what the hell he was doing, walking right up to me.

Paul has a distinctive look, as anyone who's seen him as the bandleader on David Letterman's show over the last thirty years would know. His head has always had that perfect lightbulb shape. When you stand a certain distance from him, it looks like his suit had a great idea.

So there I was on the stage as Rocky, almost naked, when Paul, looking like a cross between a maître d' on a spaceship and the world's hippest thumb, got right up in my face, a big grin on his.

"Marty! *Pssst* . . . Marty!"

I was in character, so I tried to ignore him. But he wouldn't let up.

"*Pssst* . . . Marty! Horrible news! Shakespeare's is closed tonight! Wink if Bavarian's makes sense." That was another Hamilton restaurant.

I did not wink or acknowledge Paul in any way. Inside, however, I was saying, *Paul, when I am able, I will kill you.*

As it turned out, we had a perfectly pleasant dinner at Bavarian's that night, and Paul and Eugene very charitably acted like I was halfway decent in the play. But Gilda knew the score. As soon as I came out the stage door, she wrapped me up in her arms and said, in the sweetest way, "Aw, honey, don't ever do a play like this again. Ever. Promise."

By 1976 I was feeling, for the first time in my life, a measure of professional regret. I realized that there was a hip energy in my friends' careers that was absent in mine. That year Catherine O'Hara, John Candy, Eugene Levy, Andrea Martin, Joe Flaherty, and Harold Ramis started work on a primitive version of *SCTV—Second City Television*—for Global, the network that *Everything Goes* had been on. Gilda, with whom I remained on good terms after our breakup in '74, had moved to New York and was now making it big on *Saturday Night Live*. Paul was in New York, too, as the piano player in *SNL*'s house band.

Me? Well, at the top of 1977, I was finishing up a run in Toronto in *Harry's Back in Town*, a revue of the songs of Harry Warren, the old-timey tunesmith behind "Lullaby of Broadway" and "You Must Have Been a Beautiful Baby." Not a bad show, truthfully, but . . . not exactly plugged into the happenin' zeitgeist, either. Sure, I was fortunate to have a hot and sexy live-in girlfriend named Nancy Dolman, whose beauteous and supportive presence I did not for a moment take for granted. But by February I had nothing on the employment docket: no work, no auditions, no exciting prospects. It was a career low point.

That month, absent any professional obligations, I flew out to L.A. to join Nancy, who was knocking on the doors of the record companies, trying to get a deal. (She was an amazingly talented singer and songwriter, her music not miles away from what Linda Ronstadt and Melissa Manchester were doing at the time.)

It so happened that Paul Shaffer was in town at the same time, since *SNL* was on hiatus. He was staying at the Sunset Marquis hotel—walking distance from where we were staying. Bill Murray was also in town, so Paul invited Nancy and me to join the two of them for dinner. Remember that this was the winter of 1977. Chevy Chase had left *Saturday Night Live* after the show's first season, 1975–'76. Bill was drafted in as Chevy's replacement, and he was just now coming into his own. In a couple of months, he and Paul would unleash upon the world their iconic recurring "Lounge Singer" bit, in which Bill was the smarmy crooner Nick, and Paul was his accompanist.

I, meanwhile, was stuck in a rut. There was always work for me in Toronto, but increasingly it was in the dreary safe harbor of cabaret. Having once felt like the guy who didn't need Second City, I now felt like the guy who, unlike all of his classmates, chose not to go to university because he wanted to open his own shawarma stand, but for some reason the shawarma stand hadn't worked out. So now he was behind the grade.

Nancy and I were walking along Santa Monica Boulevard, en route to our dinner with Bill and Paul, when I froze. There was a bench nearby. I coolly turned to her and said, "I have to sit down now."

"Why?" Nancy said. "What's going on?"

"I cannot spend an evening with Bill and Paul," I said. "I can't spend another evening pretending to be happy for someone else's success. I just need to sit."

So we sat. I brooded silently. I wasn't jealous of my friends, but I resented my own lack of fulfillment and momentum.

Nancy, bless her heart, sat by me and held my hand. Finally, after about fifteen minutes, she whispered, "How long are we going to sit here?"

"Boy, that's a good question," I responded. "If I only had an answer."

"Interesting," said Nan.

I gathered myself—eventually. But we didn't have dinner with Bill and Paul that night. Instead we headed east, to the Cast Theatre in Hollywood, where an improvisational comedy troupe called War Babies was performing. They were good. They made me laugh. And I finally saw the light: *That is what I am supposed to be doing.*

The next morning, I phoned Andrew Alexander, who owned and operated Second City Toronto, and boldly declaimed, "I want to join Second City." Andrew, the savior of so many of us, was, thankfully, happy to make a place for me.

And so northward I flew, ready to begin life as Martin Short, Funnyman. And forever thereafter, into our eventual lives as Los Angelenos, Nancy, whenever we drove past the corner of North Flores Street and Santa Monica Boulevard, would point to the bench and say, "Hey, look, honey, there's Breakdown Corner."

HUMBLE CELEBRITY ME

L et's jump, for a moment, to the present day. Not so long ago, I found myself onstage in the Ray Dolby Ballroom in Hollywood, about two miles northeast of Breakdown Corner, giving a speech in honor of Steve Martin. Steve was receiving a lifetime-achievement Oscar from the Academy of Motion Picture Arts and Sciences. It was a remarkable evening, and Steve was deeply moved. Kind of like how I felt when I got my CableACE Award in '87, but, you know, different.

The lifetime-achievement Oscar is not the kind you're awarded in front of a gigantic international TV audience at the big ceremony in February, but rather the kind distributed at a comparatively modest L.A. banquet called the Governors Awards—as I described it onstage, "the highest honor an actor can receive . . . in mid-November."

"Of all the people I have a fake show-business friendship with," I said in my remarks, "Steve is the star I'm fake-closest to." I also reminded Steve of the old adage: This year's honorary Oscar is a good predictor of next year's "In Memoriam" package.

A little later, turning momentarily serious, as the conventions of showbiz demand, I thanked Steve for his guidance, his wisdom, and the kindnesses he has shown me and my family. I adore Steve Martin. We've been great, close friends for almost thirty years, ever since we did the movie *¡Three Amigos!* together in 1986.

After the ceremony, a group of us adjourned to Steve and his wife Anne Stringfield's home for a celebratory binge on grilled cheese sandwiches and Dom Pérignon.

The gents of our group were standing elbow-to-elbow in our tuxedos: Steve, me, Tom Hanks, Frank Oz, and, to lower the median age a tad, Judd Apatow and Bill Hader. We must have looked uncommonly smart, for the director Nancy Meyers, who was snapping photos of us with her iPhone, kept telling us, "You look just like that picture!"

The picture to which she was alluding is the famous "Kings of Hollywood" shot taken by the great photographer Slim Aarons on New Year's Eve, 1957: Clark Gable, Van Heflin, Gary Cooper, and Jimmy Stewart gathered together at the restaurant Romanoff's, all of them in white tie, looking dashing as they laugh at some shared joke.

I had to agree with Nancy: looking around the room, I couldn't help but acknowledge that it was a pretty glamorous Hollywood night. And another thought occurred: Wow, this is a long way from Breakdown Corner, and the days when *my* Nancy and I barely knew how to navigate this city.

O ne of the great benefits of that journey—from Breakdown Corner to comic-icon status (not my words, but those of my staff)—is that I have been fortunate enough to have become friends with some fascinating people, many of whom happen to be famous. Some of these friendships have endured for so long that they've become tenured, unbreakable.

This is especially true now that we're all reaching the age where the phrase "lifetime achievement" is part of the conversation. For instance, Steve, Tom, and I, along with our film-producer friend Walter Parkes, who used to run the DreamWorks movie studio, get colonoscopies together every couple of years. Well, not *together* together—we get separate rooms at the clinic. But we actually gather for a colonoscopy sleepover at Steve's house the night before the big day. We like to make a party of it. A Hootenanny of Purge, if you will.

As anyone who has gone for a colonoscopy knows, you are required, the evening before you undergo the procedure, to cleanse your digestive system—to make it spic and span for the gastroenterologist's camera. And as much as we show business folk would kill to be able to bring hair and makeup people along for the journey, most hospitals have a real issue with that.

The goal of the evening before—Colonoscopy Eve, as we Christians call it—is to pass the time while also passing as much solid material from our systems as humanly possible. We even have the event catered, inasmuch as you can cater a gathering where the only permitted foodstuffs are water, broth, and Jell-O. At around five p.m., the four of us dutifully glug down our barium-sulfate milkshakes, made from a liquid suspension that highlights the GI tract for the doctor—and sits like molten lead in the stomach. Then we settle in for the evening and play poker.

There's an odd kind of rhythm to this poker game; oftentimes there's only one of us at the table. By midnight, the scene in the nearest of Steve's bathrooms is straight out of a disabled Carnival cruise ship circa Day 15. The following morning we drive as a group to the clinic and get our insides checked out. A few hours later, we're happily and relievedly toasting our colorectal good health over margaritas at the Ivy.

I first met Tom Hanks briefly in 1983, when he and John Candy were filming what would turn out to be Tom's breakthrough movie, *Splash*. John, always charitable of spirit, was making a video for a benefit that his old high school in Canada was holding, and he'd arranged for most of the *SCTV* cast to appear in it: Catherine O'Hara, Andrea Martin, Joe Flaherty, Eugene Levy, and me. We filmed it in some studio in L.A., and John came straight from the set of *Splash* with Tom in tow.

In hindsight, Tom, not yet a box-office juggernaut, was the one who was starstruck: not so much over me, the new guy, but over the rest of the group. *SCTV*, he later told me, was huge to him— his comedy Beatles. His eyes went wide with wonderment in that boyish way that they still do when he gets excited; if you've seen him in *Big*, you know the expression I mean.

Tom's first real memory of me is at a party we both attended in 1986 at the home of Chevy and Jayni Chase. Tom had just arrived, and was passing through the anteroom when he caught sight of me standing on top of a chair, holding forth before a crowd. He turned to his wife, Rita, and said, "Who's the loud guy?" Over the next few years our wives became close friends, and we quickly followed suit. Tom is a deeply lovely man who, in person, is exactly what you hope he would be—as funny and smart and decent as it gets.

Tom has always been obsessed with pens. Whereas many

people's retail fantasy would be to have a moment alone in Tiffany's after closing, Tom would choose OfficeMax. A couple of Christmases ago, I ran into Tom at a pharmacy near where we both live. Actually, I spotted him first. He was, of course, in the stationery section, engrossed in the variety of Post-it notes—Tom is also very particular about his Post-its— and I crept up behind him and blew a puff of warm breath onto the back of his neck, just enough to make him jump out of his shoes. "Aaaagh!" went he. Relieved that it was only me, Tom asked what I was up to. It was Christmas Eve day, and as I explained to Tom, I was heading over to the Gelson's super-market to buy ingredients for the French punch I would later be making. "Can I come with ya!" Tom said, doing his best demented, demonic smirk.

So there we were in Gelson's: me with my list, Tom at the helm of the shopping cart. "See," Tom said, "this is what it would be like if we had an apartment together. I'd be pushing, you'd be loading."

It was a busy time at Gelson's, with lots of cars in the parking lot. As I maneuvered my vehicle through the traffic, Tom and I excitedly talking about the various gifts we'd gotten people, I must have lost focus. I didn't notice a car in front of me backing out of a space, and—*THUNK!*—I slow-motion crashed into it.

Fortunately, no one was hurt, and the man whose car I'd hit couldn't have been more gracious. As I got out of my car, he im-mediately recognized me and said with a smile, "Oh! Well, I guess I don't need to see *your* ID!" Then when Tom got out from the passenger side, the guy almost had a heart attack. I went back into the car and started rooting around my glove compartment for the insurance card. By the time I'd dug it out, I found the guy engrossed in deep conversation with Tom. "Look," he was saying,

"You don't have to read the whole script. But if you can just *listen to the music* . . ."

S ometimes, like in that parking-lot episode, people are just delighted to see your face, no matter the circumstances; that's one of the upsides of fame. Generally it's fantastic to be a celebrity, an absolute privilege. By doing the movie *¡Three Amigos!*, for example, I became friends not only with Steve Martin but also with Chevy Chase. And by being friends with Chevy, I got to meet one of my all-time idols, Frank Sinatra. Like I said, I'm by and large a pre-rock guy. When our children were growing up, Nancy constantly told them, "You have to understand your father's strange time-warp approach to life. *I* did not listen to Frank Sinatra. My *parents* listened to Frank Sinatra." I can't help it; I've always loved Frank, as long as I can remember. And through Chevy I met him the night of September 17, 1992, after he'd given a concert at the Greek Theatre in L.A.

I should back up. A few years earlier, sometime in the late 1980s, I had an opportunity to meet Sinatra that didn't pan out. At the time Robin Williams, Billy Crystal, and I shared the management team of Rollins Joffe Morra & Brezner. One day Buddy Morra got word from Sinatra's camp that the three of us—Robin, Billy, and me—were invited, with our wives, to stay at Twin Palms, the Sinatra compound in Palm Springs. This, though none of us knew Frank. The gist of it was that Frank wanted to be amused, and we were the performing monkeys he had selected. The three of us were like, *Fantastic! How great will this be? Hanging with Frank and getting to show off our leisure wear?* But our wives collectively vetoed the idea. They found it degrading for us men to submit so willingly to Frank's whim—or maybe they just didn't want to be known as the women married to Frank's monkeys. In any event, it didn't happen.

Cut to 1992. Chevy called me one day and said, "Marty, do you want to be my date to see Frank Sinatra at the Greek Theatre?" I jumped at the chance.

The very process of going to the show was a big production, orchestrated, aptly enough, by a big-time TV producer, George Schlatter, the creator of, among other programs, *Laugh-In*. We all met up at George's house before the concert for drinks, a blend of what you might call old and middle-aged Hollywood: Chevy and me, Warren Beatty and Annette Bening, Gregory and Veronique Peck, Don and Barbara Rickles, Dinah Shore, Jackie Collins, Lionel Richie, and so on. Then, as if we were a senior group on a big outing from an assisted-living facility, we were all loaded onto a bus, which took us to the backstage area of the Greek Theatre.

Frank was in good voice that night, and Chevy was especially funny. Seated directly in front of us was the old-time superagent Swifty Lazar. Swifty, if you don't know what he looked like, was a hairless-little-gnome kind of guy who wore comically oversize eyeglasses that further emphasized how hairless, little, and gnomic he was. Unbeknown to Swifty, Chevy kept removing his own sunglasses and hovering them over the back of Swifty's head, effectively creating a second Swifty face. This caused Dinah Shore and Jackie Collins to titter like schoolgirls in the back row of a classroom.

After the show and the bus ride back to George Schlatter's home, I got to talking with Dinah, who had actually sought *me* out. Who knew that the 1950s big-band sweetheart, 1970s talk-show queen, and avatar of the Ladies Professional Golf Association was such a massive *SCTV* fan? We chitchatted a while, and then Dinah said, "Hey, do you want to meet Frank?"

At long last, the moment I was waiting for! He was at the party at the Schlatters' by this point, standing at the bar by himself. Dinah guided me over. I steeled myself, offered my hand, and said, "Mr. Sinatra, my name is Martin Short."

Paul Shaffer maintains that, over many years and hundreds of tellings of this story, I have embellished it further and further, and that there's no way that Frank talked like a gangster out of *Guys and Dolls*, as he does in my dinner-party recountings. But I swear that he talked *exactly* like a Damon Runyon character. What he said to me was, "I know well of you. And you're *mah*-velous."

In response, I couldn't help but gush. "Well, Mr. Sinatra," I said, "you have no idea, *no concept*, of how big a fan I am of yours." Frank just stared back at me and said, "I think I do." Sensing my nerves, he said, "Whaddya drinking, kid?" I told him, "Oh, whatever you're drinking, Frank!" He turned to the bartender and said, "Jack Daniels."

The bartender looked at me and said, "Straight up or on the rocks?" But in my nervousness, I thought he said, "Straight up or relaxed?" So I said, "Relaxed."

Sinatra, irritated at my baffling non sequitur response, turned to me and said, "He said 'Straight up or on the rocks!' "

I'd known Frank Sinatra for fifteen seconds, and already I'd pissed him off. Pretty soon, I thought, he's going to take out his gun and shoot me in the leg, and then I'll never be able to enjoy his albums in quite the same way again. So maybe it was time to split.

It's an old story for me: every time I've had the chance to meet someone I looked up to as a kid, the experience has been so profound or overwhelming that I've ended up blowing it, either by being tongue-tied or by saying something utterly silly. I don't have this problem with contemporary stars like George Clooney and Brad Pitt. Nothing against George or Brad, but it's the people who were huge to you when you were twelve who, in person, render you unsteady on your feet. They bring those youthful feelings of awe right back to the surface.

In 1976 I saw Shirley MacLaine perform her one-woman revue at the O'Keefe Centre in Toronto, and somehow I wangled my way into an opportunity to go backstage after the show. Since I knew I'd be meeting MacLaine, I actually wrote down in advance what I was going to say to her, and rehearsed my lines before going to the theater. I would tell her that she was a magnificent performer who had been brilliant in *The Apartment*, and whose elegance shone through every song she sang that night. And then Miss MacLaine would say "Thank you," and move on to the next person.

However, when I actually met Shirley MacLaine backstage and delivered my little prepared speech, she didn't merely say "Thank you" and move on to the next person. Instead, she started a conversation. "But there was so much reverb through the sound system that I could barely hear myself," she said. "Weren't you bothered by that at all?" To which, flustered, I replied, "Thank you."

Damn thee, Marty Short! thought I.

That very same year, I went to New York and scored a ticket to see the play *The Royal Family*, starring Rosemary Harris, at the Helen Hayes Theatre on Broadway. I was by myself, and the seat next to me was empty. Suddenly, before the curtain went up, I heard the unmistakable voice of Katharine Hepburn asking people to move their feet as she made her way across my row: "*Thank* you. . . . *Please* remove that umbrella. . . . Get that *leg* out of my way, you idiot!" She took the seat next to me. Determined to play it cool, I said nothing to her. But before I knew it, I was so caught up in the brilliance of George S. Kaufman and Edna Ferber's play that I had forgotten that Hepburn was even in the building. As the curtain fell at the end of act one, after Harris unleashed an astounding diatribe that culminated in her collapsing into a heap onstage, I turned to Hepburn, who I'd forgotten *was* Hepburn, and said, "Isn't she classy?"

And because I said it in a normal voice, like a normal person, Hepburn, in a very normal, conversational way, responded, "Well, Rosemary has an incredible ability to convey such deep emotions and make the audience feel that they're a part of her journey. She's always had that magic. I guess always will. So did Spencer."

At that, I was suddenly jolted back into the reality that I was having a conversation with *Katharine Hepburn*. When she finished, I said, "Well, Miss Hepburn, you're no slouch." Suddenly the conversation was over. I had burst the bubble and brought celebrity into the conversation. She turned to the person on her other side and said, "Do you mind if we switch seats?"

Damn thee, Marty Short! thought I.

Even from the grave, Frank Sinatra and his star power continue to trip me up. (Though, I must admit, these trip-ups make for good talk-show fodder.) I was fascinated by a *Vanity Fair* story from 2013 in which Mia Farrow, who was briefly married to Sinatra in the 1960s, said that her twenty-six-year-old son Ronan, long thought to be the biological son of Farrow and Woody Allen, could "possibly" be Sinatra's kid, since she continued to see Frank long after they divorced. Ronan has grown up to be a formidable young man—bright, funny, and a media star in his own right, with his own public-affairs show on MSNBC. Just recently I happened to meet him. I was in an L.A. recording facility looping some dialogue for my part in the English-language version of the Japanese animated film *The Wind Rises*, for which veteran Hollywood producer Frank Marshall had recruited me.

As it turned out, Ronan too had a part in the film, and he came in to work the same day. I'd been skeptical about the Sinatra-parentage thing, since, based on the photos I'd seen, it was entirely possible that Ronan got his blue eyes and good looks from his Farrow side. But when I saw him in person, I was utterly transfixed: *Holy cow, this kid looks exactly like a young Frank.* Obviously this was not a subject I was going to broach with him, though God knows I would have loved to.

I introduced myself to Ronan and left it at that. I went into the recording booth for a round of looping. Then, during a break, I decided to walk into the common area to get some tea. There, sitting at a desk and filling out some paperwork, was Ronan, who was also engaged in conversation with a production coordinator on the film. "Marty," she said, "Ronan and I were just talking about Frank."

Well, since you brought it up . . . "Oh my God, *Frank*," I said. "I just think he really was the greatest singer of the last hundred years. The phrasing! The passion! Who could disagree?"

The production coordinator looked at me quizzically. "Marty," she said, "we were talking about Frank *Marshall*."

Ronan looked away, and the conversation died out.

Damn thee, Marty Short! thought I.

MARTY WITH PARENTS

H ow Frank-crazy am I? Well, imagine a boy of sixteen, on the eve of the Summer of Love, with the whole world going warpedly psychedelic around him. Yet what's this kid doing? Standing solo in his attic, microphone in hand, affecting a Sinatra pose, ruminating autumnally on the swingin', sweet-and-sour life he's led:

> *One day you turn around, and it's summerrrrrr*
> *Next day you turn around, and it's faaalll . . .*

That was me in November of 1966, cutting my own faithful rendition of the title track of *September of My Years*, Sinatra's milestone LP from the year before. I actually covered the entire album. I still have the recording. It is labeled, in my adolescent handwriting, "Martin Short Sings of Songs and Loves Ago." On it, you can hear me re-creating the fiftysomething Frank's takes on such wistful classics as "It Was a Very Good Year" and "Last Night When We Were Young." Outside my attic walls, the hip sentiment was the Who's "Hope I die before I get old." Me? I was hoping I'd get old before I turned seventeen.

Martin Short Sings of Songs and Loves Ago was not a joke. It wasn't like the crooner-parody stuff I would later do on *SCTV* and Dave Letterman's show. I performed it totally straight and took it very seriously, without a trace of irony. I had my own reel-to-reel tape recorder and, of equal importance, a professional-grade microphone that came with a mic stand.

I bought a lot of this equipment with my baby-bonus money. After World War II, Canada established a program in which parents, every time they had a child, received a modest government stipend to aid in that child's upbringing. (Thank you, socialism!) Being the youngest of five kids had certain advantages, far from the least of which was that I, alone among the Short children, got to keep my baby-bonus money to spend as I pleased. I also had a huge bedroom, on the third floor, the attic level. I adored my childhood home, on Whitton Road in Hamilton, Ontario. It was a four-bedroom brick house with a spacious, flat backyard, behind which was a brick patio where my parents entertained in the summer months. Beyond the patio was a thickly wooded ravine that ran the length of our block and seemed, in my youth, to extend forever into the northern wilds.

Of the five Short children, I was not only the youngest but also the smallest even after I finished growing, and the most precocious—and without question, as evidenced by the baby-bonus money, the most spoiled. Whereas the older four all had to share bedrooms at different times of their lives, I had that attic bedroom to myself, for it had already been vacated by my eldest sibling, David, born fourteen years before me and out in the wider world by the time I was in grade school.

The hallway outside that bedroom had an amazing echoey

quality that perfectly complemented my singing—it was my own little version of Frank's beloved Studio B in the Capitol Records Tower in Hollywood. What I'd do is play the Sinatra album on the turntable in my bedroom, holding the microphone to my stereo's speakers during Nelson Riddle's rich orchestral intros. Then, just before Frank came in, I'd pause the recorder, lift the needle off the record, quickly move into the hallway so I wouldn't lose the pitch, and record my vocal where his would have been. Following that, I'd hop back into the bedroom, find the place on the record where the next instrumental passage was, record that—and then repeat the process of pausing, lifting the needle, and doing my vocals in the hallway. I managed to match Sinatra's pitch pretty well, but because I was thirty-five years his junior, my timbre was closer to a baby froglet's than a grown man's.

Outside, on Whitton Road, normal Canadian childhoods were taking place, with kids playing hockey in the street until darkness fell and the streetlights came on. Inside, little Marty was snapping his fingers and singing, "Weather-wise, it's such a cuckoo daaay!" But what was amazing about my fantasy showbiz life, and underscored how lucky I was to be a member of this particular family, was that at no point did my parents or siblings ever belittle me or make me feel foolish for what I was doing. My mother, the former Olive Hayter, was wonderfully supportive of my musical efforts. She was a superb, classically trained violinist who had served for a time as the concertmistress of the Hamilton Symphony Orchestra. When I eagerly presented her with a copy of . . . *Sings of Songs and Loves Ago*, she didn't laugh or find the gesture merely cute. She listened carefully and adjudicated each performance. I still have sheets of paper where she wrote things like "Beautifully sung; four stars" and "Some pitch issues on this one, maybe not a good selection for your voice; two and a half stars." Mom was giving me the feedback I craved, the loving encouragement that any child should receive when he's brave and willing enough to share something creative.

And was I ever creative. With my fertile imagination and trusty reel-to-reel recorder, I imagined myself not only a singer but a triple-threat entertainment juggernaut: movie star, TV host, and savvy mogul. In my mind I had my own television network, MBC, the Marty Broadcasting Corporation—the anchor program of which was, naturally, *The Martin Short Variety Hour.* I was on Tuesdays at 8:00 p.m.—well, actually, every other Tuesday, because I always made sure to leave room for my imaginary film career. My bedroom was my stage and the pictures on the walls my audience. I had a gooseneck lamp in the corner that I'd arch upward for performances; even then I understood the importance of good lighting.

I'd open *The Martin Short Variety Hour* with an up-tempo tune, something along the lines of Cy Coleman's "The Best Is Yet to Come," and then follow it with an edgy monologue.

> *Thank you, ladies and gentlemen. You're so very kind . . . and right. You know, we Canadians love living right next to America. It's like spooning with Mama Cass—you feel safe, but by morning, your spine is completely shot.*

I'd then introduce my first guest.

> *Please welcome a three-time Oscar winner: the legendary Katharine Hepburn and her spinning plates!*

I'd run over to a smaller tape recorder that played pretaped applause, record some of that applause on the bigger recorder, and

then become Hepburn, juggling plates on long sticks while saying
things like:

> *My goodness, these plates are so wobbly! I feel they're some-*
> *what precarious. If they're not going to spin properly like*
> *plates should, then to hell with them!*

Then I'd do a hard-hitting interview with Kate, playing both
parts.

> **ME**: *Miss Hepburn, what's your favorite day of the week?*
> **HEPBURN**: *I would say Sundays. Sundays are mine. They*
> *always were. I wake up very early. I then have a huge bowl*
> *of oat bran. The next few hours, I'm indisposed. And then,*
> *before you know it, it's Monday.*

My show also strived to be current. My brothers smuggled
copies of *Playboy* into the house, and I'd page through
them greedily—I swear!—for their long, serious interviews with
newsmakers. So if, for example, *Playboy* featured an interview
with Eldridge Cleaver, the author and Black Panther, I would do
both sides of the Q&A, in my own voice and in my best approximation of Cleaver's.

After that, Johnny Mathis might walk on as a surprise to sing
"Chances Are" and perhaps join me in a medley of songs that
featured the word *locomotive*. I even went so far as to type up *TV
Guide*–style listings for these shows: the guests on each episode,
what songs were being performed, and so forth.

At the conclusion of each episode, I would bid the audience
farewell:

*Well, that's our show. Good night, God bless you, and re-
member, if you must drink and drive, be sure you have a car.*

Then someone downstairs would yell, "Dinner!" and I'd put
away my taping equipment for later.

Though my eccentricities were warmly indulged most of the
time, they did occasionally cause some concern. In my bedroom,
beside the gooseneck lamp, I had an old rocking chair whose
left arm kept popping out of place, so I almost always had an
open tube of glue sitting around on my desk. At one point my
brother Michael—perhaps after hearing me in the attic shouting,
"Whoa, how did all of *you* get into my room?" to my imaginary
audience—took my mother aside and said, "I think Marty might
be sniffing glue."

"Don't be ridiculous," Mom said.

"Well," said Michael, "he just finished a medley of 'songs that
weren't nominated,' so I'm going with glue."

Still, my mother just laughed him off. She was used to doing
so, and to laughing me off, too. Once, I walked in the door from
school and jokingly shouted at her, "Owlie"—we sometimes
called her that—"Owlie, you ol' flea-bitten whore! Where are
ya?" I didn't realize that there were three additional musicians in
the house, practicing in the string quartet over which Mom was
presiding. Her eyes met mine when I made it to the living room,
and, with a combination of embarrassment and amusement, she
said, "Marty! Why don't you say hello to our guests?"

T he beauty of my "Hey, let's put on a show!" obsessiveness—
the saving grace of it, really—is that it never felt pre-
professional. With hindsight, it's easy to think, well, he was

fantasizing about having his own TV network; it's obvious where he was headed. But back then I never dreamed of being in show business. I never even performed in school plays. Show business, as I perceived it via the Sinatra albums and *The Ed Sullivan Show* (which we picked up, along with most American TV, through the networks' Buffalo affiliates), existed at arm's length, in a fantasy world. Canada at that time was further away from the United States, psychologically, than it is now. I'd see ads during *Ed Sullivan* for products not available to us—Bosco chocolate syrup, Ipana toothpaste—and think, boy, those American kids are so lucky. I'll never get to try those things. I was so taken in by those "Please don't squeeze the Charmin" toilet-paper ads that when I finally did get to visit the States, I dashed into a supermarket's paper-products aisle almost upon arrival to fondle the product, thinking, wow, it really *is* soft!

So for me to say "I'm going to be in show business someday" would have been tantamount to saying "I'm going to live on Venus someday." The Marty Broadcasting Corporation was pure imaginative play, and that was probably very healthy. Certainly music was a regular part of my life, with Mom playing violin, Michael an excellent pianist, and David a trumpet player in a swing-jazz band. But no one, including me, walked around our house with delusions of becoming a Hollywood or Broadway star.

As a kid, I assumed I'd end up a doctor—not because I was particularly interested in science, but because I found medicine a noble calling and was a big fan of Richard Chamberlain's work on *Dr. Kildare*. Becoming Dr. Short would have been very much in keeping with my upper-middle-class upbringing. My father, Charles P. Short, was an executive at Stelco, the biggest steel company in Canada, which had its headquarters in Hamilton. We were the type of family that went every weekend to the Hamilton

Golf and Country Club for dinner. We had season tickets to the Hamilton Tiger-Cats of the Canadian Football League, and, as only we Canadians can say, we had prime seats right on the fifty-five-yard line. And we faithfully attended Sunday mass at Cathedral Basilica of Christ the King.

All of these facts make us Shorts sound traditional. Believe me, we weren't. I grew up thinking that our household was the strangest on the street, bordering on insanity. I later learned that many of the other families on Whitton Road—and it was the kind of street where every family had lived there for twenty, thirty, forty years—had their own brand of lunacy, with drunken dads, sedated moms, and so on. By comparison, ours was a happy home, but it was still nuts. My father would come home from the steel company wearing that *Mad Men* fedora that all executives wore back then, and he would immediately pour himself his usual drink: gin and ginger ale, no ice. Dad didn't eat dinner with us. As we Short children convened with Mom around the dinner table in the kitchen nook, he would sit off to the side, about six feet away, sipping his gin and ginger at the little table with the radio on it, his face buried in the newspaper.

Still, his remove from the family table didn't prevent Dad from peering over his paper on occasion to insult our manners. "Marty, don't shovel the food in like an animal, dear," he'd say. Or he might jump from his chair with feigned urgency, arms wide open in a protective stance, and pretend to guard the table, saying, "Good boy, Michael. Eat even faster. I'll make sure the dogs don't get at your plate."

Later on, around 9:30 p.m., Dad would go into the kitchen and pan-fry a steak for himself, heavily seasoned with Lea & Perrins Worcestershire sauce. Occasionally he'd fry an extra one for us, sliding a piece of bread under the steak as it finished cooking so that the bread absorbed the juices. He'd bring his plate into the den, where we were watching TV, and we kids would pretend to be dogs, panting around his chair, paws out, begging for scraps. He'd say, "Here ya go, dear," and give us bites. Maybe it's sentimentality, but, to this day, I have never tasted anything more delicious.

Dad was smart, funny, and, as you might have surmised, witheringly sarcastic. His bluntness and condescending wit were hysterical as long as you yourself weren't bearing the brunt. Years later, when I was playing the celebrity interviewer Jiminy Glick on TV, I'd watch the playback of my totally improvised scenes— things like Jiminy telling Conan O'Brien, "Look at how wonderful you look; whatever cosmetic surgery you've had done, I'd say twenty percent more and then stop," or asking Mel Brooks, "What's your big beef with the Nazis?"—and think, where on earth did that instinct come from? Oh, right: Dad. (Mel's response, by the way, was, "Oh, I don't know. I find them rude.")

My father—Chuck, as we kids called him behind his back— really loved his gin and gingers, though he was careful to drink them only under our roof. Monday through Friday, he'd sip from the moment he arrived home till the moment he went to bed. Saturdays and Sundays, he sipped all day. It sounds traumatic, but it was just the normal state of things in our house. My siblings and I had a running joke: "Oh, Dad's in his drunk shirt!" He had a specific plaid shirt that he wore only on weekends, and it meant, to us kids, that Dad had had a few—and therefore it might be wise to keep a wide berth.

The five little Shorts were born, as I've said, over a fourteen-year span. David, my oldest brother, was born in 1936, followed by Nora, my only sister, in 1937. Then, a while later, came my brothers Michael and Brian, born in '44 and '45, respectively, followed, on the momentous date of March 26, 1950 (I think we all remember where we were that day), by me. We all adored our mother, Olive, who was as kind and radiant as Dad was bespectacled, plump-cheeked, and ornery. Mom was a stylish, striking woman, with blond hair and wide-set eyes; the actress Martha Plimpton reminds me a little of her. We kids considered her one of us, our ally in the ongoing battle against the benevolent household tyrant that was our father.

Make no mistake, we loved Dad, and we knew he loved us. His drinking never made him physically violent, and he was never overturning tables like Richard Burton in *Who's Afraid of Virginia Woolf?* But his words were often barbed and full of provocation. I remember that David at some point in the 1950s invited over a friend, Kent Follis, a gentle, harmless kid who happened to have an Elvis-style pompadour. My father opened the door, sized up Kent, and said, "Can I take your hat for ya, dear?" Another time a friend of mine who was half Irish and half Jewish was visiting me. My father, upon hearing of my friend's heritage, approached him and declared, "You know, dear, back in county Armagh, where my people are from, we have a name for someone who is half Irish and half Jewish. We call that person . . . a Jew."

Dad spoke with a faint Irish brogue because he was from Northern Ireland—born in 1909 in the town of Crossmaglen, one of eleven siblings. (Mom, four years younger, was born in Hamilton and was of English and Irish descent.) Dad was a self-made man, which, given the Depression era in which he navigated his new life, was quite remarkable. He first crossed the Atlantic as a seventeen-year-old stowaway, making his way to Texas before he was bounced back home for being in the United States illegally. He successfully put down roots on his second try, four years later, living first in Buffalo before finally settling in Hamilton and working his way up from traveling sales rep to third-in-command at Stelco.

Only two other siblings sought a life outside Northern Ireland. Dad's brother Tom moved to New York, and his brother Frank to Birmingham, England. One of Frank's children, my first cousin Clare Short, grew up to represent Birmingham as a member of Parliament and a tough, outspoken Labour Party firebrand who was later tapped to be Great Britain's secretary of state for international development. In other words, England got the second-generation Short who stood on principle and resigned from Tony Blair's cabinet over her nation going to war with Iraq under false pretenses, while Canada got the second-generation Short who falls over on talk shows and humps celebrities in his Jiminy Glick fat suit to get laughs.

Anyway: the other eight Shorts of my father's generation stayed in Crossmaglen, where since 1885 the family has owned and lived above a pub, Short's Bar. It's still there, and still operated by my aunt Rosaleen. When I went over and met the Irish Shorts, I began to understand how Dad's background in a big, rowdy Irish family endowed him with a quick, jousting wit, which he passed on to us. In 1997, when I was in England doing the miniseries *Merlin* for NBC, I spent two weekends over in Crossmaglen, sleeping in my father's old bedroom above the bar. My uncle Paddy, my father's youngest sibling and Rosaleen's husband, was still alive then, running the bar. One night I stayed up into the wee hours with my cousins Oliver and Patrick, Paddy's sons, talking loudly and uninhibitedly about the Shorts on both sides of the ocean. We started with beer and quickly moved on to whiskey, followed by . . . still more whiskey. I finally got about four hours of bed-spinning sleep before the sun rose and woke me up. I walked down the stairs to the pub, bleary-eyed, to find Uncle Paddy cleaning out all the empty glasses we'd left at the bar. "Soooo," he said, a glint in his eye, his voice not unlike Dad's, "how did the character assassination go last night?"

So my own family's dynamic had an ancestral context. The mealtime conversation in our house on Whitton Road, even when Dad wasn't engaged in it, was a sustained, survival-of-the-fittest verbal sparring match. The talk often became heated, but the key to it is that there was always laughter within thirty seconds of the heat. I think of this as a very Irish trait; Bill Murray and Conan O'Brien, who also developed their comedic reflexes in large, argumentative Irish Catholic families, know what I'm talking about.

I actually used my beloved tape recorder to capture some of my family's squabbling. Among my favorites is a recording of our Christmas dinner in 1966, when I was sixteen years old, and Dad was with us at the table for a change. As it opens, my brother Michael is upset at my brother Brian for wanting more dark meat from the turkey, but not a turkey leg:

MICHAEL: The dark meat is *on* the leg! You don't want a leg! Honest to God, I haven't got—I haven't got the mind to handle that problem.

MOM: Nora's, uh—

MICHAEL (*interrupting*): You'd have to take a God-damned *file* and file it off and shred it!

NORA: Just calm down.

MICHAEL: It's the only way you could do it!

DAD: He wanted dark meat, did he?

MICHAEL: Yeah.

DAD (*angrily*): Well, dark meat's all on *that Goddamned leg*!

NORA (*to Brian*): It's not worth it.

BRIAN: Now he's, now he's starting to—

DAD (*to Brian*): Pick up the leg and *chomp the dark meat*!

NORA (*to Brian*): Just close your mouth.

BRIAN: Okay. Okay, Nora.

MICHAEL: The only thing we could do is cut it up!

BRIAN (*now exasperated*): All right! All right!

MICHAEL (*surprised*): What happened?

BRIAN: Shut your mouth, Michael! Just shut your mouth and everything will be—

DAD (*to Brian*): Shut *yours*, now!

BRIAN (*defensively*): Okay! Okay. I'll shut mine, too, Dad.

DAD (*trudging off to the kitchen, speaking in a "mentally challenged" voice*): "I waaants da dark meat . . . Darrrk!" (*Returning to regular voice*) Three-fourths of the world don't have a choice between—

BRIAN (*to Dad, feeling picked-on*): Shhhh! *Shhhh!*

DAD: —dark meat or white meat.

NORA: Would you shut your *mouth*, Brian!

MICHAEL: Well, which do they eat, then?

DAD (*nattering on*): Blue meat or green meat.

MICHAEL: Well, which do they eat, then?

(*Brian and Marty start to laugh.*)

DAD: They don't have any choice of meat *at all*!

(Dad re-enters the dining room from the kitchen with the exact slices of turkey Brian wanted.)

DAD: Do you want more potatoes, dear?

BRIAN: No thank you, Dad.

MICHAEL: Are you not going to have any turkey, Dad?

DAD (*raising his voice, irritated*): My stomach is so sore right now, dear, if you mention turkey to me, I'll vomit right on the middle of the table.

(Everyone starts laughing.)

DAD: Now, if I wanted turkey, craved turkey, ate turkey, *desired* turkey—

MICHAEL: I think the question required a yes or no answer.

DAD: But I don't need a kid asking me. I don't need an immature person asking me things.

Some years ago, in the 1990s, I had this tape fully transcribed—it goes on for thirty pages—and presented a bound copy to each of my siblings. I also used to make my kids, when they were little, read all the parts every Christmas Eve. I'd always cast my youngest child, Henry, in the Dad role, just so I could hear this sweet little boy saying "Dark meat's all on *that Goddamned leg!*"

People are often surprised to learn I'm of Irish descent and was raised Catholic; there's a widespread misperception that I am Jewish. And I don't think it's just because I'm thrifty.

No, this misperception actually makes some sense, because I was pretty much immersed in Jewishness from an early age. Westdale, the neighborhood we lived in, in Hamilton's west end, had a large Jewish population. My parents' best friends, the Paikins, were Jewish. The best nursery school in the area was the one at Temple Anshe Sholom, so that's where I went to nursery school. And the friendships that I made there carried over into the rest of my childhood.

I've always been a top-feeder, drawn to the smartest people in the room, and the simple truth was that the smartest kids in the schools I attended were the Jewish ones. We had a teacher in Grade 7, as we Canadians call the seventh grade, Miss Critchmore, who seated her pupils in order of intelligence, a cruel stroke that would never be allowed now: the smartest kids (in her estimation) in the front row, the dumbest in the back. I always strove to be in that first row, where my row-mates were reliably Mitchell Rosenblatt, Shelley Lipton, Rick Levy, Debbie Zack, Alex Stiglick, and Marvin Barnett. My people: the chosen.

I dated my share of Jewish girls, too. One of these romances had to be carried out in secret, because the girl's parents were deeply observant and didn't approve of their daughter's dating a goy. After a couple of furtive petting sessions in Hamilton's Churchill Park, we tearfully went our separate ways. A sort of *West Side Story*, with blue balls.

Then there's the fact that I work in comedy, and so many of the comedic greats have been Jewish. Some of them—Jerry Lewis, Harpo Marx, and Mike Nichols—were childhood idols of mine, while others, among them Gilda Radner, Eugene Levy, and Larry David, became dear friends. So I understand why I'm often mistaken as Jewish, and I find it flattering. By osmosis, I've absorbed a lot of Jewish-comic rhythms into my performances, and when I'm doing a Jewish character, it's an easy fit. The foremost of these is Irving Cohen, the ancient, prolific Tin Pan Alley songsmith I introduced on *SCTV*, carried over to *Saturday Night Live*, and still do in my live act:

> *It's wonderful to be here representing the world of the tins and the pans and the sulfur flash pots going off here and there.*
>
> *At my age, the only time I don't have to pee is when I'm peeing.*
>
> *I just poy-chased a Maserati. I know it's ridiculous, but I'm going through a little mid-death crisis.*
>
> *You know, I have written over twenty-eight thousand songs—two thousand since lunch. Such classics as "Honey Do the Hula," "Wigwam Serenade," and who can ever forget the Al Jolson classic, "Sam, You Made the Truss Too Short"? And I feel another one coming on right now— either that, or the Metamucil is kicking in. Gimme a C! A bouncy C!*

Listen, even *I* was confused as a child about whether I was or wasn't a son of Abraham. For reasons too convoluted to get into here, I was not baptized until I was seven years old, at my family's regular church, Christ the King Cathedral. Which means that, unlike the babies who were routinely baptized there, I was fully cognizant of what was going on—physically, if not sacramentally. After the priest had done his business of ladling holy water on my head, I looked at him and asked, in all seriousness, "Am I Jewish now?"

He just barely managed to stifle his laughter into a snort, which

resonated gloriously, along with my father's laugh, through the
majestic cathedral.

My inadvertently interfaith upbringing notwithstanding, I
was never particularly stirred by the spirit of the Lord as
He or She is presented in organized religion. Nor have I ever put
much stock in the paranormal, the occult, or anything smacking
of clairvoyance. With one notable exception.

In the summer of 1962, I was twelve years old, and my brother
David was twenty-six. The age difference made him a little mysterious to me, living a life a world apart from mine. In our family
photos he's kind of off to the side, handsome and brooding in his
shades, like Stu Sutcliffe in those early photos of the Beatles as
a five-piece. But in reality David was total sunshine, a funny and
loose charmer. As a small child, I'd creep into his bedroom on
Saturday mornings around seven a.m. (he'd probably only gotten
in at five thirty) and play this game we invented called "Giant."
Basically, it was David, groggily aware of my presence, good-
naturedly pretending to be a sleeping giant while I tried to steal
the "magic pillow" from under his head without waking him. He
always tolerated my mischief and had a special nickname for me,
"Muggers-All," though none of us in the family can remember its
etymology. I just worshipped him.

At the age of twenty-six, David was justly excited about
his life. He was living and thriving in Montreal, following in
Dad's footsteps, working as a salesman for Samuel, Son & Co.,
another Canadian steel company. More important, David was
engaged to be married in the fall, to a beautiful girl named
Margaret Spracklin. His adulthood was taking off with a
vengeance.

On July 2, 1962, Dave composed a cheerful letter to me while I was away at a YMCA camp three hours north of Hamilton.

```
Dear Muggers-All:
Comment ca va ma bien frere, I am
spending this weekend in Hamilton and I
am gouging the family as usual. I was very
proud to see all the diplomas you won and
that you graduated with first class honours.
I am going back to Montreal today and
will be back August first. You can tell me
all about your adventures at camp. You
must arrange with mum and dad to spend one
week in Montreal with me and we will have
some fun.
Love dave xxxx oooooo
```

On the morning of July 18, 1962, near the end of my allotted three weeks at Camp Wanakita, I awoke in an unfamiliar, befogged state: oddly depressed, lethargic, weighted down, burdened by a sense that the whole universe was out of sync. My unease was conspicuous enough, and sufficiently out of character, for one of my cabin-mates to take notice and ask, "Are you okay? Are you sick?" I didn't know how to respond. "I'm fine," I said. "Something's just weird."

Twenty minutes later I was called down to the head counselor's cabin. After an awkward greeting, with him unable to look me in the eyes, the counselor blurted, "There's been an accident. Your brother David's been in an accident, and it killed him." What an odd way to put it.

That strange, unsettled moment of waking, just minutes before the counselor's horrible announcement, is the only extrasensory experience I can ever claim to have had. And I still can't make sense of it: why or how I knew—or my body did, or my subconscious, whatever—that something terrible had happened. Why did my twelve-year-old psyche, which otherwise seemed to exist in a perpetual state of bouncy, wired joy, feel, for the first time, a true sense of despair?

In the moment, I was simply stunned to the point of confusion. A minute later, I asked the counselor, "But is he okay?"

Up to that point in my childhood, I'd had it easy. Now, suddenly, life was a blur of sadness and confusion. My dad's good friend, Bob Lord, materialized at Camp Wanakita to collect me and deliver me back to Hamilton. The long, conversation-free drive in Mr. Lord's gunboat-size Mercury Park Lane was made more awkward still by a news bulletin that came crackling through the static of his car radio on CHML, the local Hamilton station: "David Short, the son of Stelco executive C. P. Short, has been killed in a car crash." I wouldn't learn the details until later: David had spent a late night pacing in a hospital corridor with a buddy whose wife was in labor with their first baby. At around four thirty a.m., in the Montreal suburb of Dorval, David must have fallen asleep while driving home. His car hit the back of a parked truck and flipped over, hurling him to an instant death.

Our house on Whitton Road was in a high state of angst. Dad had just flown home from Montreal, where he'd been to collect David's body. Mom was beyond bereft, upset that the casket needed to be closed rather than open, given the extent of David's injuries. "Do you want it opened? We can have it opened," said my father, heartbroken, trying to solve it all. "No, no," my mother sobbed, "it's just the idea that it can't be open."

Nora, my sister, was flying in from Los Angeles, where she

was working as a nurse. This, to me, was strangely a source of excitement—I missed my big sister and was thrilled that she was coming home. Since the airport was an hour away, I petitioned Mr. Lord, who was heroically filling in as the family driver, to let me come with him to get Nora. It was night, so he said, "Better bring a pillow." I ran into the house to get a pillow, and Mom told me in no uncertain terms that I was *not* leaving the house that night. When Nora did come home, she looked different, more grown-up, with elaborate early 1960s eye makeup and long hair— the peculiar details you fixate on in moments of crisis.

The following morning, I caught sight, from my bedroom window, of my mother talking with our next-door neighbor, Mrs. James, whose front yard was separated from ours only by a driveway. Mrs. James had lost her son five years earlier; he'd drowned in Lake Ontario. Then I saw Mom, never one to lose her temper or betray signs of aggravation, storm across the driveway and back into the house. I ran downstairs to ask her what happened. She said, "Marjorie James told me that I will get over this. I will *never* get over this."

A few days later, in the middle of the night, Mom found herself unable to sleep, so furiously were words and thoughts racing around in her head. She knew she would get no rest until she wrote them down. So she did, as a poem.

— To David —

Where is the laughing face?
The eyes so grey and tender
Looking down into my own.
The arms outstretched in greeting.

To clasp me to his side
In a bearlike hug?
Can this be all there was for him?
The few short years?
What useful purpose served?
What noble cause fulfilled?
Or was it I who was to blame?
Wrapped in my own security—
Of love and family and the joy of music.
Serenely living, until the jealous Gods
Struck with ironclad fist
To sickness and despair!
But no, if there is only one omnipotent God,
He could not surely choose—
—"You I will slay, and you protect."
In petty favoritism.
'Twas but an accident of fate.
A single moment out of time.
A tired and nodding head perhaps,
That hurled him to his death
Upon a lonely road.

OLIVE G. SHORT
(xxooxx)

This poem, and the events surrounding it, had a profound influence upon my views about organized religion. Mom's words
made complete spiritual sense. Why did David die? For some
noble cause? At some perverse whim of God? No, she concluded,
it was just a matter of a tired head on the road. Oh, and by the

way: that letter that Dave wrote to me on July 2? I didn't receive it until after his death, after the camp forwarded it to our
house in Hamilton. Its chipper tone, promising fun with me in
the future, did not suggest that there was some cosmic plan afoot
for my brother to be called to heaven. Yet in the days and weeks
after David died, well-meaning family friends and members of
the clergy constantly advised me that "God works in mysterious
ways, and you can't understand the will of the Lord."

This sentence not only failed to reassure me, it angered me.
*Yeah, well, God also created my mind, which is questioning everything,
including His will, so your theory doesn't hold.*

I had been the kind of kid who ritually said his prayers before
bedtime: "Gentle Jesus, meek and mild / Look upon a little
child," that sort of thing. But no more. I didn't stop praying or
believing, but I had no further interest in church doctrine and
unquestioning faith. My prayers changed, too. No longer did I
pray over trivial matters: "Please let me pass my history exam." I
went bigger-picture. I prayed, simply, for strength, for the inspiration to go on.

A s for Mrs. James, our neighbor, she was clearly just trying
to comfort my mother. But "getting over this"—what did
that mean? How was it done? It was a new concept to me. And
then, the night after the funeral, something instructive happened,
pertaining to this very subject. Like my mother, I too had been
traumatized by the fact that David's coffin was closed. I would
never see him again. My brain struggled to process the thought.

This trauma was fresh in my head as I went to bed that night.
And then I fell asleep, and had a dream unlike any I've had before
or since. For one thing, it was in bright Technicolor worthy of

Seven Brides for Seven Brothers. I was outside a log cabin in the woods, sitting by a scenic little stream—artificially scenic, like an MGM-backlot version of the old frontier. And while I was sitting there, David walked up and took a seat beside me. He looked handsome and strong, not remotely in need of a closed casket. He wore a vivid orange jersey that matched the scenery. And he said to me, in the most reassuring tone, "Everything's fine. It won't be long before we see each other again. I'll see you in a fleeting moment."

"A fleeting moment"—funny words for a twelve-year-old to dream.

When I woke up, I felt great, as if the veil of sadness had lifted. A spiritualist would say that I had experienced a visitation. A psychologist would say that my subconscious had manufactured this dream scenario to fulfill an emotional need for closure. In any case, I learned what would turn out to be a valuable lesson: that something terrible can happen to you, and yet, the day after this something terrible, the sun still rises, and life goes on. And therefore, so must you. I don't mean to sound facile, or to imply that David's death doesn't still pain me to this day. But I was glad of this lesson, because it would not be long before I was forced to heed it again.

INTERLUDE

A MOMENT WITH
WITH
IRVING COHEN

Irving Cohen was invented for **SCTV**, born of necessity when two of the show's writers, Paul Flaherty and Dick Blasucci, asked me to create an old Jewish songwriter character for a sketch they were writing. Paul is the brother of my friend and **SCTV** castmate Joe Flaherty. One of Joe's recurring **SCTV** bits was "The Sammy Maudlin Show," in which he played the titular star of a cheesy, clubby talk show. In this new sketch, Sammy's Ed McMahon–like sidekick, William B. Williams (John Candy), had left Sammy's show to launch his own, **The William B. Show**. My character was meant to be the kind of depressing third-tier guest to which lesser talk shows, such as William B.'s, must resort to fill their airtime.

A lot of people think that Irving Cohen is based on the prolific Tin Pan Alley great Irving Berlin, because both Irvings were/are notoriously prolific. But this is wrong on two counts: (1) Irving Berlin actually wrote **good** songs; and (2) Irving Cohen was largely inspired by Sophie Tucker, a veteran singer and former vaudeville entertainer who made frequent appearances on **The Ed Sullivan Show** when I was a kid in the early 1960s. She had a deep, mannish voice and seemed ancient (she was actually in her seventies), and whenever she came on, she'd start in with a declaration along the lines of "You know, Ed, in the old days, they had a little ting they called **vaud-dih-ville!**"

One afternoon I was idly watching the movie **Broadway Melody of 1938** on TV, and there was Sophie standing beside a young Judy Garland, telling her, "You know, in the old days . . ." Jesus! I thought. Even **then** she was talking that way! She must have had, like, one year when she was current.

At any rate, when Paul and Dick told me they wanted this old Jewish trouper, I knew precisely which influences and references to draw upon, and exactly how Irving would present himself: shriveled, irritable, smoking a huge cigar, and moving gingerly out onto the stage at a rate of about three inches a minute. Paul and Dick, not to mention Joe and John, seemed stunned by how fully I inhabited Irving right from the outset. I've been dragging him out onstage—very, very slowly—ever since.

IRVING COHEN

You know, in da old days, dey had a little ting dat dey used to call vaude-dih-ville. And it was a chance for da kids to learn their craft. Whether it was da guy with the dogs jumping through the hoop-type ting, or da Russian kid without the green card throwing cutlery at his common-law wife.

I just had a near-death experience and got to speak with God's kid, Jesu. And I'm here to announce, he says he's coming back to Earth—but first he's got to revisit da tree million planets in the universe where dey didn't nail him to a cross!

He said heaven is exactly like Earth, except up there, the outlet stores don't have so many fat people.

Then we played cards, but he's a horrible poker player. I can always tell when he's bluffing, because his hand starts to bleed.

Before dey sent me back, God, who has a much higher voice than you'd tink, confessed to me dat He's sorry about da terrorism, da hurricanes, and da earthquakes and war and famine and flood and disease . . . but den, He gets moody whenever He's trying to kick wheat and dairy.

I'll let you all in on a little show-business secret. Justin Timberlake? Third-generation octoroon.

In de old days, celebrity-type people didn't live in the world of delusion. Madonna thinks she's Jewish because she studies Kabbalah. Sorry, Madonna, you can't be Jewish if you look like every Jewish man's second wife.

If you're a singer, I don't need to hear you talk about your religion. If you're a model, I don't need to hear about your politics. And if you're a lesbian, I'm all ears.

I tink I hear a song coming on. Gimme a C! A bouncy C!

(Singing) Girl-on-girl action is my kind of ting
And if one is an Asian, my bell's gonna ring
From Gertrude Stein to Rosie O'D
Lovely lesbo loving is my cup of tea
Da da da
Dee dee dee
And whatever the hell else you wanna put in
    there

(Back to speaking) You tink you're in pain? Last night my doctor had to give me a prescription for urine softener.

Another showbiz secret: Pat Boone? Lubavitcher Jew.

I remember when Cole Porter got into dat horrible, horrible horse accident. I said, "Cole, you've always been luckier when somebody's riding you."

I don't want to say Cole was a sexual deviant, but it's da first time anybody fell from da bottom of a horse.

Den dere was the always-bickering and tight-with-a-buck conjoined Siamese twins Chang and Eng. Dey were living with me in a thirty-two-story walk-up right around da corner from da old Paramount. One night Chang, or maybe it was Eng, came into my room and said dey wanted to break up. I sat 'em both down and said, "Boys! Stick together. You need each other because you're money in da bank. You have dat special ting dat some performers work an entire lifetime trying to steal! And most importantly, you share a spleen."

Da problem with today's songwriters is, dey're just ripping off what I did years ago. "Send In da Clowns"? I wrote da same tune back in 1910 under the title "Send Up Some Towels."

Back in my day, minstrel shows were performed by white men in blackface. Not like today, with da black men in da blackface. I remembah telling Ben Vereen as he sat in his makeup chair, "Why gild da lily?"

MARTY WITHOUT PARENTS

O n the evening of September 26, 1962, two months after David's death, my mother and I were watching the very first episode of a new CBS sitcom entitled *The Beverly Hillbillies*. We were sitting in the den, Mom in her chair and me on the couch next to her. The show was all about rural hayseeds finding oil on their property, striking it rich, and moving to a mansion in Beverly Hills, but to me it was mainly about Donna Douglas, who played the daughter in the hayseed family, Elly May, unbelievably sexy in short shorts and a gingham shirt tied off at the midriff.

At one point Mom turned to me and said something along the lines of "It's so good to see Buddy Ebsen working again. Did you know that he was the original Tin Man in *The Wizard of Oz*, but they had to recast the part because his skin couldn't handle the silver paint?" Even at twelve I wondered, how could I not know of Buddy Ebsen? Today, I'd Google Buddy; then, not so easy. I was turning to respond to Mom when I saw, to my horror, that she was in the midst of a grand mal seizure—her arms and legs twitching, her eyes rolling back into her head.

I leaped out of my chair and screamed at the top of my lungs, prompting my father to come charging into the room. Neither of us knew what to do. Utter pandemonium and confusion. Michael came running down the stairs (Brian was away at boarding school), took one look at Mom convulsing, and bolted out the front door. Instinctively I took off after my big brother, and we two shoeless Short boys ran frantically down the street to fetch the neighborhood doctor. By the time we got back, with Dr. Ambrose Listen in tow, Mom's seizure had come to an end, and Dad had gently laid her out upon the living-room couch. She was hospitalized that night at Joseph Brant Hospital, and a whole new scary chapter in my young life had begun.

What I didn't know then was that Mom had breast cancer way back in 1957, and had undergone a mastectomy and radiation treatment. I don't know quite how this was kept from me, but in 1950s households it wasn't uncommon for illnesses, especially those with the word *cancer* in them, to be kept very hush-hush. Did the stress of her son's death compromise Mom's immune system, allowing the cancer to recur? It's hard for me to believe otherwise. We knew that at David's funeral, Mom had developed a nagging cough that hadn't gone away, but we had all assumed it was psychosomatic.

Mom came home from the hospital after a short stay, and she and Dad acted as if the seizure had been a onetime event, not for household discussion, especially among the children. However, by Christmastime I knew that something was terribly wrong. Mom was thinner, not her effervescent self, and clearly burdened by something she wasn't telling me.

When she eventually leveled with me, she did so, oddly, on the phone. I had called her from school about something banal, like a delayed volleyball practice, and asked her how her doctor's visit had gone. She quietly said, "Well, darling, they've found a small little lump in my breast and they think it might be cancer."

"Cancer!" I blurted out.

"Shhh, Marty," she said. "Don't say it so loudly. This will be our secret."

In 1962 a cancer diagnosis was still often seen as a death sentence. No one had yet come up with the term *survivor*—there was scarcely need for it. When I returned to my volleyball practice, I didn't know what else to do than impersonate myself acting like nothing was out of the ordinary. If I willed things to be normal, they would be. It was a little trick I'd use many more times in the years to come.

B y the spring of 1963, thanks to the many bar and bat mitzvahs I was privileged to attend in my predominantly Jewish 'hood, I was having the greatest social season of my life. Libby Stephens from down the street and I had started making out in her basement. My social life was fully abloom. But home was a different story. Mom had gone downhill quickly, her weight plummeting to 114 pounds, which was nothing, considering that she stood five-eight—that is to say, my height. All right, *fine*, half an inch taller than I would ever be. By April she was back in the hospital, and no one could say for sure when she was coming home.

My sister Nora, who had been nursing at Saint John's Health Center in Santa Monica, California, decided to take a leave of absence from her job to private-nurse our mother back to good health. When she arrived at the hospital in Hamilton, she was shocked—not by the withered condition of Mom, for which she was prepared, but by Mom's dire condition as outlined in her medical files. Dad, in complete denial about his wife's terminal prognosis, had told none of us kids, including Nora, the extent of her illness. When Nora read Mom's charts for the first time, she burst into tears and confronted the doctors. "Why haven't you told my father how ill my mother is?" she asked.

"We have," they told her. But my father had told no one. Not even the patient, his wife. Poor Daddy, keeping all of that horror to himself.

Nora was present when the doctors finally told Mom that she had no more than three months to live. After they left the room, Nora says, Mom turned to her and matter-of-factly said, "Well, that just can't happen. I have one more child to raise. Nora, pass the grapes, won't you, honey?"

That phrase—"Pass the grapes, won't you, honey?"—would be used many times in the years to come as a shorthand for Short-family determination in the face of adversity.

At that point, though, little Marty was still none the wiser as to the severity of Mom's illness. The evening of the day that Mom told Nora to pass the grapes, I could hear Nora and Dad and Michael talking heatedly in the kitchen. But when I walked in, they all clammed up.

What the hell is happening here? I thought. Even then, I was acutely sensitive to bad acting; I knew something was up. I immediately went upstairs to my bedroom, shut the door, and phoned Mom in the hospital. When she picked up, I asked her, "Mom, what's going on?"

"Well, darling," she said, in the sweetest voice possible, "I've been told that I'm not going to live my four score and twenty."

"What does that mean?"

"It means that I'm not going to live to be a little old lady."

"You're not?" I asked, aghast. "Then how long?"

"Oh, I don't know, baby. Perhaps just another ten years." Another lie, but in this case a welcome and probably well-advised one. I hung up the phone, and for the first time in my life, I felt true fear. I didn't tell anyone that I had talked to Mom. I was afraid that if I stated the cold facts out loud, then they would become real; if I kept mum, the bad news might go away. Oh, the things we learn from our fathers.

M om came home from the hospital shortly thereafter. Everyone besides little Marty—who'd been spared the awful truth by her white lie—expected her to be dead in a matter of weeks. Yet somehow she rallied. There was no stopping the "pass the grapes" chick.

Only a few days had passed before I heard Nora happily shout up the staircase, "Marty, Mom weighs one-sixteen!" She had entered a wholly unexpected remission that couldn't be explained, since she was not receiving any further medical treatment. By the summer of '63, she was to all appearances back to full health and seemed more radiant than ever. My father, who despised doctors because they never gave him the news he wanted to hear, ran into Mom's oncologist on a golf course. "Well," Dad said in his sarcastic Irish singsong when the man asked after my mother, "she's up to one-forty—and she's *dieting*."

"Well, Charlie," the guy said matter-of-factly, "that's what we occasionally experience in medicine: a pure miracle."

For the whole of my first two years in high school, Grades 9 and 10, Mom was in excellent health. But from Grade 11 to the start of Grade 13—in Ontario, in those days, secondary school lasted a year beyond the American norm—her health fluctuated. She would plummet and then pull through, plummet and pull through. Finally, though, the cancer metastasized throughout her body, and on February 14, 1968, a very sad Valentine's Day, she died at the age of fifty-five.

So many people have commented to me through the years about how sad I must have been to lose my mother at seventeen. And of course it was. But I was very aware, even as she lay dying, that I'd been the beneficiary of an extraordinary act of willpower: Mom's determination to hang in there on behalf of that "one more child to raise." To lose her at thirteen, before I was done cooking in the oven, would have been far more devastating than losing her at almost eighteen, by which time I was something approaching an adult. During those precious extra five years, Mom gave me her critical evaluations of *Martin Short Sings of Songs and Loves Ago.* Those were the years when our legendarily argumentative, preserved-for-posterity Christmas dinner happened, and when she organized our family trips to Toronto to see the great artists play the O'Keefe Centre: Harry Belafonte, Judy Garland, Richard Burton in *Camelot,* the London production of *Oliver!* on its way into New York.

And in 1965 Mom was the ringleader of the Short boys' first trip to New York City. Dad had to work, so she took Michael, Brian, and me, and we stayed at the Hotel Astor. The whole experience was magical and mind-boggling: the far-off fantasy world glimpsed in our television-watching made real. I was excited simply by the fact that we could see the giant, neon-lit Camel cigarettes billboard from our window, with puffs of smoke blowing out from the fedora'd Camel man's mouth.

The ostensible hook of our trip was the tail end of the 1964–65 World's Fair in Flushing Meadows, Queens. But Mom, ever the cultural omnivore, made sure we took in as many shows as possible. We saw Sammy Davis Jr. in the Broadway musical *Golden Boy.* Sammy broke up during the show, momentarily losing himself in laughter—something that apparently wasn't in the script—and he actually came out onstage after the final curtain call to rap with us all and make amends. Cigarette in hand, he said, "I feel like I'm cheatin' the audience, man. Let me just explain something to you cats, if I may, about what transpired . . ." (You can see how this experience *might* have had some bearing on some characters in my later television career.)

We also saw Phyllis Diller do her comedy show at the Royal Box cabaret at the Americana Hotel, and Buddy Hackett do his at the Latin Quarter. (God, how mid-century showbiz does that sentence sound?) Hackett's act was the filthiest thing I had ever heard: "How come Matt Dillon on *Gunsmoke* don't have no bulge in his pants? *No cock!*" My mother sank into her chair, mortified at what she was exposing her boys to. But overall, we had a joyous adventure. Mom was too spent to take us to Sardi's, the theater-world hangout whose walls were covered with caricatures of big stars, but Brian and I really wanted to go. Seemingly every so-phisticate on *What's My Line?* seemed to mention it: "Didn't I just see you earlier tonight at Sardi's?" So Michael stayed behind with Mom, and Brian and I went, taunting our mother and brother afterward that they'd missed out on seeing Ginger Rogers and Anthony Newley. (A complete lie, by the way.)

The point is, Mom made the most of her borrowed time with us, and gave so much of herself. Even during the making of the raunchy family comedy tapes that we Short kids recorded together on my reel-to-reel, ol' Owlie was always there. While she was a bright, sharp woman, she did not exactly have the comedic skills of Elaine May. As she was bombing when I interviewed her, you'd hear Michael in the background saying, "Jesus, *Pope Paul* could get more laughs." No one would laugh harder than Mom herself.

Her congenital happiness, her cheerful approach to life, in-formed the way our entire family operated. Our default mode was exuberant, noisy, argumentative merriment, not icy, silent, Ingmar

Bergman–movie despair. This carried us Shorts through—not only through David's death but also Mom's and, finally, in June of 1970, Dad's.

D ad's decline was more of a denouement than the final act of a three-part family tragedy. His health was already failing when Mom was in her end stages; he suffered a series of ministrokes that sometimes caused temporary paralysis in his left arm and forced him to spend the night in the same hospital as Mom, unbeknown to her, for observation. There were mornings when Michael and I, the last ones still living at home, would come down to breakfast, look across the big family table at each other, and simply laugh at the "What the hell is going on?" heaviness of it all. Humor was what kept us sane.

After Mom died, Dad was a deeply diminished man, no longer the force of nature who filled every room he entered. He was fifty-nine, but he seemed more like seventy-nine, slowed and afflicted by atherosclerosis, among other ailments. He became passive and dependent on me, the only child living in the house on Whitton Road after Brian got married and Michael got engaged. In 1969 Dad took a leave of absence from his job at Stelco. Though he told anyone who asked that the leave was temporary, it was pretty clear that he would never go back to work. That summer, after I completed my first year of college at McMaster University, he and I embarked on a cruise aboard the SS *Statendam* that departed from New York, crossed the Atlantic, and hugged the coasts of western and southern Europe. He wanted one last vacation but didn't have the stamina for hotels or restaurants, so we did it shipboard-style.

In this period I became, although the youngest, the de facto head of the Short household, administering the family's finances and being the primary contact for doctors, Dad's office, and so forth. There came a point where the bank called and asked if my father could come in and resubmit his signature; it had changed as his signing hand had weakened, and it no longer resembled the one they had on file. Rather than force Dad to schlep down to the bank in his state of infirmity, I mastered his "C. P. Short" signature and took over the books.

This played out as a natural evolution, not a power grab. I was simply doing what had to be done. My siblings didn't resent it, but they were amused and a bit baffled that little Marty, of all people, now controlled the family's purse strings. Michael got married on June 6, 1970, and I was the one who cut him the $5,000 check to cover some of the wedding costs. "You fuckin' little weasel!" Michael joked. "How the hell did you pull this off?"

Dad was well aware of Michael's pending wedding to his fiancée, Liz, but as the big day approached, it was clear that he was too ill to attend, tethered to the machines that kept him alive in the face of advanced renal failure. So Michael and I, his best man, decided to pay Dad a visit at the hospital in our formal morning coats—between ceremony and reception—to give him a little taste of the festive day.

When we arrived, though, Dad was unconscious, having fallen into a coma. We continued on to the reception hall where the wedding party was set to take place. Nora asked us what Dad thought of our suits. We told her about Dad's condition. And she, being the nurse, said, "Well, he's got no more than a day."

All the guests were there, waiting. We made the executive decision to carry on with the festivities. The party was, in customarily rousing Short-family fashion, a roaring, drunken success. At one point I got up and serenaded the crowd with "My Way" and "Ol' Man River," with Michael at the piano: unusual choices for someone my age, especially at a wedding, but then, they were among the few songs to which I knew the entire lyrics. The reception raged on and then continued into the wee hours at our house. We kicked out the last guest at 3:15 a.m. or so. And then, at 3:45, we got a call from the hospital: "We're so sorry, but your father is dead."

I was twenty years old, and parentless. I've ever since demarcated my life in those terms: Zero to Twenty, Marty with Parents; Twenty to the Present, Marty without Parents.

That said, I've always resisted people's efforts to make too much of the hard knocks I suffered in my early life. When I first became famous, and writers discovered that I'd lost my brother and parents at a young age, it became the obvious angle: *Aha! He went into comedy as a way to alleviate the pain of a tragedy-scarred childhood! Great stuff! It writes itself! Now let's go get lunch.*

It's an easy sell, that angle, but it isn't remotely accurate. My childhood was a blast. It was unequivocally happy. The difficult times were difficult, but they yielded important lessons—they gave me information about life that few guys my age had, as well as a certain fearlessness. John Candy once said to me after a particularly insane improv set at Second City (in which I'd played "Mumbo Boone," the illegitimate black son of the very, very white Pat Boone) that I had "balls of steel." Ah, but balls of steel are *earned*, I thought, not grown.

I'm also reminded of a conversation I had with Stephen Colbert shortly after he roasted President George W. Bush as the keynote speaker of the 2006 White House Correspondents Dinner. Stephen's routine had been audacious and divisive, mocking a sitting president as he sat literally inches away, and as an increasingly nervous audience withheld its laughter.

"Were you scared?" I asked him. And Stephen, who lost his

father and two brothers in a plane crash when he was a boy, said, "No. That day when I was a kid—*then* I was scared." When you're met with fire early, you develop a certain Teflon quality.

We buried Dad a few days after Michael's wedding. And so began the still-ongoing epoch that historians with time on their hands call Marty without Parents.

I n a Dickens novel, the Marty without Parents era would begin with me being cast into the street, shivering in alleyways, and falling into the clammy hands of an untrustworthy old benefactor with a name like Mr. Picklefrottage. But the truth is, I never had to worry about getting by; my father had seen to it that the family's finances were sound. I even had a legal guardian for a year, a man from the National Trust Company who I referred to as "Mr. Mooney," a reference to the uptight Gale Gordon character on *The Lucy Show*. I spent my first "orphan's relief cheque" from the Ontario government on a case of Beefeater's gin, restocking the family bar in Dad's honor. We surviving four Shorts were not rich, but our immediate concerns—most significantly in my case, college tuition and living expenses—were well taken care of.

Well-intentioned people tried to help me anyway. At Dad's funeral, the chairman of Stelco, Vincent Scully, put an arm around my shoulder and said, "Martin, I'm sure, with all that's been going on, you haven't been able to organize a summer job yet."

"No sir, not quite," I said, never in my life having desired a summer job.

"Well, consider it done, eh?" he said Canadianly.

So suddenly, despite an inheritance and no parents to tell me what to do, I found myself getting up every weekday at seven in the morning to put on a tie, drive to some godforsaken office building at the east end of Hamilton, and work in the stultifyingly boring clerical job that dear Mr. Scully had arranged for me. I'd been doing this for three days when my brother Michael, who'd come back to our house to hang out with me one night, asked, "Marty, why are you doing this job? You don't have to, you know. Who do you think you're impressing? If anything, I think less of you."

Michael the Wise made great sense. I quit the next day without a moment's guilt.

While Marty without Parents was not a phase I welcomed, I took to it easily enough. For a year I lived in our family home all by myself, with our non-live-in housekeeper, Phoebe Harris, still showing up for work every day. Mrs. Harris was a kindhearted woman who never quite understood the new parameters of things. One day she said, "Will you be home for dinner?" and I replied, "No, I don't think so, but I might bring some people back a little later." At two in morning I returned home with nine or ten beer-soaked college buddies, staggering through the front door to see a full china service for twelve set out on the dining room table. God bless confused little Phoebe.

In 1971 we Short kids finally divested ourselves of the family house on Whitton Road, and I moved into my own flat at 10 Mapleside Avenue in Hamilton, not too far from where I'd grown up. Having spent my first two years of college on a premed track, I switched my major to social work, which freed me up to do more plays. During my freshman year it had been a struggle to balance my required course load with even a mere chorus part in *How to Succeed in Business without Really Trying.* By sophomore year, given my interest in theater and growing lack of interest in medicine, I was barely squeaking by academically.

There came a point when I'd missed so many science classes, including the ones where I was supposed to dissect a cat and study its internal anatomy, that I stole a frozen cat from the McMaster biology department so I could catch up at home. While I was performing dead-cat surgery one night, in a bedroom that reeked of formaldehyde, my elderly and faithful cat Tiger, a holdover from my Hamilton boyhood, walked in on me and caught me in the act. I don't know which one of us shrieked louder. Poor Tiger. Not only was she seventeen and hanging on by a thread, but she was also roughly forty pounds overweight. The worms in her stool had Type 2 diabetes. She didn't need to see that.

Free at last my junior year from the premed grind, I became a member of the McMaster Shakespearean Players and the president of Proscenium, the club that mounted the school's musicals. Two friends I made through acting at McMaster were Dave Thomas, who was my year, and Eugene Levy, who was a little older. Dave, the son of a McMaster philosophy professor, was the most intellectual and comedically quick person I had met in my still-young life. He seemed to know every minuscule detail of the life and work of Bob Hope (and even then did the note-perfect Hope impersonation he'd later bring to *SCTV*), yet he was also fluent in the intricacies of Shakespeare's entire catalog of plays.

Eugene was a fellow Hamiltonian, the older brother of a fleeting high-school crush of mine, Barbie Levy. He was a talented and nimble actor, but what pulled me in was his dry, charismatic cool. And he was quite something to look at in those days, too, with a massive, horizontal-skewing frizz of Abbie Hoffman hair that he futilely tried to keep tucked into a little gray knit cap—or tuque, as we Canadians call them—plus a bristly handlebar mustache, uncommonly hirsute arms, and thick, Grouchoesque eyebrows that, he would later claim, "have their own agent." Eugene wasn't particularly crazy about me at first, finding me gratingly loud and cocky. The first time we met, I asked him what it was like to have the arms of an otter. He didn't quite know how to take that. Nor should he have. Years later, when I turned fifty, Eugene recalled his initial wariness of me in a birthday poem he wrote for the occasion:

What was it about this diminutive chap
That repelled me so strongly
That caused such a flap?
Was it arrogance? Well, yes . . .
And peppered with smug.
This vain little man
You could swat like a bug.

Yet we three—Eugene, Dave, and Marty—quickly developed a rapport, onstage and off. We did *The Odd Couple* together, with Eugene as Oscar, me as Felix, and Dave as Murray the Cop, and Shakespeare's *The Tempest*, with Eugene as Caliban, me as Trinculo, the fool, and Dave as Stephano. Even after Eugene graduated, I lured him back to campus to direct our McMaster production of an original musical comedy called *Benjy*, in which, of course, I starred.

Still, as my final semester of college began in 1972, I continued to regard show business as an unrealistic goal. As a teenager, I'd seen it as a fabulous fantasy world to which I enjoyed escaping. In university, it had become a fun hobby. To expect anything more seemed both naive and arrogant. I suppose if I'd grown up in Manhattan, with show business right down the street, I might have been more ambitious. But to me, making a living as an actor seemed as realistic as buying a summer home on Neptune.

My plan for the future was very set and clear, for order and clarity had always been the pillars I leaned upon in times of uncertainty. I was going to serve society and pursue a master's degree in social work. Like a lot of 1960s kids, I was very much influenced by the John F. Kennedy "Ask not what your country can do for you" ethos, and I sincerely thought I might end up in public policy or even electoral politics. (I'd have been every bit as entertaining a Canadian politician as Rob Ford, but without the "bad-tooth smell" that we know is there.)

However, Eugene wouldn't let me slip off that easily into bourgeois respectability. By that point he was living in Toronto and doing the struggling-actor thing, and he urged me to join him. More than anyone, it is Mr. Eugene Levy who deserves credit or blame for inflicting me upon the masses, for it was he who kept nudging, telling me that I had real talent and would be a fool not to give the performing life a stab. "Try it for a year," he said. "If it doesn't work out, you'll still be able to look in the mirror at fifty with no regrets."

IN WHICH I FIND JESUS

I n February of '72 I made a little contract with myself: I would give myself one year after graduation to try to get work as an actor. If by May of '73 things were going reasonably well, I would renew my showbiz contract for another year; if they weren't, I would go to the registrar's office at McMaster and beg them to hold a place for me in grad school that fall.

Counting on nothing much, I went ahead and had a student photographer take some head shots of me in different poses (Happy! Sad! Hopeful!), and I typed up a résumé fraught with lies. Then I headed into Toronto to hit every talent agency in the phone book. Most of them were uninterested, but one agency liked my "atypical" (often a kinder word for "homely") looks and sent me off on my first casting call, for a credit-card commercial—which, to my shock, I actually got. On March 17, 1972, I worked my first day as a paid actor, playing a talking credit card in a woman's purse. She opened it, and there I was, miniaturized, in this placard-like costume, sitting on top of an oversize compact mirror and explaining my virtues as a Chargex card, the Canadian version of Visa.

My second audition—and really my first as far as proper acting was concerned—was for the musical *Godspell*. Talk about a cattle call: every young person with show-business aspirations in Toronto, Eugene and I included, turned out for it, and for good reason. The show was a massive off-Broadway hit in New York, and its composer, Stephen Schwartz, just twenty-four years old at the time, was on hand to personally select the cast for the Toronto production.

Godspell is, essentially, the gospel according to Matthew as told by clowns—as *sung*, really, by hippie Jesus and his hippie apostles in a wildly original rock-opera musical idiom. Paul Shaffer has long said that in the early 1970s, the theatrical community was obsessed with two things: "full-frontal nudity and the Lord Jesus Christ." *Godspell*, mercifully, fit only the latter description.

Eugene and I made it through the initial round of auditions and got a callback for March 25, at the Masonic Temple in Toronto. That day was like an entire season of *American Idol* compressed into one twelve-hour slog. You'd go up in groups of sixteen, each sing a song, wait an hour, and then eight of you would get called back. Then your group of eight would be called upon to improvise a parable. And then maybe four of those eight would get called back. And then two of the four. And then one of the two. The air was thick with nerves, anticipation, and the sound of longhairs strumming guitars and humming Carole King and Neil Young songs. It was 1972, and not a soul in the room was over twenty-eight. I had never seen so much patchwork denim and rampant bralessness in my life.

There was one girl for whom I immediately felt a pang of pity. She was wearing loose-fitting bib overalls and had her wavy hair tied off in two goofy ponytails that stuck out from either side of her head. She launched into the Disney song "Zip-a-Dee-Doo-

Dah," which she sang like a demented child at the peak of a sugar rush. Oh, that poor thing, I thought, she's so desperate.

But when she finished, to my amazement, Schwartz and the show's director, Howie Sponseller, jumped out of their seats and broke into spirited applause for this skinny, daffy girl—as did pretty much everyone else in the hall. This was my first sighting of Gilda Radner. Gilda later explained to me that she had actually seen the off-Broadway production of *Godspell* in New York, and therefore she knew exactly what Schwartz was looking for: a certain looseness, an emphatic lack of Broadway polish. But believe me, advance knowledge alone did not account for the way this talented girl took control of that room.

Earlier in the day, two girls performed their audition pieces not with the house accompanist but with a piano player who had tagged along with them: a bopping Elton John kind of guy with oversize goggle-like eyeglasses and a ferocious, rockin' approach to his instrument. This was the young Paul Shaffer, though, truth be told, Paul never seemed young, just as he doesn't now seem "old."

Paul was not auditioning for the show himself. He was there to accompany his girlfriend, Ginny, and another of his friends, Avril. As I'd soon learn, Paul was, like me, on a one-year contract to make it in show business. Unlike me, however, his contract was with an outside entity: his father, an eminent attorney named Bernie Shaffer. If the music thing didn't work out soon, Bernie was going to insist that Paul follow in his footsteps and go to law school. At the time of the *Godspell* auditions, Paul was playing a Hammond B-3 organ in the house band of a Toronto strip club, and had mere weeks left on his contract with Shaffer senior.

After Paul's two female companions finished their auditions, Stephen Schwartz summoned him to the edge of the stage.

Schwartz expressed to Paul how frustrated he was with the regular accompanist's dainty, traditional piano playing, and how much he admired Paul's pounding, rockier style. Would Paul, Schwartz wondered, be willing to take over for the rest of the auditions? Though he didn't know how to read music, Paul said yes. He has the entire catalog of popular music in that brilliant head of his, and he proved himself able to play anything asked of him that day, including Gilda's "Zip-a-Dee-Doo-Dah."

M y fashion concession to the times was a jive-turkey newsboy cap—on John Lennon or Sly Stone, it would have been called a pimp cap—that I wore slightly askew over my now-shaggy hair. But my audition piece was pure throwback: a variation of Frank Sinatra's version of "My Funny Valentine" that I put over with just enough in-on-the-joke self-awareness to connect with the counterculturists who surrounded me.

Nearly everyone else auditioned with a song from the rock or folk idioms, and one, a tall guy with the golden ringlets of Art Garfunkel and the face of Michelangelo's *David*, did an actual *Godspell* song, "Save the People," which left the rest of us envious of both his cunning and his singing talent. This was Victor Garber. I would later learn that, though he was my age, Victor had already had a 1960s career as part of a Mamas and Papas–like folk-pop group called the Sugar Shoppe, which had made a couple of appearances on *The Ed Sullivan Show*. Victor had subsequently toured as part of a revue called Canadian Rock Theatre, which was basically a bunch of young singers covering songs from *Godspell* and *Jesus Christ Superstar*—a symptom of the Jesus mania that Paul had diagnosed.

Victor, his quavery voice gentle yet strong, like the fluttering of butterfly wings, delivered his song beautifully, to the palpable awe of everyone in the hall. Jesus had come to the Masonic Temple. Poor Eugene had to go next, singing "Aquarius" from the aptly named (given the singer in question) *Hair.* To this day, he shudders at the thought of having had to follow Victor.

When it was all over that day, Schwartz picked ten people to form the original Toronto cast of *Godspell.* Victor was a shoo-in as Jesus. Gilda, despite my initial misunderstanding of her approach, was an obvious yes also. As for Paul, Schwartz gave him the break of his life by offering him a job as *Godspell*'s bandleader and musical director. The Canadian bar's loss was showbiz's gain. Honestly, can you imagine how different David Letterman's show would be if it was just Dave sitting there alone, unable to make all those asides to the guy at the keyboard who looks like the love child of Howie Mandel and James Carville?

Eugene and I made it, too. We couldn't believe it—close friends, getting our first big break, *together.* He was twenty-five, and I would turn twenty-two the next day. We went to the back of the Masonic Temple, where there was a pay phone, and took turns calling everyone we knew to share our happy news. I hadn't even graduated from college yet, and already I was exceeding the terms of my self-imposed contract.

Before rehearsals began, Howie Sponseller, our director, threw a cast party so that we apostles of Christ could better get to know one another. It was just a gathering of callow theater geeks drinking jug wine, but to me it was the most amazing party I had ever been to. Why? Because I was in a room where *everyone was making a living by being in show business.* That fact floored me. I didn't want the evening to end. Avril Chown, one of the girls Paul had accompanied, was one of the chosen (though his girlfriend, Ginny, wasn't) and was sexy as hell. Jayne Eastwood, another woman in the cast, had a quick wit that I instantly took to. Gerry Salsberg, who had been cast in the role of Judas, was sweet yet intense, a perfect foil to the chipper Paul and the chipperer me. By the end of the evening, it was like we'd all fast-forwarded two years in our relationships and become old friends.

The life of the party, however, was Gilda, who jovially worked the room, making conversation with everyone. She did this, however, while very conspicuously holding the tip of her right index finger to her forehead, even as she was walking around and maneuvering between people. When I asked Gilda why she was doing this, she lifted her finger for a moment to reveal a pimple that she didn't want anyone else to see. I found this hilarious and charming. Gilda was a rare event, hard to explain if not experienced in person. I had never met a woman so comfortable in her strangeness.

With one possible exception: Andrea Martin. Andrea wasn't at that first party, because she didn't make the cut at the March 25 auditions. I saw her get the bad news that day. Her face fell almost as if in slow motion, in so nakedly expressive a fashion that I had to suppress a laugh; there was nothing funny about her not getting the job, yet there was something inherently funny about Andrea. Then, a few weeks later, a woman who *had* made the cast dropped out for personal reasons, creating an opening. Eugene lobbied Stephen Schwartz and Howie Sponseller to hire Andrea.

A petite Armenian-American force of nature from the great state of Maine, Andrea had briefly dated Eugene, and the two of them had recently shot a low-budget horror-film spoof called *Cannibal Girls*, whose director was another guy who had been a few years ahead of me at McMaster, Ivan Reitman. Howie threw another party, and Eugene and I brought Andrea. She turned it on at the party and just *killed*, winning everyone over with the same manic energy that she later brought to *SCTV*. She was in. I've known a lot of funny people in my life, but no one matches Andrea for sheer in-person, on-contact funniness.

Throughout the months of April and May, I commuted from Hamilton to Toronto to rehearse between classes and finals. Rehearsals were an exercise in collective euphoria, because, as Paul likes to say, we were all so happy that we didn't have to go to school anymore, and we were free of that soul-crushing burden of classes, homework, and thinking about getting "real" jobs. We were working on this hip show, a job that everyone in town wanted but didn't have, and on top of all that, we were getting *paid*.

By the end of May, having finished my last exam, I bade the city of Hamilton good-bye, never to live there again. Eugene and I, along with our friend John Yaffe, rented a house at 1063 Avenue Road in Toronto. (Tom Hanks, by the way, thinks the name Avenue Road is hilarious and acutely Canadian. He brings it up whenever the subject arises: "Hey, Marty, when you were a kid in Toronto, did you ever wish you lived on Street Lane instead of Avenue Road?")

Godspell opened at the Royal Alexandra Theatre on June 1, 1972. Our good feelings about what we had were ratified by the audience, whose members, dressed up in black tie for opening night, bought in from the moment the curtain went up, laughing and applauding beyond our wildest expectations. My big song was "We Beseech Thee," what I would learn is known in theater as the eleven o'clock number—a showstopper that occurs late in the second act. This one was a vamping, up-tempo gospel-style song that, in our version, built and built and built to a rousing finish.

It unfolded so perfectly, with my voice gliding so effortlessly along, that I momentarily levitated outside myself—I was up in the rafters, watching me singing down there, enjoying the show.

The reviews in the papers the next day were ecstatic. Most of the writers' attention focused on Victor, but I was delighted that my hometown paper, the *Hamilton Spectator*, singled *me* out. The reviewer noted, perceptively, that at the conclusion of "We Beseech Thee," my face had "the look film directors try to capture in movies about young stars breaking into the theatre." He also wrote that Eugene looked "like a well-fed Frank Zappa." Again, very perceptive.

Your first major work experience tends to be formative, something you remember vividly for the rest of your life. That's what *Godspell* was for our cast. To this day, Paul, Eugene, Dave Thomas (who joined the cast later in the run), and I can, and on occasion will, run through the show's score in its entirety. Sometimes Paul will phone me up in L.A. from New York, and, without so much as a hello, say something like, "Why would Avril open that number that way? It's such an odd choice"—as if we were still living in 1972. This is a continuation of the obsessiveness with which we lived and breathed the show, all of us involved. Our cast operated as a sort of gestalt—all for one and one for all, more like the Beatles than like Elvis. When we weren't performing together, we were hanging out together, oftentimes at the Short-Levy digs on Avenue Road, more frequently still at a theater-folk bar called the Pilot. John Candy, with whom many of us fell into friendship at that time, joked that he hated hanging around with the *Godspell* people because all they ever talked about was fucking *Godspell*.

In late June, a few weeks after we opened, there was a birthday party for Gilda at Global Village, a little avant-garde theater where we rehearsed *Godspell* and where Gilda had held a part-time job selling tickets. There was this bizarre couple there, the same age as the rest of us, who spent the entire evening in character as Gilda's Jewish parents from Detroit. At no point in the night did they ever break character. I eventually found out that they were not in fact a couple, but friends of Gilda's and a working comedy team to boot. Their names were Dan Aykroyd and Valri Bromfield.

In the weeks to come I started hanging out with them, and with Gilda, as much as possible. I would drive Gilda's white Volvo around town with her in the front passenger seat and Danny and Valri in the back—deliberately getting lost en route to wherever we were going because I didn't want my time with these inspired freak-geniuses to end. We would be at a stop sign, and while an elderly couple slowly, deliberately crossed the street, Danny and Valri would *become* the couple, bantering back and forth.

VALRI: I'm telling you, I'm lactating! I'm moist where I shouldn't be, and it's not from drooling.
DAN: Dearest, you're eighty-seven. It seems so unlikely.
VALRI: You're calling me a bloody liar?
DAN: Sweetie, not so much as calling you eighty-seven.
VALRI: Oh, piss up a rope.

I was also becoming close with Andrea, whose ritual of initiation for new friends was to whip out her breasts in a public place and say, "You've seen these, haven't you?" Andrea had an original, manic comic energy that rivaled Gilda's. Preshow at the Royal Alexandra Theatre, Andrea would do things like walk past us with her hair in curlers, belch loudly, and then yell at herself, "You *whore!*" in this coarse, guttural voice, as if channeling some babushka'd Transcaucasus ancestor. Gilda would turn to me, laughing so hard and shaking her head, and say, "What the—who does that?"

But Gilda was the one I fell for. She wasn't a conventional beauty, with her skinny build and untamed brown hair, but her charisma made her irresistibly sexy. Above all, she was *funny.* To me, there is nothing more seductive than a funny woman. Her every eccentricity turned me on. The zany, ray-of-light loopiness of her smile. The giant bows she put in her hair. That guileless, children's-theater-lady speaking voice. The way she walked into a room and filled it, with both her big personality and the bags she encumbered herself with. Gilda typically carried two bags, ones that she'd knitted herself. The bigger one contained her knitting materials and personal effects. The smaller one, more like a little pouch, contained her bingo chips and cards. Gilda loved her bingo and indulged in it with the zeal of a retiree, bundling off to bingo halls whenever she could to get her fix, sitting among all the old folks and smoking her Virginia Slims cigarettes. Her great pride was that she could keep eighteen bingo cards going at once, her mind agile enough to maintain her grids no matter how fast the caller barked out the numbers. It's like she had a retro-hipster pastime before retro or hipsters existed.

When we started on *Godspell* in June, I still had a Hamilton girlfriend, and Gilda was dating a guy named Marcus O'Hara. But by September, Gilda and I were more or less living together full-time at her place on 77 Pears Avenue, and I was madly in love. First time living outside of Hamilton, first job, first love—*heady* is a clichéd word, but it accurately describes the whirlwind of *God-spell's* early months. Speaking of which, the show was originally only supposed to be in Toronto for three months before going on tour, with stops in Boston and Chicago, but it kept doing such great business that it never left the city. As Gilda and I were getting serious, *Godspell* relocated from the Royal Alex to the Playhouse Theatre, where it ran until August 1973, for an ultimate total of 488 performances. ("Playhouse Theater," now that I think of it, is almost as ridiculous as "Avenue Road.")

So Gilda and I basically put down roots and played house. When we weren't getting conjugal on Pears Street, we were hanging around with Eugene and Paul at the bachelor apartment on Avenue Road, partying and laughing, impervious to fatigue because we were all so young. I treasure a tape I have of the four of us, plus Michael Shepley, *Godspell*'s company manager, in conversation at three a.m. some night that autumn. My kids like to listen to the tape because they love Paul, and it's perhaps the earliest known recording of that off-camera laugh that generations of *Letterman* watchers would come to know, the signature Shaffer "*Haaaah*-hah!" The laughter began that night because of how I reacted to the sound of Eugene's voice, which was shredded from performing eight shows a week.

MICHAEL: Should we have the microphone, like, on the table?

EUGENE (*rasping*): Can't do that, the sound is terrible. It has to be good.

MARTY (*in hoarse Louis Armstrong voice*): Gotta be as crisp as Eugene's voice. "Sound is terrible!"

PAUL (*hysterically*): Haaaah! Ha-ha-*haaaa*-ha! *Haah*-haah-haah-ha! That is so-o funny . . .

MARTY: Paul, why is it funny?

PAUL (*helplessly, in tears*): Oooh-hooo . . .

(Everyone now laughing at Paul's laughter.)

GILDA (*mimicking Paul*): Oooh-hooo!

PAUL: For a number of reasons!

MARTY: For a number! Of reasons!

PAUL (*slurring a bit*): There'zh the obvious reason. In addition to the reason that he sounded so terrible. There's also the reason that you sounded like Louis Armstrong when you came in.

GILDA (*still mimicking Paul*): Oooh-hooo!

PAUL: And the *choice of words*! "Gotta be as crisp."

GILDA: "Gotta be as crisp." It's true. 'Cause "crisp" is an unused word.

PAUL: But gee, it's going to be fun listening back to this, isn't it?

The beauty of listening back to that laughter is that it could just as easily take place today between Paul, Eugene, and me. The poignancy of it is that Gilda is no longer around to take part in it with us. She was spectacular, and I was smitten with her. I am told by Catherine O'Hara that the first time Catherine and I met—for she is the little sister of Gilda's ex, Marcus O'Hara, and Gilda was the type of girl who stayed friends with her ex's kid sister and took her out to dinner—I barely cast a glance in Catherine's direction. She was a mere girl of eighteen, as was her school friend who tagged along, Robin Duke. (Robin would later, like me, perform in the casts of both *SCTV* and *Saturday Night Live*.) Catherine and Robin both say that I was utterly indifferent to them in the restaurant that night. But to Gilda, they say, I was a gallant gentleman, lavishing upon her all of my attention—mooning over this enchanting, funny girl.

G*odspell* was a springboard, giving us all new work opportunities even as the show's run continued. Victor was plucked from the cast almost immediately, summoned by Columbia Pictures to star as Jesus in the movie version of the show. He was replaced by a young actor named Don Scardino, who was almost as angelic looking, and years later would distinguish himself as a film and TV director and one of the executive producers of *30 Rock*. After Don's departure, it was finally Eugene's turn to play Jesus, though Eugene's hairiness almost derailed that plan. In our production, Jesus made his entrance wearing only boxer shorts. The producers were concerned that Eugene's woolly Ashkenazi Jewish chest pelt might frighten the small children who came to matinees, so he was asked to shave or submit to a waxing. Eugene refused. Career disaster was averted when Eugene and the producers agreed to a compromise: Christ would appear before his apostles wearing a tank top. And lo, it came to pass.

Late in '72, I landed a gig hosting a CBC teen variety program (in my off hours from the show) called *Right On*. It aired live at 5:00 p.m., and the show's announcer was a rising Canadian personality named Alex Trebek. Though *Right On* lasted only a few months, it wasn't lost on me how great and surreal it was for me to be hosting my own live TV show with an actual band, just seven years after I had play-acted pretty much the same scenario in my attic.

And then, when word got out that Chicago's Second City improv theater was starting up a sister company in Toronto—in June 1973, just as *Godspell* was winding down—the better part of my social circle banged down the door to enlist. For reasons I've already detailed, I elected not to audition, but Gilda, Eugene, Jayne Eastwood, and Gerry Salsberg from our show did, as did Danny Aykroyd and Valri Bromfield. And they all got in! Second City Toronto's first cast was supplemented by two veterans of the Chicago operation, Joe Flaherty and Brian Doyle-Murray. Meanwhile, John Candy moved to Chicago to take a slot in Second City's cast there, alongside Brian's brother Bill Murray. John came back to Second City Toronto the following year, by which time Catherine O'Hara was also a full-fledged member, soon to be joined by Andrea Martin and Dave Thomas.

Does it seem like I'm blatantly name-dropping here? Yes, it does—and with good reason. Toronto at that time had a Paris-in-the-'20s thing going on. Not in the sense that anyone was sitting around and self-consciously declaring, "Take a good look around, my friends, for someday all of us shall be prominent players in the captivating business of show!" No, it was simply that we were all young and like-mindedly creative, in the same place at the same time. I don't think of it as a magical "What did they put in the drinking water?" scenario. Rather, I think that so many of us went on to bigger things because we were there for each other early: friends and friendly competitors, pushing ourselves to heights we never would have reached individually.

And remember, at the time, none of us had any idea that we were anything more than very fortunate, very happy young performers. No one was sitting around pointing a finger and saying, "Hey, you're Gilda Radner! You're Eugene Levy! And you're Dan Aykroyd!" We were in Toronto, you see, so we still thought of ourselves as minor-league compared to the *real* actors who plied their trade in New York and Hollywood.

Paul Shaffer was the first of our circle to leave Toronto more or less for good, moving to New York City in '74, when Stephen Schwartz beckoned him to be the piano player for a musical that Schwartz had opening on Broadway, *The Magic Show* (whose star was yet another McMaster alum of my generation, the magician Doug Henning). Gilda and I were so thrilled for Paul, and one day, sitting in the kitchen at her place, we were excited to receive a phone call from him. "Paul," Gilda asked in wonderment, as if he had bounded over the rainbow and into the land of Oz, "what are New York actors like?" As we cradled the receiver together, Paul, in his kindly Paul voice, said, "Well, maybe it's just 'cause you're my friends, but I think you guys are just as talented."

Gilda turned to me and said, "Aww, isn't that so sweet?" And then, jokingly, to Paul: "Liar!" Because we found it daunting, the very idea: *New York actors*. In a year and a half Gilda would be a household name, starring in *Saturday Night Live*. But on that day, we couldn't fathom that New York would ever want anything to do with us.

NANCY'S BOY

G ilda and I were a couple, on and off, for almost two years. The first few months were bliss, but overall we had a tempestuous relationship, with multiple breakups and rapprochements. Basically, our happiness kept running aground upon the same argument, which we had over and over again. Gilda, for all her exuberance, had lots of dark moods and neuroses. I'm not being indiscreet here, because she acknowledged these issues in her own memoir, *It's Always Something*, including her struggle with eating disorders. I could never fathom, in our time together, how a woman of her talent and advantages could get so down on herself. It hadn't been that long since I'd buried my mother, who died before her time and was desperate to stay happy and keep living—who clung to the slightest bit of positive medical news as a cause for celebration.

So for Gilda not to appreciate her good fortune—with her burgeoning career, her well-to-do Detroit upbringing, and her natural gift for making every guy have a crush on her and every girl want to be her best friend—well, it was just beyond what my inexperienced young man's brain could comprehend.

And that was part of the problem. I was twenty-two years old to Gilda's twenty-six when we started dating—a significant difference in age at that point in life. I was unworldly and immature, simply too unsophisticated psychologically to understand that a person could have all the blessings that Gilda had and still be burdened with unhappiness and an enormous need for people to demonstrate their love for her, all the time. I had a joke on this subject that amused even Gilda: that one time I'd walked into her kitchen and found her on the phone, saying, "Okay . . . So all right . . . Love you! . . . See ya! . . . Bye! . . . Love you! . . . Call me!" After she'd hung up, I asked her, "Who was that?" and Gilda said, "Wrong number."

Gilda channeled some of her need for love into her pets, which were suitably eccentric. She had a three-legged cat named Muffin and a morbidly obese Yorkie named Snuffy. I was saddled with the responsibility of dog-sitting the Snuff Machine, as the pooch was alternately known, when Gilda traveled home to Detroit to visit her mother, Henrietta. While she was gone, I decided to take Snuffy to visit my brother Brian and his wife, Gwen, in Ancaster, a little village near Hamilton. I checked in with Gilda from their house, watching as my three-year-old niece fed the podgy little dog slice after slice of Kraft American cheese. "How's my Snuffy girl doing?" Gilda asked. Suddenly I noticed that the dog was no longer moving. Right at that moment, Gilda said, "Remember, Snuffy's allergic to dairy, so make sure she doesn't get any." I made my excuses and got off the phone. I raced over to Snuffy and collected her near-lifeless body . . . just in time for her to explode all over me, from every orifice.

By the time I picked up Gilda from the train the next day (she was afraid of flying), I had already rushed Snuffy, whose coat had resembled an aerial view of Dresden, to Anita Chapman's Dog

Boutique, where they scrubbed and shampooed her to the best of their ability and adorned her with little Rose Marie hair bows. Gilda eyed the woozy dog suspiciously.

"Why does she look so out of it?" she asked.

"She missed you, baby," I responded.

A fter *Godspell* had been running for several months, the cast started to turn over. Victor Garber was the first to leave, having been tapped to do the *Godspell* movie. A few months later Jayne Eastwood left, and Andrea Martin shifted into Jayne's role. Taking Andrea's old part—as Robin, the girl who sings "Day by Day," the one *Godspell* song that every human being knows—was a young woman named Mary Ann McDonald. And when Eugene finally graduated to playing Jesus, our McMaster friend Dave Thomas came in to take Eugene's old role, as an apostle named Herb.

There was turnover in the understudy ranks, too. One day all of us—all of us guys, anyway—were struck by the new girl who'd been brought in to cover Gilda and Avril Chown. Her name was Nancy Dolman. She was forbiddingly attractive, with Joni Mitchell cheekbones and long, long, straight blond hair that fell halfway down her back and swooshed in a sexy way behind her as she walked. As Ed Grimley would say, "She made your heart beat like a little distant jungle drum."

Victor, though he was no longer in the show, had already worked with Nancy: the two of them had performed together in that Jesus-rock revue he'd been in, Canadian Rock Theatre, the vehicle through which he learned the *Godspell* songs ahead of the rest of us. Nancy, much to her parents' horror, had dropped out of her college, Western University in London, Ontario, at the end of her freshman year to join Canadian Rock Theatre. This was just in time for their U.S. tour, which turned out to be a semi-traumatic experience. The producers hadn't taken the trouble to secure the rights to do the songs they were doing, and by the time the revue got to Las Vegas, the music publishers had caught wind of it and issued an injunction forbidding Canadian Rock Theatre from performing further. While in limbo in Vegas, the cast was invited to attend some random hip groovy person's random hip groovy party. Another disaster: Nancy and Victor spent the evening clinging to each other in terror in a hot tub, riding out a bad trip after someone surreptitiously slipped them acid.

Another person who knew of Nancy pre-*Godspell* was Eugene Levy's new girlfriend, Deb Divine, who would become (and remains) his wife. Deb and Nancy grew up on the same street in Toronto and went to the same high school, York Mills Collegiate Institute. Deb, two years younger, had looked up to Nancy as York Mills's golden girl, a blond beauty who, in her mind, was always speeding off with some cute jock guy in a convertible. Nancy was industrious, too. Unbowed by the unraveling of Canadian Rock Theatre, she used her remaining time in the States to raid its thrift shops for secondhand clothes, which she smuggled across the border and sold at a handsome profit at a carefully curated vintage-clothing shop she opened in Toronto with the very much of-its-era name Reflections of Ambrosine.

I knew none of this at the time. All I knew was that Nancy, per her job as the understudy, came to the theater every night, signed in, checked in to see if anyone was sick or otherwise indisposed, and, if not, went on her way. We guys would stand there watching this ritual with our mouths agape, doing everything short of muttering "Humina, humina!" This chick, lissome in her antique capes and filmy dresses, was way out of my league.

One day, though, Paul invited me to join him and Mary Ann McDonald, who was by then his girlfriend, for a night out at a jazz club. Mary Ann and Nancy were friends, so Nancy was coming along too. Gilda and I had just been through one of our "Well, then fuck *you*, idiot!" fights earlier in the day, and as I had nothing better to do, I agreed to come along. That's all I thought of it as: me going to the jazz club with Paul and Mary Ann, who happened to be bringing her friend Nancy.

But at our table for four, it became a different situation: my unconsidered "Jesus, she's beautiful" take on Nancy evolved into genuine feelings for her. It was that thing where you finally talk to the pretty girl and discover that she's not only pretty but also funny, smart, and simpatico. The chemistry is right, and the hang is great. And as we discovered, we had people and places in common. Nancy's godfather had worked for my father at the steel company! Her mother was a native Hamiltonian, and she herself had been born in Hamilton! What were the odds?

Still, the night ended innocently. I went home to Avenue Road, and Nancy had a boyfriend at the time named Paul Ryan. (Not the congressman from Wisconsin and 2012 Republican vice presidential candidate; his then three-year-old ass I would have kicked easily.) I was barely in my apartment two minutes when the phone rang. It was Gilda, somehow all-seeing and all-knowing.

"You've been with someone!" she said.

"I've been with no one!" I protested.

"Tell me the truth, Marty!"

"I'll tell you exactly what happened: Paul and Mary Ann went to the jazz club with Nancy Dolman, and I happened to go along. That's all that happened. I swear to you."

That turned into a huge headline in *Godspell* land. Gilda, pissed off and vengeful, the next day arranged for all the women in the cast to cut Nancy dead when she walked in. For a few days Nancy was a pariah. Then, as if it had been nothing, the hard feelings evaporated and everything was okay again. Gilda and I resumed being a couple. A while later, I heard, through the high-school-style grapevine endemic to all theater companies, that Nancy had admitted to someone that she had a crush on me. An ego boost, to be sure. But still, I was with Gilda, and Nancy was with non-congressman Paul Ryan.

Gilda and I split for good in July 1974, eleven months after *Godspell* closed. We didn't do so with the foreordained finality that the words above suggest; it's just how things panned out. Not a few days after what, at that time, was simply our latest breakup, I was drinking at my usual haunt, the Pilot bar, when Nancy happened to walk in. Yes, this girl can wear a top, was all I could think at that moment. We began talking. I mentioned to her that I was looking for a new place to live. She told me that there were some nice flats available in the Beaches, her neighborhood, in east-central Toronto. Also, she had just broken up with her boyfriend.

We arranged to spend the next day, a Sunday, looking at apartments together, followed by a round of tennis, since we both played. Before Nancy left the Pilot that night, I said to her lasciviously— I don't know what possessed me—"Have you ever tried a comedian before?" Which was either very sexy or very creepy, depending on your opinion of me. She just stared at me, betraying no emotion, and said, "I hope you have a racket. I'm pretty good."

Our tennis date was such fun that I invited Nancy to come see me that night in the show I was doing, *What's a Nice Country Like You Doing in a State Like This?* "I'm Haldeman / I'm Ehrlichman / I'm Klein / Ze three sour Krauts from ze Rhine!"

You know, speaking from experience, I can tell you that there's no aphrodisiac more potent than Watergate-themed cabaret music. Well, in my case, anyway. By night's end, Nancy and I were making out while pressed against my Volkswagen convertible in the theater's parking lot. Boy, were we both easy.

Since I am a decent sort of chap, I wasted no time in asking Nancy out again, and brought her to a cast party the very next night. At the party we were holding hands. Andrea Martin, who was in the show with me, cornered me for a moment and asked, with typical Andrea forthrightness, "When did you start having sex with Nancy Dolman?"

I told her that I had not, in fact, started having sex with Nancy Dolman.

But Andrea was adamant. "You two have the intimacy of a couple," she said. "I can see it! You're having sex!" We truly weren't, but hey, it wasn't the worst idea.

That very night, after the party ended, I took Nancy to the Hyatt Hotel in Toronto. Bear in mind that it was summer. I was wearing cutoff shorts and a T-shirt. Nancy was wearing very short shorts and a halter top. She was twenty-two years old, and I was twenty-four—though I looked about fourteen. We had no luggage. I walked up to the clerk at the front desk and announced, "My wife and I would like a room, please!" He looked us up and down, burst into laughter, and then very kindly gave us a key.

We opened the door to our room, pulses racing, pheromones pumping. Nancy teasingly told me, "I'll be right back," and went into the bathroom to powder her nose. Now, this was the first time I had ever been in a hotel room that featured movies on demand. As I waited for Nancy, sitting on the bed, I turned on the TV and saw that Mel Brooks's *Blazing Saddles* was available for viewing. I couldn't believe it. How could such things exist? So I ordered the movie and started watching.

Nancy emerged from the bathroom, astonishingly, beauteously naked. She saw the movie playing, and her face momentarily fell. "This is a joke, right?" she said. "Are you serious?"

"I'm gonna turn it off! I can't tell you how quickly I'm gonna turn this off!" I said, desperately waving my hands in the international I-mean-no-harm gesture.

"Oh, yes, Marty," she said. "I think you're going to turn the movie off."

N ancy and I were a couple from that day forward: July 8, 1974. We wouldn't marry for another six years—it was the '70s, *maaan*—but we were instantly in love. On paper, she was the classic rebound girl, the woman into whose arms one conveniently falls after an epic heartbreak. But the miracle of Nan and me is that once we started, we never stopped; we remained forever devoted to each other. There was never a blow-up I'm-packing-my-bags! moment. Whatever did come up, we dealt with.

In the early days, I admit, there was a fair amount to deal with emotionally, mostly on my end. Falling deeply in love with Nan didn't instantly obliterate what I'd felt for Gilda, which had been no mere schoolboy crush—it too had been love, real love.

Gilda always had her ear to the ground, and she called me as soon as word got out about Nancy and me. "You're going out with Nancy Dolman?" she asked, not accusingly, but shocked. "But, but . . . we're supposed to get back together again! That's our pattern! We weren't done." But we were done.

For a year or so I had some difficulty juggling the roles of good boyfriend and good ex-boyfriend. By the end of 1974 Gilda was living in the States again, part of the touring stage show that *National Lampoon* magazine had put together. Nancy and I took a trip to New York to check out the show, and we were there for opening night. The director was Ivan Reitman, and the cast was extraordinary: Gilda, John Belushi, Bill Murray, Brian Doyle-Murray, Harold Ramis, and Joe Flaherty.

In one sketch, Gilda played Jacqueline Onassis as a panelist on a *What's My Line?*–style show. The host, the John Charles Daly figure, fired a starting gun to begin the games. At this, Gilda, in her Jackie suit, jumped out of her chair and started crawling over the other panelists toward the back of the studio. Bill Murray, as Daly, would say, "No, no, Mrs. Kennedy! We're just starting the game!" In another sketch, Gilda played a blind woman on a date with John Belushi. As John kept jumping Gilda's character, forcing himself upon her, he assured her that it was her dog trying to "jazz" her, not him. It played better than it sounds—the kind of classic sick humor for which the *Lampoon* was notorious.

Because we knew nearly everyone in the cast, Nancy and I were invited to the after-party, which was something of a reunion-slash-fusion of all the people who had ever met through *Godspell*, Second City Toronto, and Second City Chicago. Ivan Reitman still talks about that party as one of the greatest nights of his life, a sort of here-we-are moment for a generation of comedy people on the cusp of fame. Paul Shaffer was playing piano, and as was the wont of our group, each of us got up to do a little performance.

When it was my turn, I got up and sang "You and I," the song I'd muffed in front of Tony Bennett on Canadian TV. This time I nailed it, hitting all the notes just as Stevie Wonder had intended them to be sung. My peers greeted me with rousing applause. Then I made a dumb mistake. Nancy was watching from stage left, and Gilda from stage right. When I stepped down to be congratulated, with all these smiling, familiar faces before me, I went . . . stage right, to Gilda. More or less out of force of habit, but still. Nancy was not thrilled with me for a couple of days thereafter, and wondered out loud whether we had a future. I had little to say. I'd already inadvertently revealed too much.

think it's true of most relationships that the first year, you have the best sex, but there is some confusion and unsettledness about intention: *Does this person really love me the way he says he does? Is this for real?* Nan and I were no different. Our first year, we had a lot of fights over things like me spending too much time at parties talking to other people and not paying enough attention to her. I was accustomed to Gilda, who was naturally outgoing and schmoozy, and who ran in the same circles as me; I never felt the need to check in on her in social situations, since she took control of every room she was in through sheer force of personality. Nancy, not an extrovert, expected more of me, and it took a few chilly nights where I got the silent treatment until I figured out that I had to grow up a little and pay her more mind.

Over time, as it became evident to all parties that Nancy and I were a bona fide, in-it-for-the-long-haul couple, the triangular tension drifted away. In fact, when I decided in early 1976 to embark on a career-advancing expedition southward to New York City—auditioning, taking meetings, putting myself out there, so to speak—Gilda and Nancy had a very civilized, adult telephone conversation in which they worked out that I would stay at Gilda's place on the Upper West Side for the duration of my trip. They did this independently of me and presented the plan to me as a fait accompli.

Gilda's apartment was painted almost entirely blue and was very *her*, a combination of expensive furniture that reflected her upbringing and thrift-shop bric-a-brac that represented her funky, wayward spirit; it could just as easily have been Annie Hall's apartment.

It was an exciting time, because *Saturday Night Live* was still in its first season, and the novelty of its and her success had not yet worn off. Years later Steve Martin and I had a discussion about how exhilarating that first season of *SNL* was, even to those of us who were mere spectators. Steve was living in Aspen at the time, and when he saw those first few episodes, his reaction was, "They've done it. They did what was out there, what we all had in our heads, this new kind of comedy." Meaning that someone (Lorne Michaels) had finally worked out a way to channel our comedy generation's loose, weirdo, hairy, nontraditional bent— Belushi's manic energy, Aykroyd's subversiveness, Chevy's smart-ass leading-man thing, Gilda's woman-child daffiness—into something that could be presented on network television.

Victor Garber was also in New York at the time I was staying with Gilda, so he and I made a plan to watch *SNL* at her place while she did the show. As she headed out to 30 Rock, Gilda told me, "There's some grass in that top drawer if you want to get high before the show."

So at around 11:10 p.m., I got out some of Gilda's pot, rolled it into a spliff, lit it, and took about five hits. It was potent stuff. Maybe just a tad too potent. By 11:20 I was having a massive anxiety attack: heart pounding, body sweating, hands shaking. Oh, boy, I thought. Papa's got to sit down.

At 11:25 Victor arrived. In my panic-mindedness, I decided to put up a cheerful front. My logic was that if I articulated to Victor that I was having an anxiety attack, then that would make it real. Whereas, conversely, if I pretended that I was fine, the attack would *not* be real.

So Victor came in, and in this insane, overly jovial way, I

started rat-a-tatting all these upbeat sentiments at him: "Victor! How are you? You look great! Isn't this exciting? Can you believe Gilda's on *Saturday Night Live*? I mean, isn't it just tremendous to see a friend who's starting to do so well, and—"

And then, all at once, I could contain myself no more. "I'm too *high*, Victor!" I wailed. "I smoked some marijuana and I'm having a nervous breakdown! Oh, Jesus, what do I do, Vic? I'm scared! Bad, bad scared!"

Like a surgeon in the field, Victor calmly and completely took over. "Sit down," he said, and sat me down. Then he went into Gilda's kitchen and brought back a little dish of honey and a Coca-Cola. Victor is a diabetic. "You're having the same reaction to the pot that a diabetic has from a blood-sugar crash," he told me gently. "Everything's going to be fine. Here, take this." He fed me a spoonful of honey like I was a sick child. Then he had me drink the Coke. And he was totally right. I was back to normal within minutes.

The first few days of my stay at Gilda's were fun. I was sleeping on her couch, which wasn't all that comfortable, so one night Gilda said, "Don't be silly, come into bed with me. Nothing's gonna happen." I said, "It *used* to happen, though. A lot." She waved me over with a good-natured *C'mon* motion. I joined her under the covers.

And indeed nothing did happen, apart from some warm reminiscing. I said, "Isn't it fun that we had those couple of years together? And you were *sooo* much older!" This sent her into hysterical laughter—that great inhale-wheeze laugh of hers. It was a lovely night. At lights-out, all we did, literally, was sleep together.

But one day, a week into what was meant to be a three-week stay, I was sitting at Gilda's kitchen table, stuffing envelopes with my head shot and résumé, when she barged through the apartment door and made a beeline for the bathroom. I could hear her vomiting. Dick Cavett, she explained to me when she came out, was that week's host, and as she perceived it, he had been rude to her. Her feelings hurt, she had binged on Snickers bars.

I am not giving myself any points for sensitivity here. I lost it. "Honest to fucking God, Gilda," I said, "this is the same shit. Nothing changes. I'm pathetically and pointlessly licking envelopes that will never be opened, and you're on *Saturday Night Live*, and *you're* vomiting." We had fallen back into the same old argument—and we weren't even a couple anymore.

Paul Shaffer was at that point the piano player in *SNL*'s house band, and he had a bachelor's hovel up in the West 100s, near Columbia University. "Fuck this, Gilda, I'm going to Paul's," I told her.

"Please don't go," she said, starting to cry. "I wanted to do this for you, to help you out by having you stay here. I wanted this to be something I could give you." But I stormed off and headed uptown.

A night later Nancy came down from Toronto to join Paul and me. Late, around one thirty in the morning, Gilda called, not knowing that Nancy was in town. "Is Morden there?" she asked Paul. That's what she used to call me. Paul, speaking loudly, so both Gilda on her end and I on ours caught his drift, said, "Ahhh, Gilda! Marty and *Nancy* are here with me!"

Realizing that I was not available for an emergency heart-to-heart, Gilda meekly told Paul, like her character Emily Litella, "Never mind."

Gilda and I, I'm pleased to say, eventually grew up into grown-ups about our relationship. We remained good friends to the end of her life. In 1983, when Nancy and I adopted our first child—our daughter, Katherine—Gilda sent over an embroidered wall hanging with Katherine's name on it, only it read KATHARINE, the Hepburn spelling. Since Gilda and I were never ones to hold back from each other, I told her, "Thanks, Gilda, but honest to God, talk about self-centeredness! Even Hitler knew how the Eichmann kids' names were spelled!"

She insisted that I put Katherine, a baby, on the phone. I could hear Gilda yelling through the receiver, "Tell your dad he's an asshole and that he spelled your name wrong! You want it spelled with an 'A'!"

In 1985, by which time Gilda was happily married to Gene Wilder, the four of us—Nancy and me, Gilda and Gene—had dinner together in London, where we all happened to be at the same time. Nancy and I couldn't help but notice a touch of concern in Gene. A few times he asked Gilda, "How are you feeling?" To which Gilda replied in sprightly fashion, "I feel great! I feel perfect!"—the takeaway from which could only be that Gilda had *not* been feeling well.

A year later I was doing a press junket with Steve Martin and Chevy Chase for *¡Three Amigos!* in Tucson. We kept getting pestered with questions about Gilda's health, which we kept deflecting, since we didn't know anything. But by the end of the day, after the three of us nervously called friends from Chevy's hotel room, we found out that the reports were true: Gilda had been diagnosed with ovarian cancer.

She and I talked about it over the phone a few times—her condition, her blood numbers, and her chemo. She had a nice period of remission where, she told me, she was contemplating adopting a child herself. I remember seeing her on the cover of *Life* magazine in 1988, with shorter hair but looking great. The headline was "Gilda Radner's Answer to Cancer." But not long after that, while I was helping arrange a benefit show for Cedars-Sinai, the hospital in L.A. where Gilda had received treatment, I heard through a woman I knew that Gilda was sick again. I called Gilda and told her exactly what I had been told. I wanted her to tell me it was bullshit. She indulged me. "I'm fine!" she said. "In fact, I just hiked up a mountain. So tell that cunt that I just climbed a mountain, okay?"

That talk—aptly defiant, funny, and obscene—was one of our last. Gilda's cancer had indeed returned, and she passed away in 1989, when she was only forty-two. I found out through Steve Martin, who phoned me with the bad news in the morning. It was a Saturday, and he was hosting *SNL* that night.

On the show, Steve abandoned his planned monologue and introduced an old clip: a wordless, poignantly funny sketch that he and Gilda had done on the show in 1978, in which they spotted each other across a crowded room at a disco and launched into an MGM-style dance routine, to the tune of "Dancing in the Dark" from the Fred Astaire–Cyd Charisse musical *The Band Wagon*. Both Steve and Gilda wore white, and alternated between genuine grace and total comic spazziness: so committed, so perfect.

L ife with Nancy, as we settled in, was a wholly different experience from life with Gilda. Which is not to say that Nan was a shy, retiring little lady who existed at the service and pleasure of her man. (Though I'd love to try that someday.) She was a force of nature in her own right; I am attracted to strong women, if that's not already evident.

Yet Nancy was a very different type of force. Though she too was an enormously talented singer, songwriter, and actress, she ultimately didn't "want it" as much as the real strivers do. She didn't have that "Look at me, laugh at me!" need for approbation that many performers have. (Gilda and I were probably too alike in that regard.) In fact, Nancy was quite the opposite: fiercely individualistic and private—evocative, in a way, of Katharine Hepburn. I realize now that I've already mentioned Hepburn several times in this book, and that it may seem like I have a perverse Kate Hepburn fetish. But it's kind of an odd coincidence. My impersonation of Hepburn came about serendipitously, because I discovered my voice was in the right register to do late-period Kate and she was so imitable to begin with. Nancy was more akin to early-period Kate, in her beauty, outdoorsiness, and independence. And she knew it. *The Philadelphia Story* was her favorite movie, and she had watched it dozens of times.

Years later, when we became U.S. citizens and Los Angeles residents, Nancy's women friends—who included Deb Divine, Rita Wilson, Catherine O'Hara, Laurie David, Carolyn Miller (wife of Dennis), and Laurie MacDonald (producing partner and wife of Walter Parkes)—nicknamed her the Mountie: a nod to both her roots and her no-bullshit, no-frivolity, no-disloyalty "If you've got buck teeth, either be a clown or get them fixed!" spirit.

But Nancy reigned over the domestic sphere, too. As a new couple, we moved into a little flat for two on the top floor of 44 Binscarth Road, a beautiful old Victorian house in a leafy neighborhood of Toronto. We Canadians have our Thanksgiving in October—like logical people, when the harvest is still in effect and therefore the whole "harvest festival" idea makes sense. (We also stuff our turkey through the beak, but I'll discuss that later.) On Canadian Thanksgiving 1975, I learned the meaning of domestic bliss, until then a theoretical concept that existed outside my adult experience. Returning home exhaustedly from whatever show I was doing, I was enticed up the staircase by a lovely, wafting aroma of roasted turkey. That was wondrous enough, but here's the little detail that made my heart swell: As my key turned in the door, I heard Nancy scurrying to the record player, dropping the needle on Frank's rendition of "Autumn in New York" so it would be playing as I walked in.

We even did a show together, a cabaret version of *The Apple Tree*, a Jerry Bock–Sheldon Harnick musical that had played on Broadway in the 1960s. The original production was a big to-do, directed by one of my idols, Mike Nichols. Our version was bare bones: just the two of us and a pianist in the dinner theater of Anthony's Villa, an Italian restaurant in an out-of-the-way corner of Toronto whose main dining room featured singing waiters and waitresses in clown costumes. Needless to say, this gig came during a bit of a professional lull for both of us.

There was one warm, muggy night when only two people showed up, despite the theater's two-hundred-seat capacity. It is a maxim of the theater—which I have since discovered is simply an invention of lazy actors—that if the size of the audience is equal to or lesser than the size of the cast, the performers have the option of not going ahead with the performance. So I walked right up to the solitary couple in attendance and said, "We'll pay for your dinner if you just want to eat. Don't you think it seems a little sad to do the show for just you guys?" But the guy said, "No, not particularly. We kind of want to see it." (There's the kind of enthusiasm that can get a depressed actor over the hump!) So Nancy and I performed it. The man and woman stared at us blankly the whole time, offering up no reaction whatsoever.

Still, Nan and I were so in love that we had a blast. We even somehow managed to get a terrific review from the *Toronto Sun*, written by this mustachioed fuddy-duddy English-expat critic named McKenzie Porter. He was something else, infamous for having written a column in the mid-1970s bemoaning the indecency of people who defecate in bathrooms at work, rather than in their home loo. ("Defecation in any place where it is difficult to wash the anus is unhygienic," he wrote.) But Mr. Porter loved our little-seen production of *The Apple Tree*. Or, at least, he loved Nancy. He described her in the review's first paragraph as being "as luscious and curvaceous as a dish of prize melons." And it went on and on—this old man's extended, lustful tribute to my future wife's body. "When men reflect on those firm arcs of flesh and large melting eyes that are inseparable from the ideal cuddle," Porter wrote, "it is almost certain they have Dolman in mind." I really couldn't agree with him more—though I was a little wounded that he made no mention of my beautifully sculpted balls.

N ancy and I established a policy of never going to bed mad at each other, or with unspoken, unresolved issues. Our commitment to talking things out began when, one cold January day early in our time together, Nancy received a phone call that upset her. Without explanation, she ran into our bedroom, shut the door, and pulled the covers over herself. I barged in after her and demanded to know what was wrong. "I don't want to talk about it!" she said. So I—in a real asshole move, by the way—angrily pulled the covers off her and threw them to the floor. It was my Short-family upbringing coming to the fore: leave nothing alone, and everything in the open.

My sensitivity was wanting, but the ultimate goal was noble: I didn't want Nancy to suffer whatever she was suffering all by herself. So she opened up: her mother, Ruth, had just told Nancy that her father, Bob, a doctor, had left, and her parents were getting a divorce. It truly was news worth crawling under the covers for. But, as I said to Nancy, "This is not going to be our relationship." Locked rooms and emotional shutdowns were precisely what caused her parents' marriage to fail. We were not going to repeat that history.

We skewed in the other direction—we bantered back-and-forth, like Nick and Nora Charles in the *Thin Man* movies. One summer, when I was still merely a very, very minor Canadian celebrity, Nancy and I were invited to be judges in the Miss Prince Edward Island beauty pageant. One of the contestants, in the talent segment of the pageant, opted not to sing but merely *recite* the lyrics to the Barbra Streisand song "Evergreen," William Shatner style: "*Love—soft as an easy chair!*"

Nan and I were convulsing as we tried to hold back our laughter. And remember, we were the judges! But what truly delighted me about that moment was that the two of us found the same things so hysterically funny.

But don't misunderstand me: there were fights, too, often springing from moments when my natural instinct to push things too far managed to push even Nancy too far. There was, for example, the night of the French Laundry, the Napa Valley restaurant that many critics consider America's best. They really poured it on for us, literally: I think Nan and I had drunk three glasses of complimentary wine before we even ordered. The staff was incredibly solicitous—"Oh, good evening, Mr. and Mrs. Short"—but in a formal way that I found amusing, especially as the wine started to kick in. I became obsessed with getting at least one of the waiters to laugh, but I was bombing miserably, like a tourist trying to get a rise from one of those fur-hatted Queen's Guards in front of Buckingham Palace.

Finally the wine steward approached our table and asked Nancy, "Would you like to talk about the wine?" Nancy replied that he was free to choose for us, since we knew very little about fine wines.

That's when I interjected, "Yeah, I just pulled her out of the chorus!"

Nothing. Crickets. "In fact, on the way here," I went on, dauntlessly, "it was a struggle for me just to get her to spit out the gum!"

Still nothing. I was bombing badly at the French Laundry.

After the guy walked away, I'd started chuckling about my comic strikeout when I noticed that Nan was staring at me with disgust. "Well, that . . . was . . . *embarrassing*," she seethed.

"What?"

" 'I pulled her out of the chorus'? What the hell was that?"

"It was a *joke*!" I said.

"Well, you know what the problem with that joke is, Marty? It's not *funny*. Jokes are supposed to be funny, you know."

Now the fight was starting. "Oh, c'mon!" I said. "Why do you care what some waiter would think?"

"I care that you act like a *moron*," Nancy retorted.

I noticed at that point that we were attracting attention: other diners in America's most revered restaurant were looking up from their plates to watch us bicker. So, in my most whispery approximation of a shout, I said through clenched teeth, "Stop it! We *cannot have this fight*!"

"And *why is that?*" Nancy asked.

"Because the *bill* is going to be *thirty-three hundred dollars!* So we have *got to have a good time!*"

Nancy slumped back in her chair. "You're right," she said.

We didn't speak for the next two minutes, merely eating the fine courses that had been placed before us. At last, after the waiters cleared our plates to make way for yet more plates, Nancy quietly said, "Marty?"

"What?"

"I'm over it now."

From that point forward, we enjoyed our dinner and found our earlier squabble hysterical. Nancy still deemed my behavior unclassy—"God forbid we should act like we *deserve* to dine in an elegant restaurant," she later told me—but the night became a part of our mental scrapbook, a concentrated snapshot of the Marty-Nancy dynamic.

Nancy wasn't shy about putting anyone—not just her husband—in his place. To bring things full circle back to *Blazing Saddles*, the movie that nearly dashed our first night of passion, here's one of my favorite Nan stories, from when we were in Washington, DC, for the 2009 Kennedy Center Honors. I was there to take part with Matthew Broderick, among others, in a tribute to one of that year's honorees, Mel Brooks. My job, in fact, was to sing the *Blazing Saddles* theme song on horseback, surrounded by a bevy of chorus girls.

Afterward there was a formal dinner in one of the Kennedy Center's ballrooms, attended by the honorees, along with President and Mrs. Obama and various luminaries from politics and show business. I was seated beside Matthew, with Mikhail

Baryshnikov to his left. Nancy, some distance away, was seated next to a prominent if notably pompous intellectual.

Nancy, from the moment I met her, was a stickler for manners, chief among them that one must *make* conversation with one's neighbor at the dinner table. What do you do when you're seated next to someone you don't know? You ask him questions. You ask him about his life. And then, after the conversational wheels have been greased, your neighbor reciprocates and asks you some questions about *your* life, or maybe the two of you fall into a fantastic discussion on some completely new topic. But none of this script worked with Nancy's dining companion, who was known to be socially intimidating and accustomed to deference from all those around him. Nan got nothing from him. She sat there determinedly asking him question after question, but received only bland, perfunctory responses.

Finally, after the umpteenth conversational dead stop, Nancy lost her composure. She said to the man—sharply—"Okay, you know what? At some point, you're going to have to throw me a bone."

I was oblivious to the situation until Matthew, who had observed the whole thing, nudged me and pointed in Nan's direction.

"Ask me something," Nancy said. "Form words and ask *me something.* Just for the experience."

Startled and looking a little ashen, the man thought for a moment before finally coming up with a question. "Do you like L.A.?" he said.

Nancy suddenly extended her arms out in front of her, planted her hands on the table, and flopped her head down in exasperation. Then she looked back up, turned to the man, and said, "Okay, you know what? We're done." And at that moment she turned her attention from him to the woman sitting on the other side.

The guy was probably sitting there thinking, What a bitch. But for me, it was hilarious: my wife, at the Kennedy Center, in full Mountie mode.

INTERLUDE

A MOMENT WITH ED GRIMLEY

People always ask me which of my characters I would save if they were all drowning? My heavens, that's like asking Hugh Hefner which of his registered nurses he prefers to cut and pre-chew his food for him. It's almost an impossible thing to answer. But I suppose that if I had to choose, it would probably be a toss-up between Jiminy Glick and—oh, give me a break, Ed Grimley, and that's no lie!

Born in 1977 on the stage of Second City Toronto, Ed not only helped me through some fraught moments with Nancy early in our relationship but also went on to have "a very decent time, I must say" on **SCTV**, **Saturday Night Live**, and even his own very hip Hanna-Barbera animated series, **The Completely Mental Misadventures of Ed Grimley**, which ran on NBC for a year. For a time Ed was also available in toy stores as a Tyco talking doll; you'd pull the string in his back and he'd say things like "Gee, **that's** a pain that's going to linger!" (A mint Ed doll in its original packaging fetches a fortune on eBay. By the way, I don't really know if that's true, but that's what I tell people.)

As I've already detailed, Ed's peculiar manner of speaking was a combination of how my school friend Patrick and my brother-in-law Ralph spoke, and his shirt was salvaged from my teenage 1960s wardrobe (and eventually replaced with a series of look-alike shirts). But his signature verbal tic—"I must say"—was not there from the beginning. At first Ed simply punctuated his sentences, as many Canadians do, with the expression "Eh?" I have in my personal archive a rare clip of early Ed, circa the late 1970s, from a Canadian TV show I did for a season called **Ferguson, Short & Ross**. In it, Ed's still wearing my actual childhood plaid shirt, which is in complete tatters at the elbows, and he says "Eh?" where you expect him to say "I must say": "Sometimes people can be rude, eh? It seems sad when they are, but sometimes people can be rude, eh?"

But by the time I got to **SCTV**, Rick Moranis and Dave Thomas had hit it big with their "Great White North" sketches as Bob and Doug McKenzie, ultra-Canadian brothers who called each other "hoser" and finished their sentences with "Eh?" And, you know, there just wasn't room for yet another **SCTV** character who said "Eh?," eh? So Ed's "Eh?" became "I must say." **Oh, and I suppose it didn't!**

ED GRIMLEY

Oh, give me a break! I couldn't be more excited to appear here in this literary memoir, I must say. Just the thought of it is making me go completely mental and my heart is beating like a distant little jungle drum.

What if this book goes on to win a National Book Award, I must say, or a Pulitzer in letters, or even the Nobel Prize in literature? I think I would be found dead amongst my own mental excitement, and my head would be, like, exploding with untainted elation. Oh, and I suppose meeting His Majesty Carl XVI Gustaf, King of Sweden, wouldn't be the best. Give me a break! Like, I suppose life could get better than that. No way! 'Cause it's sad, in a way, but royalty have that special glow that commoners just can't muster.

(SUDDEN SWITCH TO EXCITABLE ENERGY.)

What if we became best friends? Best friends **ever**, so that I could just like phone him and say, "Oh, is Gustaf there? Well, just tell him it's me."

(SUDDEN DESPAIR.)

Oh, and I suppose that would ever happen! Like the King of Sweden doesn't have, like, a million billion friends already.

(SUDDEN BURST OF OPTIMISM.)

But then again, maybe he **doesn't**! It's difficult to always know!

Some of you have perchance been wondering where I've been aboding for the last thirty years. Well, it's like, I've been dwelling in the "Characters Who Were Popular in the '80s for an Hour" Home in Trenton, New Jersey. Don't pity me. My rock bottom is still your wildest dreams.

(OVEN-TIMER BELL GOES OFF.)

Gee, my gingerbread cookies are ready! How pleasant.

(ED RUSHES TO OPEN THE OVEN DOOR. A HUGE CLOUD OF SMOKE BLASTS OUT.)

Could be a tad overdone.

(ED PULLS OUT THE COOKIE TRAY.)

Gee, they do look very decent—and yet I can't help but wish that I'd worn some sort of oven mitt.

(ED DROPS THE TRAY IN PAIN.)

Gee, that's a pain that's going to linger.

(SUDDENLY LEAPS INTO THE AIR WITH EXCITEMENT.)

But I don't care, 'cause I'm in a literary memoir, I must say. Oh, and I suppose being in a literary memoir isn't the best. It's like a joke!

(THE STRAINS OF A HUNGARIAN CZARDAS FILL THE AIR. ED GRABS HIS TRIANGLE AND BEGINS TO DANCE.)

Yes, it's time to dance the dance of merriment, for joy is my new middle name, I must say.

TOP Me at age two . . . with a little more Botox.

MIDDLE The Short kids *(from L–R)* Michael, Marty, Brian, Nora, and David at Southampton, Ontario, 1956.

BOTTOM Having never been nicknamed "Ol' Washboard Abs," age thirteen with my parents at Southampton, 1963.

TOP With Mom, Brian, and Michael at the Latin Quarter in New York City, awaiting Buddy Hackett's filthy set, 1965.

MIDDLE Sultry at sixteen.

BOTTOM At age seventeen in the original Grimley shirt (with family at a Christmas gathering).

TOP LEFT AND RIGHT   Me and Nancy in *Godspell*, 1972.

BOTTOM   The Toronto *Godspell* cast, 1972 (*from L–R*) Andrea Martin, me, Jayne Eastwood, Avril Chown, Rudy Webb, Victor Garber, Valda Aviks, Eugene Levy, Gilda Radner, and Gerry Salsberg. *(Lansbury Productions)*

TOP With Eugene Levy, Paul Shaffer, and Dave Thomas backstage at an awards show in Toronto, 1985.

MIDDLE Besotted with Gilda during *Godspell*, 1972.

BOTTOM The '82–'83 cast of *SCTV* (*from L–R*) Andrea Martin, John Candy, Joe Flaherty, me, and Eugene Levy. *(Courtesy of The Second City Entertainment, Inc.)*

TOP With John as Divine (and me as pirate David Steinberg) on *SCTV*. *(Courtesy of The Second City Entertainment, Inc.)*

BOTTOM With Meg Ryan in *Innerspace*, 1987. *(Warner Bros./Everett Collection)*

TOP AND BOTTOM Nan and me at Andrea Martin's family home in Maine, July 1976.

TOP Making it legal at St. Basil's Catholic Church in Toronto on December 22, 1980.

MIDDLE Baby Katherine visits *SCTV* as I film the epic sketch "Oliver Grimley," February 1984.

BOTTOM Two-year-old Katie visits Dad on the set of *Innerspace*.

TOP "Gimme a C!": getting touched up as Irving Cohen for my talk show, 2000.

MIDDLE With Billy Crystal in *SNL's* "Kate & Ali" (i.e., Hepburn and Muhammad) sketch, 1984. *(Al Levine/NBC/NBCU/Getty)*

BOTTOM The motley "Steinbrenner Season" *SNL* cast surround guest host Ringo Starr, 1984. (*top row from L–R*) Harry Shearer, Barbara Bach (Ringo's wife), Billy Crystal, Gary Kroeger, Ringo Starr, Julia Louis-Dreyfus, Mary Gross, Christopher Guest, (*bottom row from L–R*) Pamela Stephenson, me, Jim Belushi.

THE NINE CATEGORIES

O ne of the paradoxes of my early, crazy-in-love years with Nancy is that they coincided with my lowest ebb professionally. As successful as my debut in *Godspell* had been, and as many opportunities as it afforded, it didn't fast-track me to any particular destiny or destination. Though I seldom lacked for work, my choices were simply the jobs that were available.

In Canada at the time, there was no real star system that built up actors to the point where any of us were in a position to mull the merits of one job over another. There was never a question of whether you said yes or no when offered work; you simply asked, "Do I need to bring a suit?" In the course of a day, you ("you" meaning me) might do a radio commercial for Chrysler and an audition for a role in a CBC radio production of *The Merry Wives of Windsor*, and then, at night, appear in a cabaret show such as *Cole Cuts: The Music of Cole Porter.*

Although I made little headway in mid-1970s Toronto in terms of gaining fame or making serious money, I did get to experience life as a working actor and to grow with each job, which I consider a blessing. At that point, had I been thrown into the bigger showbiz ponds of Hollywood or New York, I don't think I would have survived. My one-year contract with myself would have lapsed, and I'd have found myself back in Hamilton as a social worker, handing out checks to the needy and gently cautioning them, "Now, don't spend this all on booze."

The array of jobs I had back then was staggering. There were some good ones, such as working with Andrea Martin in an Elaine May play called *Not Enough Rope*. But there were a lot of strange, misbegotten choices, too, more akin to *Fortune and Men's Eyes*, my ill-fated gay-prison fantasia. I played rough trade for a second time in an episode of a mid-1970s CBC anthology program called *Peep Show*, a showcase for daring theater. My costar was Saul Rubinek, excellent as a buttoned-down classical pianist who picks up a ragged, thrill-seeking rent boy: yours truly. I was trying to convey the coiled menace of a young Brando, but I delivered something closer to the young Jerry Lewis, especially as I barked at Saul, "I'm twice as Jewish as you are! And I ain't never wore a beanie, either! You know why? I been circumcised twice!"

In a completely different direction, I did a guest spot on an ecology-themed children's TV show called *Cucumber* as Smokey the Hare, a character who sang downer songs about the rape of the planet:

Where, oh where is the polar bear . . .
He's hard to find, and getting more rare

I did my best to sell the lyrics, but it was no easy task, given that I was outfitted in giant ears, long whiskers, an argyle sweater, and skinny jeans with a white cottontail sewn onto the ass.

Even after I found my calling at Second City Toronto—after that fateful moment with Nancy in L.A. on Breakdown Corner, and my consequent rebirth as Martin Short, Funnyman—my career, while full of fun and creativity, remained rather middling. Not until 1982, when I joined *SCTV* and was in my thirties, would I achieve what I'd call lasting professional success.

Thankfully, though, my happiness was never predicated first and foremost upon my career. It's an outlook that has served me well. I did a joke recently on Conan O'Brien's show in which I said that on my gravestone, there will be but one word: ALMOST. I *almost* made it big as a movie star in the 1980s, except that none of my string of high-profile movies from that period did well at the box office. I *almost* caught the wave of talk-show mania that gave people like Rosie O'Donnell and Ellen DeGeneres huge second careers in daytime television, but my talk show ran in so many different time slots in so many different places (this was in 1999–2000) that it had no chance of taking hold.

I have a whole list of almosts and coulda-woulda-shouldas. I *almost* joined the cast of *Bosom Buddies*, the early 1980s sitcom that launched Tom Hanks (I'd have played his cousin or something), but the timing wasn't right, and I turned down the chance. I *might have* ended up on *SCTV* sooner than I did, but Nancy and I decided in the late 1970s to leave Toronto and try California for a while. And I perhaps *could have* been on *Saturday Night Live* years earlier than I was, in the original Lorne Michaels era, but the stars were not aligned.

Though my friendship with Lorne didn't really take flight until the 1980s and *¡Three Amigos!*, he was someone with whom I'd been vaguely acquainted since the *Godspell* days. He was already a big deal then, a homegrown Canadian hotshot who had starred in his own CBC variety program, *The Hart and Lorne Terrific Hour*, and worked in L.A. as a writer for *Laugh-In* and Lily Tomlin's TV specials.

I had a formal meeting with Lorne in New York in December 1978, in which he offered me what is known in our fabulous business as a holding deal, wherein I would agree, in exchange for a modest sum of money, to give him the right of first refusal if I got an offer for some other job, such as a sitcom pilot.

There was a lot of speculation at the time that John Belushi and Danny Aykroyd were going to leave *SNL* after the '78–'79 season. The premise of the holding deal was that I'd put other opportunities on hold until the situation cleared up; if Lorne needed reinforcements, I would be one of the people he might call upon. But I was hardly the only actor on his list—I still suspect that Lorne took the meeting with me only as a favor to Gilda, who generously remained a staunch Marty advocate—and there was no guarantee of me making the *SNL* cast. Besides, I was at a point then where I wanted to check out this thing they had in L.A. called pilot season. (And, indeed, I got cast in a good pilot—more on that in the next chapter.)

So I never signed the holding deal with Lorne. As it happened, John and Danny did, in fact, leave *SNL* in the spring of '79, to make *The Blues Brothers*. I might have had a shot after all. The new person that Lorne ended up bringing in for the '79–'80 season was the ingenious, deeply talented Harry Shearer—with whom I'd work in the '84–'85 season, by which time Dick Ebersol was running the show.

I do sometimes wonder what might have been if I'd made it into the tail end of *SNL*'s mystique-laden Original Era. Would Ed Grimley have impacted the outcome of the Carter-Reagan election? Would late 1970s fame have warped me in a way that mid-1980s fame somehow didn't? Would I be the bestest of bestest chums with Garrett Morris?

The truth is, I'll never have a clue, because it didn't happen. In my heart of hearts, I know I wasn't ready for *SNL* then.

And if it had happened, I probably wouldn't have been a part of *SCTV*, unequivocally my most satisfying professional experience. As I said earlier, I was never career-driven to the exclusion of all other factors, so I lost no sleep over missed opportunities. I stayed happy.

This wasn't purely the result of my contentedness with Nan, nor was it wholly a consequence of the perspective that my early family losses gave me, though both of those factors were huge. It was, to me, a simple matter of logic. On that subject, permit me a brief detour into an atypical period of unhappiness. In October of 1975, after three packed years of consistent acting employment, the work suddenly and inexplicably stopped for about three months. This was a new experience for me: a frustrating state of professional limbo. I resented that, as I saw it, my fate was somehow no longer in my own hands. It really felt as if the world was conspiring against me. For example, every time I took the subway during that period, my timing was off. Whether I ran to catch the train or slowly took my time getting to the station made no difference; inevitably, as soon as I descended to the platform, I'd find a train closing its doors and pulling away.

I was in a funk. The way my mind was working at that point, I decided that my career wouldn't get moving again until I started having better luck with the subway. And when, for reasons just as mysterious as those for the lull, I started getting acting work again, I looked back at those three months in limbo as utterly wasted time. I had accomplished little besides sitting by my telephone and sulking. And from that day forward, I resolved to never again fritter away my precious hours.

Recognizing that prolonged periods of unemployment are part of an actor's lot, I devised a rigorous self-evaluation system that I call the Nine Categories. I know, it sounds like some sort of scary Illuminati initiation gauntlet, but to me it was merely my benign, orderly way of taking personal inventory: objectively weighing the good against the bad. I wanted to see if I could use logic to overcome emotion.

I decided to systematically compare my performance in that one specific category of my life—work—with my performance in the other important life categories, and to give them all equal importance. My mind has always worked systematically to begin with. For example, I still operate according to the school-year calendar, where September heralds a new start and May/June the conclusion of another grade; as I write this, in the spring of 2014, I am finishing up what I think of as Grade 59.

Since I was already thinking of time in school-year terms, I decided to think of life in course-load terms, with the main objective being to maintain a credible GPA. I might be getting a D in career, I thought, but if I got good marks in some of the other subjects, I could bring my average up. After thinking long and hard, I drew up what I thought of as the course load of life, aka the Nine Categories.

CATEGORY 1: SELF

The logical starting point. Without a highly functioning self, nothing else works. It can be anything from "Have you had your yearly physical?" to "What's your current weight?" to "Any blood on the pillow this morning?" Everything else in life unravels if you're not perpetuating your own survival. You have to take care of yourself, and when you do, try and lock the door so no one walks in on you.

CATEGORY 2: IMMEDIATE FAMILY

The proverbial wife and kids. This category is about gauging how your family relationships can be made stronger. When was the last time you sincerely told your kids you loved them—even the chubby redheaded one you don't really care for?

The important thing with children is to ask them questions.

Like, How was school? How are your friends? Am I fat? Do your friends think I'm funny? Should I fire the gardener? Is Mommy getting it on with the gardener? Why does Mommy seem so distant in bed? She's getting it on with the gardener, isn't she? You would tell me if she were, right? If you didn't know me, how old would you say I look? Did I ask you how school was?

And it's not just your kids; you must always be sensitive to your wife's needs—and make sure your personal assistant fulfills them.

When I am fortunate enough to have grandchildren, they shall be included in this category as well. I was heavily influenced, while devising this system, by the 1973 kidnapping of J. Paul Getty III, the teenage grandson of the Getty oil tycoon. The grandson was taken captive while living in Italy. His abductors told his mother that they were going to send her one of his fingers as proof that the boy was still alive. But Old Man Getty, unmoved, refused to get involved. Even after the kidnappers cut off one of the boy's ears and sent it to a Roman newspaper, the senior Getty would pay only the amount of the ransom that his accountants said was tax-deductible; he made his adult son, the poor kid's father, borrow the rest of the ransom from him at 4 percent interest. I was struck by how profoundly skewed the old man's values were. By my system, no matter how high his grades were in finance and career (Categories 5 and 6), his family grade would have been so fathomlessly low that his GPA would have been screwed. You simply *must* balance career with family.

Unless, that is, you have an amazing, unstoppable career. Then, I agree: who needs family? They'll just get in the way.

CATEGORY 3: ORIGINAL FAMILY

How are you getting along with the people you grew up with: Mom, Dad, and your siblings? In my case, since I no longer have living parents, I like to phone up people who have played my parents in movies, such as Richard Kind (*Clifford*), just to let them know I still care.

CATEGORY 4: FRIENDS

Are your friendships in a healthy place? Are you keeping in touch with everyone adequately? Are there any seething undercurrents of resentment that need to be put on the table and worked out? As a wise woman named Bette Midler once put it, "You've got to have good friends and good lighting."

Speaking of Bette: In 2005 Tom and Rita Hanks had a spectacular New Year's Eve party at their home in Sun Valley, Idaho. Around eight p.m., as Nan and I were driving there, the snow was coming down unrelentingly. It continued to do so throughout the evening, never letting up. At one thirty a.m., I was gazing out the window at the continuing blizzard, and Bette Midler was standing beside me. I said, "Jeez, Bette. If this snow continues like this, we're going to end up eating each other."

To which Bette replied coquettishly, "Why, thank you!"

CATEGORY 5: MONEY

Beatrice Kaufman, the wife of the playwright George S. Kaufman and a fellow member of the Algonquin Round Table, once said, "I've been rich and I've been poor. Rich is better." I'm with Beatrice. I believe it was also Beatrice who said, "Money can't buy you happiness, but at Exotic Thai Massage, it can buy some relief." Or was that Donald Trump?

CATEGORY 6: CAREER

As it says on my answering service, "I'll take it."

In my business, there's a traditional career path: TV, movies, Broadway, your own reality show, Chabad Telethon performer, the Palm Springs Follies, and writing your autobiography. So what grade do you give your working life?

At this very moment I'd give mine a solid grade, although,

cumulatively, I still feel that I'm two films short of making the Oscars-night memorial reel.

CATEGORY 7: CREATIVITY

Beyond the *amount*-of-work aspect, is your work creatively fulfilling? Innate creativity is a wonderful blessing. But when I look at George W. Bush's paintings, I wonder if a pill could be invented that causes something called painter's block.

CATEGORY 8: DISCIPLINE

Not just the simple imperative of self-preservation as addressed in Category 1, but having the self-control to actually implement your goals. In my underemployed-actor days, I used this category as motivation: *I'm not working, but I'll use this time to get into the best shape of my life. Or to read more, or write more, or do more of what I feel I should do so that this fallow period jobwise won't be wasted time.* Discipline is essential to life, whether you are administering or inflicting the spanking.

CATEGORY 9: LIFESTYLE

Put aside all the usual yardsticks of success and well-being: Oscars, Tonys, Emmys, deals, yachts, beach houses, penis length. Are you actually enjoying life? Are you having any *fun*? And, God forbid, are you doing something to make the world a better place?

The Nine Categories have been a part of my life for more than thirty-five years now. Every Monday I assign myself a grade in each category, augmenting the grades with comments. I used to do this by hand, in a spiral-bound notebook, but now I do it on the computer. Some categories have subcategories. In Category

1, for example, I keep track of my weight using color-coded classifications based on the old Tom Ridge Homeland Security alert system. So let's say my ideal weight is 142 pounds. (I'm not a tall man.) That means that the 142–44 range would be blue ("Looking Fine"), 145–47 would be yellow ("Guarded"), 148–50 would be orange ("Elevated—subject must go on diet"), and 150 and up would be red ("Severe—subject no longer requires fat suit to play Jiminy Glick").

Green ("Low") would denote that I'm fasting for a role à la Jared Leto or Matthew McConaughey, or perhaps dying.

I also maintain week-at-a-glance files, the upcoming week detailed in red lettering, the week just past recorded in black: yet another way to review my activities in total and see how they will impact, or have impacted, my overall well-being. I'll note, say, that I deserve an A in career for the week I've spent prepping for a Broadway show, but I'll also see that I've failed to return Eugene Levy's call, or that my children are no longer speaking to me, and I'll think, hey, Marty, you'd better put that right.

My manager, Bernie Brillstein, who passed away in 2008, was convinced that the Nine Categories system was my ticket to untold riches as a self-help guru. "Kid, I'm tellin' ya," he'd say, "you're sittin' on a fuckin' self-help *bible!*" (Bernie looked like a Jewish Santa Claus and talked like a Hoboken stevedore.)

"The color-coded weight, the Nine Categories . . . it's a God-damned *life philosophy*," Bernie told me. "You do the book and we'll book you on *Oprah*. It's real simple."

Bernie's idea was tempting, but ultimately, I'm no evangelist. The Nine Categories are a tremendous aid to me, but they are not something I push on other people, not even my own kids. I preside over a cult of one.

O ne of the crucial benefits of the Nine Categories is that they've gotten me through the many uneven periods of my career and kept in focus the true priorities of life. Maybe, at times, the inconsistency and iffy quality of some of the work I took on held my "career" grade down, but this would only encourage me to push my "creativity" grade as high and fearlessly as I could. In the 1970s, for example, audiences weren't yet conditioned, as they are now, to laugh at the very sight of me, so I could do straight drama, like a production of Clifford Odets's *Paradise Lost* for Canadian television. On the flip side, I had nothing to lose by trying my hand at stand-up comedy, so I did. Once.

I had a friend named Carole Pope who fronted a punk band called Rough Trade. In 1978 she asked me to open for her band at a club in Toronto called Egertons. Rough Trade's lyrics dealt with bondage, homoeroticism, and other taboo subjects; they had a song called "What's the Furor about the Führer?"

For whatever reason, I agreed to do a stand-up set before Rough Trade went on, despite having zero stand-up experience. I decided that, as a stand-up, I'd position myself as a cerebral, observational comic, making references to Camus and Kierkegaard. I wasn't so much concerned with getting laughs as I was with seeing audience members turn to each other at any given moment and say, "*Exactly!*" The fact that I was opening for a band whose members wore jockstraps and chaps onstage didn't dissuade me from pursuing this direction, for some reason.

The audience was terrifying from the moment I got up onstage: punks, goths, and people who had crudely carved the words ROUGH TRADE into their skin with razor blades. There was one scary man done up as a priest—who I later learned actually was a priest. I was booed and screamed at, it seemed, before I even left my house. Yet with the balls of steel that John Candy had once attributed to me,

I bounded onstage undaunted and launched into my material: "To-night is eerily reminiscent of Truman Capote's infamous Black and White Ball in 1966—as well as his infamous Black and Blue Ball from that unfortunate dismount off Sal Mineo in '72."

Nothing.

"People constantly want to know what religion I am. I find that rude. It doesn't matter. Whether you're Christian, Jewish, or . . . you know . . . help me out here—Who are those crazy people constantly blowing things up for no reason? Americans! That's it!— we're all God's children. Some of you are his bastard children. I think the Turks in the audience know what I'm talking about."

Nothing.

"I recently saw Mel Brooks's film *Silent Movie* with an all-black audience, and they were signing back at the screen."

Nothing still . . . except crescendoing boos, shouted obsceni-ties, and harassment. One member of the audience even started bleating at me, like an enraged sheep.

Suddenly, a Jack Ruby–type guy came out of the shadows and threw a beer in my face, momentarily stunning the audience into silence. I used this opening as my exit: "Hey, that was a light beer," I said, "and I don't have no weight problem! Well, good night!"

After my set, Carole came up to me and said, "I'm so sorry, Marty, I promise that tomorrow night will be different."

I told her, "Carole, I *know* it will be different. Because I won't be here. I'll be home, watching Jack Klugman chew up the scen-ery on *Quincy.*"

O ut of the ragtag array of acting jobs during this period came some good things: signposts leading the way to *SCTV* and

Saturday Night Live. In 1976, shortly after my fruitless job-hunting trip to New York City, the one where I stayed with Gilda first and then Paul, I was cast in *The David Steinberg Show*. David, eight years older than me, was and is a Canadian comedy godhead, the man who proved to his countrymen that one of us could make it in America. He was raised in an Orthodox Jewish home in Winnipeg, the son of a rabbi, but he broke from the rabbinical path (no doubt infuriating Old Testament God, the more volatile and Sinatra-like of biblical deities) to join Second City Chicago in 1964. He zoomed to success in the 1960s as a stand-up comic and frequent guest on Johnny Carson's *Tonight Show* and on *The Smothers Brothers Comedy Hour.*

David's new show was pretty much what Garry Shandling's *Larry Sanders Show* would be on U.S. television fifteen years later: a behind-the-scenes look at a dysfunctional variety show. What's significant about David's show now, though we didn't know it then, was that it served as a sort of test run for *SCTV.* Joe Flaherty played David's stage manager. Andrea Martin was David's secretary. John Candy was the show's Doc Severinsen–like bandleader. Dave Thomas was the studio's security guard. And I was Johnny Del Bravo, David's annoying cousin, who he was forced to hire due to family pressure although he was ashamed of him. We had all worked together before in different combinations, but this was the first time that the five of us were collected in one place.

David wanted Johnny Del Bravo to be a lounge singer because he found them unbearable and tacky. The mid-1970s were fertile ground for the mockery of such crooners, because rock had taken over and there wasn't yet a new generation of Harry Connicks and Michael Bublés to bring verve, youth, and style back to the Great American Songbook. The guys plying their trade in Vegas and the dinner theaters of Jupiter, Florida, in those days were generally pale imitations of Frank Sinatra and Tony Bennett—all the mannerisms and none of the talent. In early '76 *Saturday Night Live* ran a short film by Gary Weis called "Play Misty for Me" that intercut between performances by an array of such singers as each of them, in their various toupees and ruffle tuxes, sang "Misty," the Erroll Garner standard.

Even some of the big-time entertainers of the old guard were having a rough time fitting in during that period. The Murray brothers of Second City, Bill and Brian, were obsessed with the train-wreck syndicated talk show that Sammy Davis Jr. hosted for a couple of years in the mid-'70s, *Sammy and Company*: an unintentionally hysterical spectacle of rococo wardrobes and overcooked production numbers, with Sammy rappin' Very Sincerely with such guests as Liza Minnelli, Lola Falana, Chita Rivera, and Suzanne Pleshette. The Murrays, along with Paul Shaffer, organized what they called the Sammy Club for their like-mindedly hip and funny friends: everyone would gather at either Bill's or Brian's place for a laugh-along viewing party of *Sammy and Company*.

Equally obsessed were the Flaherty brothers, Joe and Paul, and Paul's writing partner, Dick Blasucci. When *SCTV* first reared its head, it was not for nothing that Joe's variety-show send-up was called *The Sammy Maudlin Show*, and that its guests included "Lorna Minnelli" and "Lola Heatherton," and that Maudlin's sidekick had the exact same name as Davis's, William B. Williams. (Though John Candy looked nothing like the real Williams, a slender New York radio personality.) Sammy Maudlin and Bill Murray's lounge singer, Nick, were products of the time—of our generation's fascination with the showbiz entropy taking place before our eyes.

But first—for the historical record—came my Johnny Del Bravo.

Johnny wore chest medallions, chunky rings, shiny, wide-collared shirts, and a cream-colored suit with rhinestone studs. His hair (a wig) was wavy and thick in a way that to him probably evoked virile masculinity but to the audience evoked Rue McClanahan. His mannerisms were more explicitly Sammy-influenced than Bill's Nick—I greeted the audience with the exhortation, "Peace, love, and grooviness," and pulled the occasional wonky eye. I said smarmy things like, "You know, in my business, or, in *our* business, when a song *lingers* for many many years, man, it becomes what we like to call *a standard*."

Johnny was basically a less extreme version of my future *SCTV* character Jackie Rogers Jr. Doing *The David Steinberg Show* was a step toward the fulfillment of my comic destiny. Alas, it lasted only one season on CTV, its network. They replaced us with something called *Stars on Ice*, because, as David put it mournfully, "In Canada, anything 'on ice' is better."

INTERLUDE

A MOMENT WITH

WITH

JACKIE ROGERS JR.

"Well, Marty's done it again," said Joe Flaherty in the **SCTV** writer's room. "Created yet another disgusting, unlikable character!" Jackie Rogers Jr. was basically a version of the Johnny Del Bravo character I created for **The David Steinberg Show**, dialed up to the point where he made the entire **SCTV** cast and crew go "Eww!" every time I did him.

Jackie Jr. was supposed to be a one-off, a footnote gag. Early in my tenure at **SCTV**, circa 1982, I used to go into the writer's room and do this stylized freak singer who I called Jackie Rogers. Dick Blasucci, Paul Flaherty, and my brother Michael, all then writers for the show, suggested that I play this character in a sketch, but I resisted. "Cheeseball lounge singers have been overly satirized at this point," I said. "Nothing fresh there."

However, it occurred to me that if I introduced the character of Rogers and then had him killed off in the same piece, we could have some fun without overdoing it. So the four of us—Michael, Dick, Paul, and me—wrote a piece in which the SCTV Network was promo-ing an upcoming Jackie Rogers special called **Old Mother Nature, She Loves Me**. In the promo, Rogers was shown bantering with various creatures of the forest and singing upbeat standards to them: "Pardon me, miss, but I never done this with a real live squirrel!" You get the idea.

Abruptly, the promo cut to a shot of a lurking cougar, who lunged at Rogers in mid-song and fatally mauled him. At the very end, Jackie Jr. popped up in a little inset circle on-screen and said, "Hi, I'm Jackie Rogers Jr. In 1970, my dad gave his life making this special. . . . I miss my old man. I hope you don't—Saturday nights at nine on **SCTV**."

I had recently seen a picture in a newspaper of Mickey Rooney Jr., a musician son of the famous actor who, for some reason, struck me as albino. (He was merely blond.) So I rather randomly made Jackie Rogers Jr. a cross-eyed albino. And as the character gained legs on **SCTV** and **SNL** (legs encased in silver-lamé tights, that is), I made Jackie Jr. this grotesque vehicle for the idea of a child using a famous parent—a dead parent, no less—as a way to gain credibility in show business.

Jackie's facial tics were a nod to Sammy Davis Jr., and his laugh—a dorky **thhh-thhh-thhh** emitted by raising my tongue to my upper teeth and breathing through them—was taken straight from Andrew Alexander, the head of Second City Toronto and executive producer of **SCTV**.

Andrew for years denied that he laughed this way, but then he got married, and among the wedding pictures was a shot of him caught unmistakably in the middle of a **thhh-thhh-thhh** laugh. He sent it to me with a note that read, "Dear Marty: Fuck you."

JACKIE ROGERS JR.

(ENTERS SINGING.)

I'm Jackie Rogers Jr.
And I'm like "this" with all the high flyers
Yes, I'm Jackie Rogers Jr.
My show's hipper than Seth Meyers'

Jimmys Fallon and Kimmel
Had better best beware
'Cause the Jackie Rogers Jr. show
Is on the . . . airrrrrrrr!!!!

Thank you, thank you, ladies and gentle-men! Oh, aren't you kind. Aren't you sweet. Aren't you everything I'd hoped you would be. And even though I wasn't your first choice as a performer tonight, it doesn't really bother me, because Gary Busey is such a different type.

Interesting story: I was getting some plaque removed from teeth that had already been bonded—which is not supposed to happen, by the way. At any rate, this cute little dental hygienist with magnificent hooters says to me, "Mr. Rogers Jr., sir, what are the Pointer Sisters really like?" And here I'd just been with those dudes two nights before, in the South Shore Room at Harrah's Lake Tahoe—

(SUDDENLY THE PRERECORDED VOICE OF AN ACTOR DOING JACKIE'S LATE FATHER EMANATES FROM ON HIGH.)

"Jackie!"

(LOOKING SKYWARD.)

Wh-what the f-hell? Who be you?
"I am your father, the late Jackie Rogers Sr.!"

(IN WONDERMENT.)

You . . . are my father? I . . . am your son?

**(SNAPPING OUT OF IT, ADDRESSING THE
AUDIENCE.)**

Gee, is the Holy Spirit nearby? Because with
three you get egg roll!

**(BREAKS HIMSELF UP LAUGHING, SLAPPING HIS
THIGHS.)**

I'm sorry . . . so sorry. . . . Please, let's bring
up the lights. Someone get a shot of this tele-
prompter. Ladies and gentlemen, I must explain. That line that I just laid on you, about
the Holy Spirit—who can be lots of fun, by
the way, when you get him alone—**cannot** be
found withinst the confines of the script. It was
a **totally** spontaneous addition. I have no idea
where that came from. But, you see, **that** is
what you call . . . improvisation!
  (**The prerecorded voice of Jackie Sr. booms
back in.**)
  "Jackie."
  Yes, Papa?
  "So you know the Pointer Sisters?"
  Does anyone, really?

WORKPLACE NIRVANA
AT *SCTV*

I spent twenty-one months with Second City Toronto, improvising throughout. We did all our shows in a handsome redbrick Victorian building known as the Old Fire Hall, which had the main theater downstairs and a restaurant upstairs. On Fridays and Saturdays we'd have dinner in the restaurant between the two shows, right alongside the customers we'd be performing for. Their presence didn't restrain us from drinking and carousing and in general having a great, noisy, swear-y time in each other's company. I think it was at one of these dinners in the summer of 1978 that I, overcome by our collective good fortune, turned to one of my castmates, Steven Kampmann, and declared, "Look at us. We're eating steak for dinner. We're twenty-eight years old. We're a hit. The house is full for every show. *This is as good as life can ever get.*"

My experience at Second City was tremendously important in helping me develop a unique (some would say "off") comedic voice. What we all learned at Second City was to trust the concept that our comedy wasn't about jokes. Rather, it was about situations and characters—the peculiar moments that we encounter in life, the peculiar people that we meet, and how we (and they) react to these moments and meetings.

I think this approach was particularly Canadian, and especially emphasized in Toronto. While Second City Chicago's comedy was often more pointedly topical and satirical, Second City Toronto's material tended to be more character-based and just plain strange. Canada is a sparsely populated nation, a mere 34 million people across a vast expanse of land. Consequently, as you grow up there, you encounter more weirdos who have been given a wider berth to stew in their weirdness and become gloriously eccentric. These are precisely the kinds of folks who served as our comic muses in Toronto. On top of this, the performers in Second City Toronto were a particularly nice, un-mean group, so the characterizations were sweet and empathetic rather than cruel; an oddball as played by Catherine O'Hara or John Candy was an unusually agreeable oddball.

Soaking up all this influence, I began obsessively studying the sorts of odd people to whom I hadn't previously paid much attention. There was a guy named Marion who worked behind the counter at my dry cleaner. I became fascinated by him. I was never quite sure if he had a bad hair weave or just really bad genetic luck, but his coiffure resembled something you'd chase out of your garden in the early morning as you were picking up your newspaper. With his madras clamdiggers and midriff tees, cut high to showcase his utter lack of abdominals, he was the type of guy who, if I had pitched him as a character at *Saturday Night Live*, anyone in the room would have said, "Too broad; divide by three." But Marion wasn't a character on *SNL*, nor was he trying to be funny. And yet, as he earnestly tried to explain why the shop had failed to remove the ink stain from my shirt, he was utterly priceless: "Mr. Shorm, I tried to get dat ink stain from yer outerwear, I did. But dat fucker didn't want to come out from where it had made a home, it didn't."

As broad as Marion was as a character, his pure sincerity made him totally believable. (Which was good, given that he was a real person.) The innocence with which he inhabited his eccentricities struck me. Don't telegraph, don't oversell—*that* was how you created an absurd yet three-dimensional character.

Now don't get me wrong. As anyone who has seen a reel of my work will attest, I'm also not afraid to explore the world of "Going Big." But even this world has to be rooted to some extent in reality. As a child, my parents took me to something called the Canadian National Exhibition, an old-fashioned summertime expo that featured everything from amusement-park rides to reputable nightclub headliners. My favorite part of the exhibition, though, was the freak show. We'd go into a tent and pay our quarter to see such memorable acts as Schlitzy the Pea Head (take your right hand, form a fist, and that was Schlitzy's head); Spike Boy (a temperamental fifty-six-year-old guy who belligerently told the audience, "I can't work with all this talking! May I have a little respect for my craft?"—and then shoved a two-foot-long spike up his nose); and my personal favorite, No-Middle Myrtle, whose measurements were 37-0-36. There was also Bones the Defensive Fat Man, who upbraided the audience by shouting, "What're you lookin' at?" These folks proved to be the underpinning of one of my most cherished showbiz philosophies, "More is more."

N ancy and I had become homeowners in my Second City period, with a lovely house on Indian Road in the High Park section of Toronto. Provincial Canadian celebrity was ours for the taking: a lifetime of contentment doing husband-and-wife shows like *Love Letters* and *The Gin Game* in summer stock. Perhaps I could even become a spokesman for Tim Hortons! All damned tempting. But in my heart, I knew I wanted more. The reality at that time—and it's different now—was that there was a low ceiling to Canadian show business. Really low. A Munchkin would have had to crouch.

Nancy and I were determined to try our luck out on the West Coast while we were still young. And we both did pretty well, considering. I landed a part in a pilot very quickly, for a sitcom called *The Associates*. This was 1979. The show was about a group of young lawyers who are new hires at a prestigious white-shoe firm in New York City. Its creator was James L. Brooks, the man behind *The Mary Tyler Moore Show*, *Lou Grant*, and *Taxi*. Actually, it was better than a pilot. Jim Brooks's track record was so good that ABC let us film thirteen episodes, half a season's worth, all at once, sight unseen. An unheard-of deal. Nancy, who had always found steady work as an actress and jingle singer in Toronto, saw her good fortune continue in Los Angeles, quickly getting signed to a holding deal at CBS, which would culminate in a pilot the following year.

The Associates was a joy to do, with great writing and a great cast, including Alley Mills, later the mom on *The Wonder Years*, Joe Regalbuto, later of *Murphy Brown*, and, as our boss, the wonderful British character actor Wilfrid Hyde-White. (He played Pickering in the movie version of *My Fair Lady*, singing "The Rain in Spain" with Audrey Hepburn and Rex Harrison.) Nancy and I rented a furnished house in the Hollywood Hills with views of the Valley. Our first night, we stood there giddily, looking at all the twinkling lights below, while the sound of two gay men arguing—one saying spitefully to the other, "Randy, everything I do is wrong! *Everything!*"—echoed through the canyon.

Ahhh, I thought. Canyon views, same-sex domestic spats, and the smell of jacaranda trees in bloom. I could get used to this. Even the Dobermans that got loose from the house down the street and scared the shit out of us were kind of exciting, because they were *Bill Shatner's Dobermans.*

You can probably figure out, since you've never heard of *The Associates*, that it didn't become the massive hit we all assumed it would be. It was actually a pretty good show, worthy of the Brooks pedigree, and it won positive advance reviews in *Variety* and other publications. But the show just didn't take with viewers. It was pulled from ABC's lineup after four episodes. While it got a second shot in the spring of 1980, with five more episodes airing, no one particularly wanted to be associated with *The Associates* anymore, and off it went.

Still, I forged onward in L.A., undaunted. I was growing to love the place. Wilfrid Hyde-White, an endless font of show-business lore who had worked with everyone from George Bernard Shaw to Marilyn *Mon*-roe, as he pronounced her name, was nominated for a Golden Globe award—as was *The Associates* itself—so Nancy and I got to attend our first L.A. awards show. On top of that, Robin Williams, who was on fire at the time with *Mork & Mindy*, asked me to accept his award for him, since he couldn't make the ceremony. I'd gotten to know Robin a bit from doing work on the side at the Comedy Store on the Sunset Strip, in an ad hoc group that he and I occasionally joined called the Comedy Store Players. Robin was staggeringly fast on his feet onstage and a truly considerate guy. His trick, when he wasn't sure of your name, was to address you as "Doctor": "*Hell*-o, Doctor! What's goin' on, Doctor? Ha-*ha!*"

That first Golden Globes was a dazzling affair for the likes of little Marty and Nancy Short from Ontario. We shared a table with Marilu Henner and her date for the night, John Travolta. We met Dustin Hoffman after his win for his performance in *Kramer vs. Kramer*. At one point I went up to Al Pacino, of whom I was a huge fan, and babbled on endlessly about what his work meant to me, and how every Al Pacino film is a master class in acting, and so forth. When I finally took a breath, he looked at me quizzically for a moment and said, "I ordered a vodka about twenty minutes ago. Can you find out what happened to that?" To be fair, Al was thirsty, and I *did* look like a kid waiter!

The following TV season, 1980–'81, Nancy was cast in *Soap*, the hit nighttime soap-opera parody that was pretty daring for the time; Billy Crystal was in it as Jodie Dallas, one of the first regular gay characters on television. Nancy's character, Annie, was the second wife of one of *Soap*'s two patriarchs, Chester Tate, a WASP twit expertly played by Robert Mandan. I, meanwhile, was cast in *I'm a Big Girl Now*, a sitcom vehicle for Diana Canova, one of *Soap*'s young breakout stars. Both shows were on ABC and had been created by Witt/Thomas/Harris, a highly successful production team, so it felt like we were being well taken care of by the industry.

Well, it seemed that way until we encountered a slight hiccup: in July 1980, our union, the Screen Actors Guild, went on strike, temporarily halting production of our shows and every other scripted network TV program. Nancy and I figured that since we were stuck in a holding pattern, we might as well fly back to Toronto and resume living in our beloved house on Indian Road until the situation resolved itself. I arranged to return to Second City Toronto for an open-ended engagement as a member of the cast.

Shortly before we left L.A., I ran into Robin Williams at a party. He asked me, "What will you do during the strike?" I told him of my Second City plan. With a mischievous glint in his eye, he said, "Can I come and visit? Perhaps do a set or two?" I said absolutely, never expecting him to act upon my encouragement.

Cut to August. It was night, I was onstage performing, and who comes bounding into the Old Fire Hall, rumpled yet bright-eyed, but Robin himself. Bear in mind that *Mork & Mindy* was about to begin its third season and that *Popeye*, Robin's first big movie, was coming out later that year. He still had most of his fantastic film career ahead of him, but never again would there be a moment when Robin was hotter. The Second City crowd went utterly insane at the sight of him, the audience members suddenly up on their feet.

Robin proceeded to do a set with us and totally killed. The speed of his mind, and the ease with which words, characters, and comic ideas poured out of him, was jaw-dropping—and, for the rest of us in the cast, both inspiring and intimidating. That night, Robin and I played Shakespearean father-and-son haberdashers, competing drunken choreographers with a bitter interpersonal history, and a two-headed man from Newfoundland singing gaily of the glories of Canada.

At one point, in his merry exuberance, Robin, unfamiliar with the dimensions of the stage, tumbled right off it and onto some delighted patrons. He was fine, though the white-linen pants he was wearing got smudged up pretty badly.

Only after the set did I learn from Robin the circumstances under which he had arrived at the theater. He had impulsively decided, in L.A., to take me up on my offer for him to visit. So off to LAX he went—with no cash and no luggage, only a credit card and the clothes on his back. He landed in Toronto, rented a car, and, in those pre-GPS days, drove around confusedly, getting lost a few times, until he finally pulled up at the Old Fire Hall.

We had Robin stay with us at Indian Road. While he slept, Nancy kindly took it upon herself to wash the clothes that he had arrived in. (I loaned him some of my clothes to tide him over until he bought some of his own the next day.) What Nancy didn't realize was that Robin's linen pants were dry-clean-only. After they'd been washed and dried, they looked like culottes, four inches shorter than they used to be. When Robin put them back on he immediately said, "When I get home, I'll say to my wife, 'I swear, I didn't fuck anybody! I have no idea why my pants are four inches shorter!'"

Robin was our guest for a week. It was sort of like having an agreeable, very funny teenager in the house; he slept till about two or three p.m. every day. I was never privy to Robin's wild nights out and the compulsions that underpinned them—he never went there with me, nor did he take drugs in my presence. For as long as I knew him, which was pretty much until the end of his life, I witnessed only his sweet and kind side—well, that, and the manic, unceasingly inventive comic side that everyone else witnessed, too. And here's the other thing about Robin: he was such a tremendous audience to other people being funny. He so loved to laugh, his booming "Ha-*hah*!" filling the air. (Robin was later a very good sport about the "Ha-*hah*!"-heavy impression I did of him on *SCTV*.)

But, as we've all learned, the flip side to "manic" is "depressive," and I did see in Robin, that week in Toronto, a certain melancholy. Our guest bedroom was up in the attic, and in the afternoons, he enjoyed simply staring out the room's street-facing window, watching the local kids play road hockey as he sat quietly. "*Ohhh*," he'd say in that vaguely Irish-sounding, wonderment-tinged Robin lilt, "they're so *won*-derful, Marty. So utterly carefree. I wish I could stay here and watch them all day!" He reminded me of Saint-Exupéry's Little Prince: wistfully surveying a world to which he felt he didn't quite belong.

T he actors' strike was finally settled in October. Nancy and I returned to L.A. and plunged right into work, our Hollywood careers seemingly ascendant. Near the end of the year, with both of us raking in sitcom dough, we decided that we deserved a celebration. So on December 22, 1980, after six years of living in sin, we were married in St. Basil's Church in Toronto, in the midst of a whirling, swirling snowstorm. Weather aside, our wedding reception, which was held at the Palais Royale, a gorgeous old waterfront dance hall where Count Basie and Duke Ellington had once played, was as raucous and sloppily fun as we'd hoped. (Though we did have one of those towering, elegant croquembouche cakes.) We'd booked a honeymoon suite in the swanky Windsor Arms Hotel, but as we were driving there, Nancy said, "Marty, do you realize that all the Shorts are back at our house right now, having one of the greatest post-wedding after-parties imaginable—and *we're missing it?*" My bride, the genius! I made a quick illegal U-turn on Bloor Street and headed straight back to our place on Indian Road to swing with the Shorts. After all, Nan and I had already done the "consummation" thing years ago, that night I'd nearly blown it with *Blazing Saddles* interruptus.

Upon our return to L.A., Diana Canova and another of my *I'm a Big Girl Now* castmates, the bawdy, sexy Sheree North, organized a celebratory wedding dinner for us. When it came time to open our gifts, it was clear that someone—I suspect Sheree—had mandated that they all be pornographic in nature. I can tell you from experience that there's nothing more awkward than listening to your waiter announce the night's specials while you are unwrapping a brand-new set of Ben Wa balls. The presents only got filthier from there: vibrators of all shapes and colors, a potpourri of flavored lubricants, and, to cap it all off, a monstrous two-foot-long rubber dildo attached to a pair of rubber testicles. When the night was over and we got home, Nancy and I laughingly stashed our sex-toy haul into an unused bottom drawer of our dresser in the house that we were renting at the time.

We wouldn't have given these wares another thought (I swear!)

were it not for what happened a month later. We were back in Toronto on break during our shows' hiatuses when we got a call from our landlady, Mrs. Vogel. She was a kindly German woman who lived three doors down from us. She was calling to inform us that our house had been broken into. "All da drawers in da bedroom vere pulled out," Mrs. Vogel reported, "and their contents vere scattered around da bedroom."

I said, "When you say all the drawers, do you mean *all* the drawers?"

"Jah, all da drawers," she said. "And all da contents of da drawers vere dusted for fingerprints." Normally Mrs. Vogel was very friendly, but there was an uncharacteristic coldness to her voice. Suddenly I understood why.

"Were the contents put back in the drawers?" I asked.

"No," she said, even more coldly than before. "Ve vill leave that for you."

Nancy and I wasted little time in flying back to L.A. We hurried from the airport to our robber-tossed crime-scene house, and when we got there, lo and behold, spread out on the floor for all of the LAPD to see were our carefully fingerprint-dusted wedding gifts.

A s it turned out, our high-riding L.A.-sitcom days were short-lived. *Soap* was on its last legs by the time Nancy joined up, and the show was canceled after her one season on it. *I'm a Big Girl Now* fared no better. I played one of Diana Canova's professional colleagues, Neal Stryker, the office whiz kid at a Washington, DC, think tank. But by the season's eighth show, the writers found the think-tank setting too limiting so they decided, without any explanation to the audience, to turn our workplace into a newspaper. Needless to say, *I'm a Big Girl Now* was not renewed. On the plus side, I did get to meet Danny Thomas, who played the father of Diana's character and had been a childhood favorite of mine on his 1950s TV show *Make Room for Daddy*. Danny was very nice to me, though, discomfitingly, he wore a holstered pistol on his person at all times. Diana would feel it pressing against her stomach when they would hug on-camera as father and daughter. Diana said that if the series had been picked up for a second season, she wouldn't have asked for more money, but, rather, for Danny to lose the gun.

Eventually the chanciness and highly variable quality of television work chased Nancy and me out of town. Another pilot I did, between *The Associates* and *I'm a Big Girl Now*, was so bad that I was rooting for it to fail almost from the start. *White and Reno* was loosely based on the veteran black comic Slappy White's experiences as part of an interracial comedy team called Rossi and White. In our show, Slappy played the manager of a young comedy team composed of me (Reno) and his nephew (White, played by William Allen Young). Reno and White were not only partners but also roommates whose friendly, foxy neighbors were played by the real-life sisters and *Playboy* models Audrey and Judy Landers. Audrey's character was a nurse, while Judy's was—and here, the word *stretch* comes to mind—a stripper with a heart of gold. Dick Martin of *Rowan & Martin's Laugh-In* fame directed the pilot, and the humor was on the level of me saying to Slappy's character, "Ben, jokes like this won't get us a spot on *The Tonight Show* with Johnny," and Slappy replying, "Yah, but jokes like this will keep you from going *down* the—*Johhhh-nnny*!"

Every time Slappy said that line during the run-throughs, I'd suddenly feel the sharp knife of a migraine ripping through my brain. Mother's balls, I'd think, what if this horrid thing actually goes? About a month after we filmed the pilot, while we were awaiting word on the show's future, I was at the Crocker Bank in

Studio City when I noticed a familiar NBC executive standing in line. He saw me and beamingly flashed me a thumbs-up, as if to say, *Looks like your show is getting picked up, kid.* Me, the star of the freshman NBC sitcom *White and Reno*! It was a future I found so appalling that I had the audacity to walk right up to the guy and say, "Look, I don't run your network, but I'm here to tell you that you're making a terrible mistake." To my relief, *White and Reno* went down the *Johhhh-nnny* shortly thereafter.

Nancy and I moved to New York for a spell after our respective sitcoms died. We had no jobs lined up, but we could afford to take the risk, because we had earned dual network incomes in L.A. and were childless, so the financial cushion was there. Nancy was already pulling away from show business. Though she never had trouble getting cast in TV pilots, she disliked the process more and more—the idea of driving over that hill into Burbank to sit, yet again, in a waiting room with a bunch of other girls who all looked alike and all wanted it so badly, even though the pilots she was reading for made *White and Reno* look like *The Wire*. Plus, we were trying to get pregnant, and Nancy saw segueing into motherhood as a natural way out of the performing phase of her life.

And me? I wanted to take a shot at Broadway. I auditioned to be a replacement in a hit musical that had been running for a while, *A Day in Hollywood / A Night in the Ukraine*. Didn't get it. The Nine Categories served me well at this point, the early 1980s. I didn't panic as I had on Breakdown Corner, but, rather, I started contemplating the reality that most people don't make it as actors—and maybe I wasn't going to, either. I was thinking about pursuing a more backstage involvement in show business, the way that my friend Harold Ramis had, brilliantly refashioning himself as a writer, with *Animal House*, *Meatballs*, *Caddyshack*, and *Stripes* already to his credit. Sure, the fact that I couldn't really *write* gave me slight pause—but then, that hadn't stopped a lot of successful screenwriters in Hollywood, so I remained upbeat.

As all these thoughts were churning in my head, Andrew Alexander, for the second time in five years, descended suddenly from the rafters with harp in hand, my guardian angel. He called me in New York and asked if I would be interested in moving back to Toronto and joining *SCTV* as a writer-performer. I had to think about it for, like . . . oh, I don't know—zero seconds?

S*CTV* was, it's not hyperbolic to say, the hottest thing going in comedy at that moment. The show had been on Canadian TV sporadically between 1976 and 1981, bouncing from commercial to public television. By its 1981–'82 season, though, NBC had picked up *SCTV* as a ninety-minute program that aired Friday nights after *The Tonight Show*. Its ratings were never particularly high, but it was during that season that *SCTV* really took off among the comedy cognoscenti—in marked contrast to *Saturday Night Live*, which was then in its post-Lorne period, with Dick Ebersol trying to salvage the show after a bad season with Jean Doumanian at its helm.

Andrew Alexander was the Lorne of *SCTV*, and he faced an issue not unlike the one that Lorne had discussed with me when Danny Aykroyd and John Belushi were poised to leave *SNL*: Rick Moranis and Dave Thomas were on the verge of departing to do, among other things, a Bob and Doug McKenzie movie called *Strange Brew*. Catherine O'Hara was thinking of leaving at season's end, too. But Andrew wanted me to come north right away, to work on the remaining three 90-minute episodes of the 1981–'82 season alongside Rick, Dave, and Catherine, as well as Eugene Levy, Andrea Martin, John Candy, and Joe Flaherty.

These people, with the exception of Rick, who had never been in Second City Toronto and had come aboard *SCTV* via his friendship with Dave (and, needless to say, his obvious talent), were all old friends. Not only were the performers and writers of *SCTV* like family to me, but in some cases they *were* family: Andrea was now my in-law, married to Nancy's brother, Bob Dolman, who was working at the show as a writer . . . as was my own brother, Michael.

All that said, my exhilaration at being tapped by Andrew quickly turned into intimidation. It's entirely possible to be awed by your old friends. While I had been away doing my L.A. thing, they had all honed and perfected their craft to a point where they were now doing work way beyond anything we ever did onstage at the Old Fire Hall. *SCTV* was so brilliantly realized: a sketch TV show organized around the premise of a fictitious network (the Second City Television Network) that operates out of a fictitious town (Melonville) and offers its own slate of dodgy programming, populated by its own constellation of demi-stars. Far away from the meddling hands of American network executives, Joe, John, Eugene, Catherine, Dave, Rick, and Andrea, along with Harold Ramis, who was the show's original head writer and a cast member for *SCTV*'s first season, had created something stunningly layered and original.

Joe was Guy Caballero, the station's owner, as well as the talk-show host Sammy Maudlin and the howling horror host Count Floyd. Andrea was unrelentingly hilarious as Edith Prickley, the network's horny, leopard-print-clad station manager. Catherine was spectacular as the steely-needy-leggy showbiz survivor Lola Heatherton. John and Eugene were comic perfection together as the polka duo the Shmenge Brothers, and, individually, especially adroit at parodying low-budget local advertising (John, in snake face paint: "Hi, I'm Harry, the guy with a snake on his face!"; Eugene, with beard and flailing limbs: "Hi, my name's Phil, and

I got a warehouse full of nails!"), while Rick and Dave were great not only as Bob and Doug but as impressionists, their Woody Allen–Bob Hope homage, "Play It Again, Bob," astonishingly well-realized. And those characters are just a fraction of those that every cast member wheeled out week after week. Everyone was acutely versatile, equally capable of playing broad or subtle.

And *SCTV* placed great faith in the intelligence of its audience, assuming that its viewers were as bright as or brighter than its creators. The nuance that its writers and cast brought to their parodies of showbiz made watching the show feel like a very smart, very insider experience. Conan O'Brien has told me that he and his brother, when they were very impressionable (and very pale) teens, would watch *SCTV* and say, "*They're* saying the things that we just *think*!" It was almost disappointing, Conan says, when the brothers O'Brien discovered that people besides them knew of *SCTV*, because they considered it *their* show.

I felt the same reverence. I couldn't believe how good *SCTV* was. And now I had to plunge in and become a part of it. But my nervousness swiftly fell away after the first read-through, where, to my surprise and delight, two pieces I'd written with my brother Michael not only got laughs but were actually approved to be filmed. One was a bit in which I played the paparazzo Ron Galella, who was known for pursuing Jackie Onassis everywhere she went, and the other was a takeoff on Richard Pryor's then-massive *Live on the Sunset Strip* concert film—only ours was a promo for *Martin Scorsese's Jerry Lewis Live on the Champs-Élysées*. After the read-through, Joe Flaherty congratulated me by saying, "Well done—and next time, write cheaper!"

I got my first sketch lead in a piece that Rick didn't want to do, a parody of a 1950s-era Red Scare movie called "I Was a Teenage Communist." I also made a positive impression in a Paul Flaherty–

Dick Blasucci piece called *Battle of the PBS Stars*, in which I, as Fred Rogers of *Mister Rogers' Neighborhood*, squared off in a boxing ring against Julia Child, played, inevitably, by John Candy. (Mister Rogers won dirty, by decking Julia with his King Friday puppet.) I did a lot of flipping and tumbling as Mister Rogers, which excited Paul and Dick, who happily exclaimed, "Ah, a physical-comedy guy!" If nothing else, that was a niche I could occupy.

But what made me truly earn my *SCTV* stripes was *Martin Scorsese's Jerry Lewis Live on the Champs-Élysées*. Having idolized Lewis my whole life, to actually play him—and to "run around like a monkey," as Dave Letterman once described my Lewis shtick—was as fulfilling a moment creatively as I'd ever experienced. I appeared not as early slapstick Jerry, but as mid-period auteur Jerry, with the slicked hair, the blockish oversize eyeglasses, the attitude of superiority, and the legions of adoring French faithful. In one scene I wore a child's sailor suit while smoking a cigarette and lecturing the crowd: "And the point is, they're terrified of a perfectionist. And if a *Jerry Lewis* ain't gonna get a distribution deal, because of some fakakta twelve-year-old with the pimples on his face who's head of the studio . . . *this* week . . . who doesn't know from *Hardly Working* or *The Errand Boy* or *Cinderfella* . . . where are you, the public, expected to find the *love* and the *caring* and the *feeling* and the *good* and the *nice*? And even if you did, it wouldn't be the good kind, because of the difference caused by the earlier thing."

My Jerry was a temperamental fellow who broke down while singing "You'll *Jamais* Walk Alone" and went ballistic at his conductor (played by Dave) for not picking up this breakdown as a musical cue: "When I do the cry, you do the cue! Cry? Cue! You like your job? *Do it!*"

It was during this Jerry bit that one of the show's producers, Nancy Geller, called people over to the TV monitor showing the live feed in her office and said, "Is everyone watching what's going on here?"

I was in; I had proven that I was attuned to that not easily located *SCTV* frequency where each sketch, and each characterization, was rife with subtle, unexplained touches that lent the comedy unusual texture, even if they didn't always make apparent sense. (This sensibility would also serve me well in working with Christopher Guest in the years to come.) It had all been pent up in me, these ideas, these characters, this *energy*. For the first time my career trajectory was coinciding with the hip energy in comedy. At thirty-two, I was finally able to give the world the Full Marty.

R ick, Dave, and Catherine did indeed leave the show at the end of that season, in May '82. As I've said, I still think in terms of the school-year calendar, and the *SCTV* schedule neatly coincided with my mind-set: we didn't have to go back to work until the day after Labor Day. I was beside myself with joy. It had been a long time since I'd had the perfect actor's summer: two months off, with the guarantee of a good job in the fall.

It was daunting to carry on with *SCTV* with a mere five performers—John, Joe, Andrea, Eugene, and me—but the atmosphere that next season was total bliss. Collectively, the five of us were in great spirits and creatively fertile. We would go on to win an Emmy that season for Outstanding Writing in a Comedy or Music Program. There was literally no way for us to lose: all five nominees in the category were *SCTV* episodes.

John Candy—how fabulous was it to finally collaborate creatively with this man? Though he and I had known each other ten years, we'd never truly worked together closely, unless you count the time he (unintentionally) broke two of my ribs while we were roughhousing with a football on the set of *The David Steinberg Show*. The two of us just looked funny together, given our size difference, whether it was the Fred Rogers–Julia Child thing or him playing Ed Grimley's evil, manipulative brother Skip Grimley in *What Ever Happened to Baby Ed?*, our homage to the Joan Crawford–Bette Davis kitsch classic *What Ever Happened to Baby Jane?*

A typical John writing session took place at his huge house north of Toronto. John always radiated prosperity and magnanimity; he had movie roles in real movies way ahead of the rest of us (in *Stripes*, *The Blues Brothers*, and even Steven Spielberg's *1941*), and he loved playing host and picking up the check. Actually, we never really got much writing done at John's. We'd drink a bunch of rum and Cokes, watch some delivery men load a new pool table into his rec room, eat dinner at around eleven thirty, and then I'd clap my hands and say, "John, we have got to write this scene." "And we *will*," he'd say, "but first, how dare your glass be empty, you bastard!" And there would go the night.

Which isn't to say we didn't work hard on *SCTV*. But it was all so idyllic. As a little boy, I'd watched *The Dick Van Dyke Show* and romanticized its view of show business: the way Rob Petrie's job was to go sit in a room all day, write jokes with Morey Amsterdam and Rose Marie, and then be home in New Rochelle in time for dinner with his sexy wife. *SCTV* was really like that. Every episode was labor-intensive, but we kept civilized hours. And the conviviality of our writing sessions was unlike anything I've experienced since—even when things got contentious.

One time, Andrea was pitching an idea that Eugene didn't get. Now, Eugene was *SCTV*'s most prolific and selfless writer, generating more material than anyone else and giving himself the least flashy roles in the cast pieces he'd write. He was and is the sweetest human being ever created; I still address him by the nickname his mother bestowed upon him, Lamby. (Mrs. Levy was that rarest of specimens, an Orthodox Jew reared in Scotland; "Oh, my wee Lamby," she'd tenderly say in her unique Yiddish-Scottish accent as she served Eugene an extra helping of brisket.) But in the writers' room, Eugene could get very professorial. And in his slightly serious, analytical way, Eugene said, "Andrea, I wish I could understand the humor of that scene, but I just can't." Andrea, who was sitting next to Eugene, stared at him for a beat and then reached over with her pen and marked an X on the crotch of his pants, where his penis would be. "I'm just putting that there so Deb can find it later," she said.

The working pace at *SCTV* was so civilized. We'd take six weeks to write and then six weeks to shoot, followed by another cycle of six weeks writing and six weeks shooting. The writing breaks were crucial, for they allowed inchoate ideas to develop, mature, ripen, and, on occasion, ferment into total, utter originality, all without the *SNL*-style pressure of "Whaddaya got for *this week?*" And when Catherine came back to do our Christmas shows, we had even more fun. (Catherine, I think, had the most unique, brilliant comic instincts of any of us—a fearless Canadian individuality coupled with a magical changeling's ability to morph into any being her fertile, freaky mind could conjure—while Andrea was the most instinctively funny of us as a performer.)

The unsung heroes of *SCTV* were its hair, makeup, and costume people. Our head of makeup was Beverley Schechtman, whose constant refrain to me was "Give me the look"—meaning, show her the signature facial expression(s) of whichever character I was trying to formulate. So, for Jerry Lewis, I'd do a series of Jerry faces, and I'd have a robe on, to which Bev would tape photographs of the real Jerry while trying to achieve the ideal synthesis of what he looked like and what I was doing with my face.

For Jackie Rogers Jr. I did my palsied, cockeyed Sammy Davis Jr. face, and Bev did her magic with makeup to bring out Jackie's full albino grotesquerie. Our hair and wig designer, though that title barely covers the full extent of her gifts, was Judi Cooper-Sealy. She would not just hand me a wig but present me with five albino-white versions of Jackie's hair—among them a Veronica Lake swoop, a Farrah Fawcett shag, and a pageboy—and I'd try them all on before deciding, "Judi, let's go with the pageboy."

Our costume designer was a man named Juul Haalmayer, who was almost like another comedy writer. I could say to him, "Jackie should be Vegas-y, but *low* Vegas-y, bordering on Reno," and he'd intuitively get it, without any rigmarole. I'd show up the next day, and there on the costume rack would be the shimmery silver tunic and leggings: the Jackie look as horrified viewers would come to know it.

S*CTV* deliberately veered away from any comedy concept that seemed too obvious, e.g., a note-for-note parody of some current show like *Three's Company*. Eugene and I, for example, did this routine in which we donned tuxedos and painted our teeth white to play Sandler and Young, a real-life nightclub singing duo (I was the Belgian-born Tony Sandler, and Eugene the American-born Ralph Young) who were a constant presence on TV specials in the 1960s and '70s. Sandler and Young specialized in performing hopelessly dull, hopelessly square duets. Surely no human being in North America was clamoring for a parodic rendering of Sandler and Young, yet we plowed ahead, and it worked, regardless of whether the viewers had ever even heard of the act. (Sandler and Young were occasional guests on *The Sammy Maudlin Show*—Eugene singing "Feelin' Groovy" in counterpoint to me singing "Alouette," that sort of thing.)

Ed Grimley, my old Second City stage character, was someone I'd initially resisted bringing to television, because I thought he was just too weird even for *SCTV.* Well, that, and because he had by that point become a very intimate figure in my personal life—the character Nancy summoned to mediate our arguments, and whose face I sometimes pulled as I walked out of the shower, dripping wet and naked, just to get a laugh out of her. You know, you put together the concepts of "naked" and "marital aide" and "Ed" and you start to think, this is way too personal for anyone besides Marty and Nancy Short to see.

But there was a call at the end of the 1981–'82 season, before Rick and Dave left, for one-off low-budget pieces that could be shot quickly, against a wall, and I came up with the idea of Ed being a guest lecturer on "Sunrise Semester," a recurring *SCTV* bit that parodied dull early-morning educational television. It was pretty simple: Ed talking about snakes—"The snake is a hypnotic thing, I must say . . ."—and then falling under the sway of a cobra with whom he comes face-to-face: "Yes, master . . ." No one was particularly taken with the piece in the writers' room, but I filmed it anyway, barely having any idea what I was doing.

SCTV was filmed at Magder Studios in Toronto. The way it was laid out, the writing offices were upstairs, and you had to walk down the stairs and across the actual studio floor to get to the dressing rooms and hair-and-makeup area, as well as to the Italian restaurant on the ground floor that we all frequented. Dave Thomas was passing through the studio while I was filming Ed's *Sunrise Semester,* and I showed him the playback, asking him how I could make the piece better. Dave regarded the screen for a moment and answered, "Just do it. Keep going. I have no idea what you're doing, but I think you do."

The lead producer of *SCTV* that season, Don Novello, best known as Father Guido Sarducci on *Saturday Night Live,* didn't know what to make of the "Sunrise Semester" bit and didn't slate it for an episode. That might have been the end of Ed right there. But the following season, a new producer, Pat Whitley, found the snake piece sitting on the shelf and thought it was hysterical. So Ed finally made it to network television on Friday, November 19, 1982, and, for reasons no one on this planet can fully explain, connected with viewers. Dave was right: I just had to keep going and trust that someone would find these dispatches from my odd little mind appealing.

From there, Ed became a regular, an actor who worked at the Second City Television Network, appearing with John in *What Ever Happened to Baby Ed?*, as a lovelorn dweeb in the Jerry Lewis–movie takeoff *The Nutty Lab Assistant*, and as the star of the after-school special *The Fella Who Couldn't Wait for Christmas*: "This waiting is, like, making me mental, I must say. What time is it now? Aw, two oh four, this is a *joke*!"

G oing home from work late one night, I picked up a copy of *New York* magazine to read on the subway. Leafing through its pages, I was flabbergasted to find an article by James Wolcott, the future *Vanity Fair* columnist, that was basically a two-page paean to me. "Short has brought to *SCTV* the elfin twinkle he had on *The Associates*," Wolcott wrote, "but he's also chipped in something novel and unanticipated—a brash, cavorting, crazy-legged kickiness."

I'd learned long ago not to put much stock in reviews, but this was something different: an unsolicited love letter to what I personally had brought to *SCTV*. I can't tell you how good it felt, how validating. Of my Jerry Lewis impression, Wolcott said that it played as "a pitilessly detailed piece of caricature," but "when Short vamped with the orchestra, braving whiplash as he flung back his head in mad abandon, he reminded us of how much fun Jerry Lewis was in his bounding prime, when his anarchistic exuberance threatened to burst his seams." Yes, exactly. I wasn't above poking fun at Lewis, but I brought affection and a sense of tribute to my Lewis bits too. I considered them the performance equivalent of Al Hirschfeld's pen-and-ink caricatures. Yes, you had to show the warts, but you also had to prove why the subject was worthy of your attention.

What *SCTV* was for me, I came to realize, was the culmination of all those routines I did as a child in the attic on Whitton Road—right down to the idea of an imaginary television network stocked with imaginary programming. The way I see it, you spend the first fifteen years of your life as a sponge, soaking up influences and experiences, and the remainder of your life recycling, regurgitating, and reprocessing those first fifteen years.

Ed Grimley owed a lot to the Harpo Marx routines I saw on TV in old Marx Brothers movies. Harpo was my favorite of the Marx Brothers. To me, his movements, facial expressions, and unpredictable sight gags (effortlessly positioning his thigh to hang from a lady's arm, reaching deep into the folds of his trench coat to produce a full glass of water) were infinitely funnier than any punch-line-driven joke.

There was some Jerry Lewis in Ed, too. What I loved most about Lewis was his penchant for the absurd. There's a lesser-known film in his canon, *Three On a Couch*, in which he has to pose as an experienced cowboy to impress a girl. When they go to a rodeo, she, trusting him to know what he's doing, pushes him out into the ring when the emcee asks for volunteers. You don't actually see what happens next. You see the rodeo audience's impressed reaction turn into shock, and *then* the camera cuts back to the ring, where Lewis is lying on the ground with his arms and legs trussed up, the cow standing calmly beside him.

In the best Lewis bits, as in the best Harpo bits, you can't just sit there passively, waiting for a cue to laugh—you're a participant in a ping-ponging comedic journey that ends up somewhere completely different from where you expected to be.

Jonathan Winters, Lucille Ball, Jackie Gleason, Dick Van Dyke—all were also huge influences. What they had in common was that their comedy was more about the character than the joke. That, and the fact that they were on television. My favorite TV show of them all was probably *The Jack Paar Program*, the Friday-night variety show that Paar reemerged with from 1962 to 1965 after he had given up the nightly grind of *The Tonight Show*. (Another parallel between childhood and *SCTV*: the joy to be found on TV at the end of the week, when you got to stay up late.)

Among Paar's regular guests were the comedy team of Mike Nichols and Elaine May, whose true gift, as with everyone I've mentioned above, was for layered, fully inhabited characters. I sat awed as I watched May, as a Jewish mother, place a phone call to her rocket-scientist son, played by Nichols, and via an unrelenting onslaught of guilt and manipulation, reduce him in five minutes from an annoyed, busy professional to a jabbering, infantilized toddler.

I've since gotten to know Mike, and he's the one person, of all the many famous figures I've met, of whom I'm still in awe when I'm with him. I mean, I keep a vintage vinyl LP of the album *An Evening with Mike Nichols and Elaine May* in my office as a kind of aspirational talisman—and yet I actually have Mike Nichols's e-mail address! In fact, whenever I get an e-mail from Mike, I want to print it out and have it framed. He's as funny in person as he was on TV in the 1960s, too. A few years ago David Geffen invited us both onto his spectacular yacht, the *Rising Sun*. As we sat down to dinner one night, I took in the sight of all David's guests—each one famous and accomplished—and decided to initiate a game called

"Who Has Met Whom?" Surely at least *one* member of this crowd had met just about any great twentieth-century figure you could think of. "Did anyone here ever meet Eleanor Roosevelt?" Warren Beatty responded, "Actually, *I* met Eleanor Roosevelt." From the far end of the table, Mike called out, "Did you fuck her?"

S *CTV* was where I got to emulate these comedy heroes, to bring their influences to bear—often, ironically, in the service of playing delusional non-talents like Jackie Rogers Jr. or Irving Cohen. The name Jackie Rogers, by the way, was a borrowing from my TV-obsessed childhood: a stage name I thought up for myself in my teens, when "Martin Short" seemed too pedestrian. I was totally intent on becoming a doctor back then, but for the sake of dotting all the i's and crossing all the t's of my imaginary show-business career, I needed to have the stage name nailed down too.

I never wanted to leave *SCTV,* or for it to end. After the 1982–'83 season, Dick Ebersol approached me about joining the cast of *Saturday Night Live,* and I turned him down. For a moment this looked like a foolish decision; NBC dropped our show in the spring of '83. But *SCTV* received a stay of execution when Cinemax, the premium cable network, stepped in to underwrite and air another season. By that time the show was down to a four-person cast, since the siren call of Hollywood had become too persuasive for John Candy, ever beloved and in demand, to ignore. Joe, Eugene, Andrea, and I banded together for the negotiations with Cinemax, and with the aid of expert management secured an absurdly lucrative deal—the biggest payday any of us had ever experienced.

There was another reason to stay with *SCTV,* besides the fact that it was the best job I'd ever had: Nancy and I were about to become parents, and we didn't want to disrupt what had become a pretty perfect life in Toronto. We had struggled for a few years to get pregnant the usual way, with no luck. Then we tried in-vitro fertilization, and still no luck. Nancy was eventually diagnosed with endometriosis, in which the cells that form the uterus's lining (the endometrium) also grow outside the uterus, where they're not supposed to—a condition that, in some women, causes infertility. So we decided to pursue adoption, and in December of '83 we welcomed into our home our first child, the most beautiful baby girl maybe ever. We named her Katherine Elizabeth. She was joined in '86 and '89 by, respectively, her dashing brothers Oliver Patrick and Henry Hayter.

By the good graces of Cinemax, Nancy and I enjoyed one last season of *SCTV* bliss, joined midway by little Katherine. My three castmates and I carried on happily for eighteen new forty-five-minute episodes, with guest appearances from John, Catherine, and Dave, our ranks occasionally augmented by such friends and Second City associates as John Hemphill, Valri Bromfield, Jayne Eastwood, Mary Charlotte Wilcox, and, as Ed Grimley's love interest in the fairy-tale fantasia *The Fella Who Was the Size of Someone's Thumb*, my own bride, Nancy.

As a now-confident core member of *SCTV*, I pulled off some work I'm truly proud of in that final season, even if hardly anyone saw it, since Cinemax was not as widely available as it is today. The weirdness of Jackie Rogers Jr. reached its apogee in *Gimme Jackie*—a send-up of the controversial Rolling Stones documentary *Gimme Shelter*, the one that depicted the concert at Altamont Speedway in which a spectator was killed by Hell's Angels who had been hired as security. In our version, Jackie's Australian manager (played by a visiting Dave Thomas) had hired fez-capped Shriners to be the security goons. Jackie promised an outdoor-concert experience that would be "about music, good weed, and some heavy-duty balling," but his decision to open his set with the theme from *The Love Boat* incited a riot. In typically serpentine, nonsensical *SCTV* fashion, this eventually led to a scene in which Jackie had to submit to a lie-detector test administered by the attorney F. Lee Bailey (Eugene), where Jackie ended up admitting through tears that he was still a virgin.

SCTV folded its tent for good in the spring of 1984, with Ed making one last appearance in the network's futile pledge drive, offering a copy of his new concept album, *Did She Call?*, to viewers who pledged $60 and up.

Once again, after the season had wrapped, Dick Ebersol called to see if I would join the cast of *Saturday Night Live*. This time I said yes.

INTERLUDE

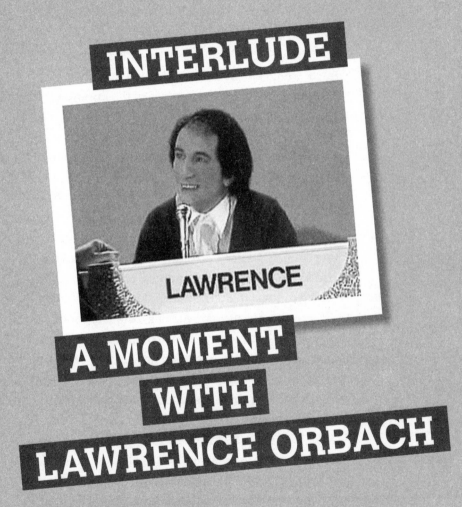

LAWRENCE

A MOMENT WITH WITH LAWRENCE ORBACH

Lawrence was one of the more unsung carryover characters to travel with me from **SCTV** to **Saturday Night Live**. He began his life as a simpleton I played in a sketch written by Eugene Levy called "Half-Wits": a game show whose contestants were slow people. I'd been toying with the idea of a character who had never gotten his second teeth—his first teeth never fell out, so he was an adult with baby teeth. Bev Schechtman, **SCTV**'s endlessly inventive makeup wizard, would simply blacken the bottom halves of my upper teeth and the top halves of the lower teeth. It worked brilliantly. For Jackie Rogers Jr., Bev started painting my teeth white, giving them a cheesy bad-cap look. Years later I met Carol Burnett and told her about this trick, and she loved it. "How could I have been working in comedy all these years," she said, "and no one told me about **painting my teeth**?"

So that was the beginning of the character, Lawrence Orbach. I wasn't planning to go particularly broad with Lawrence's appearance, because we'd received a request from hair and makeup to tone down the massive looks to spare **SCTV**'s exhausted staff. But one day I walked into the makeup room and saw this huge honker of a prosthetic nose sitting on one of the molds. "Who's that for?" I said. Judi Cooper-Sealy, our hair and wig chief, responded, "Oh, it's for Joe. He's gonna wear that in 'Half-Wits.' "

Well, that did it. If I'm competing with that nose, I thought, I've got to amp it up. It had always made me laugh, in a sad kind of way, when I'd see guys in their late twenties going prematurely bald. So as Lawrence I would wear a bald pate covered by a receding hairline. I also requested pockmarked skin, just to add a certain je ne sais quoi. As for Lawrence's demeanor, I knew a TV writer who had a nervous, slightly mouth-breathing way of talking—I'm leaving him nameless because he's actually handsome, successful, and not a moron—that I borrowed for Lawrence.

Lawrence gained his greatest fame in the very first episode of **Saturday Night Live** I did, appearing in a pretaped segment with Harry Shearer in a sketch about two brothers going for the gold in the Summer Olympics.

HARRY: **My brother and I know it's not going to be easy. Men have never done synchronized swimming in a sanctioned competition in this country. Officially it's got, like, zero acceptance.**
LAWRENCE: **I don't swim.**
HARRY: **My brother doesn't swim. So no one is going to walk up and hand us a gold medal, especially since men's synchro isn't even in the Olympics . . . yet.**
LAWRENCE: **But that's okay, because we could use the time. 'Cause I'm not that strong a swimmer.**

LAWRENCE ORBACH

High-lo. I am talking into a recorder that is inside my portable telephone. It is my understanding that this will be transcribed.

Although I have a strong command of the English language, I can neither read nor write. So words like **transcribed** are such a mystery to me.

My morning glass of milk comes from cats. Even though I'm in my mid-twenties, I'm having some degree of difficulty getting through high school. But I'll do it, because I have certain goals in life I feel compelled to achieve. One of which is becoming a circuit court judge, and the other is to perhaps play professional hockey.

FAST TIMES AT 30 ROCK

I wish I'd enjoyed *Saturday Night Live* more. I wish I hadn't felt so perpetually under pressure when I worked there. But I think that's just what the show does to some people. I certainly knew that I was at a pivotal moment in my career, and that if I made this *SNL* thing work, it would open doors for me that would have otherwise remained closed.

And don't get me wrong—I really enjoy the show *now*. I've been back to host three times, I'm friendly with roughly 90 percent of everyone who's ever worked there, and I've kissed Lorne Michaels on the mouth on national television. But my one season in the cast of *SNL* was a roller coaster of elation and anxiety. With thirty years' perspective, I now recognize that I should have allowed myself to step back for a moment and simply exult in the privilege of doing that show.

I had trepidation about *SNL* from the moment I told Dick Ebersol that I was in. (As a reminder, Dick, not Lorne, was the executive producer of the show in 1984.) I'd had as perfect a life-work setup imaginable on *SCTV*, and whatever followed was going to have a hard time topping that experience. To complicate matters further, Nancy and I rented a house in Pacific Palisades right after *SCTV* wrapped its final season, and I found myself falling in love with the California way of life; I couldn't get over the rush of seeing the ocean on my left as I drove up the Pacific Coast Highway. I put off the decision to join *SNL* for as long as possible, sitting outdoors in the sunny Palisades with a notepad, listing the pros and cons of doing the show.

The cons, to me, were many. One was essentially the same fear factor that had dissuaded me from auditioning for Second City Toronto in 1973: I didn't like the idea of being funny on demand. While by 1984 I was a proven sketch performer, I had grown accustomed to *SCTV*'s gentle, if laborious, pace. After each take, we'd all crowd around the monitor and watch the playback, and everyone would discuss how to recalibrate the scene for the next take: "Okay, maybe a little less from John, a little more from Andrea, and a lot less from Marty." (Incidentally, Mitch Hurwitz, the creator of *Arrested Development*, works the same way, which is why I had such a spectacularly fulfilling time working on that show in 2005, playing Uncle Jack, an elderly, Jack LaLanne–like fitness legend who can no longer move his legs—another in my gallery of what Joe Flaherty calls "Marty's disgusting, unlikeable characters.")

But on *Saturday Night Live*, naturally, there would be no second takes, much less third, fourth, and fifth ones. And I'd heard many a horror story about its unrelenting pressure, and what it could do to one's psyche. Plus, was it even a hip show anymore? *SNL* is such an unbreakable institution now that it's hard to remember how tenuous its future was in 1984. Eddie Murphy had given the show a much-needed boost in the early 1980s, but now he was gone, and so was Joe Piscopo. NBC was giving serious consideration to just canceling the show outright. I remember being stunned, when I finally did arrive, that *SNL*, unlike the low-budget *SCTV*, had no wig department—they still just rented stuff on a season-to-season basis, as if they were never sure if there would be a next season.

Dick Ebersol deserves a lot of credit for his crazy gambit the season I joined: shell out a bunch of money, George Steinbrenner style (that was the metaphor he used), to hire proven veterans, and let it be a somewhat different show—maybe a little more grown-up, a little more ready for primetime. It was due to the amazing people he had already recruited that I was swayed to say yes.

Billy Crystal, who had hosted the show twice the season before, agreed to come aboard, along with Christopher Guest and Harry Shearer, who were red-hot from their mockumentary *This Is Spinal Tap*, the comedy event of the year. Dick also hired Pamela Stephenson from the British sketch show *Not the Nine O'Clock News* and the stand-up comedian Rich Hall, who had his own cottage industry with his *Sniglets* books of wordplay.

Like a lot of high-priced dream teams, this one didn't always gel. There was also the separate issue of the people retained from the previous season—Julia Louis-Dreyfus, Mary Gross, Gary Kroeger, and Jim Belushi—who now had to take a backseat to the newcomers who very quickly emerged as the focus of the '84–'85 season.

Billy I knew a little from our days as Witt/Thomas/Harris actors, when I was in *I'm a Big Girl Now* and he, like Nancy, was in *Soap*. I had immediately taken a liking to him—so smart, fast, and versatile. Harry I also knew a little, because we had a friend in common, Paul Shaffer. Chris Guest I didn't know at all. But at our very first *SNL* read-through he struck me as a kindred spirit, both in his sense of humor and his own ambivalence about having enlisted. During Dick's tenure, there was a little stage in the writers' room where, if you were so inclined, you could get up with your script and act out a sketch idea rather than just table-read it. At the read-through for the first show, Jim Belushi and Gary Kroeger got up to act something out. Everyone, me included, pivoted their chairs toward the stage to watch them—everyone, that is, except Chris Guest, who sat stock-still, his back to the stage, the whole time Jim and Gary were doing their thing.

When I turned back around, I saw that Chris had written three flight options back to L.A. on the top of my script: UNITED 274, AMERICAN 117, AMERICAN 133. Pure Chris. I now knew that I was not alone in my fretfulness, and that I was in the presence of a very dry wit. Years later, he would ask me, "Martin"—Chris is one of the few people who addresses me by my full name—"tell me, what is your new film *Captain Ron* about?" I said, "Well, it's about a man with three children who inherits a boat." Without emotion or hesitation, Chris replied, "I didn't say spoil it for me."

Chris, Billy, and Harry were a formidable trio, three major comic talents in full bloom. I was simultaneously intimidated and stimulated by their collective presence.

Though the first live show of that season didn't air until October, a bunch of us newcomers got together two months in advance to write and shoot some pieces. We members of the Steinbrenner brigade were keen to make our influence felt, and we pushed for the show to embrace more elements of *Spinal Tap* and *SCTV*: from the former, a deadpan cinema verité feel, and from the latter, more pretaped bits and a heavier reliance on prosthetics and makeup. No more Chevy Chase playing Gerald Ford while looking and sounding nothing like Gerald Ford. If Harry Shearer was going to play Ronald Reagan, he would spend hours in a makeup chair to look not just a little, but *exactly like* Ronald Reagan—to visually match the accuracy of Harry's verbal impersonation.

Late in the summer of '84, Chris, Harry, Pamela, and I filmed a piece that Harry and I had written about a pair of brothers trying to make the Olympics as a synchronized swimming team—even though there was no such Olympic event as men's synchronized swimming. Harry was the older brother, a sort of determined but delusional everyman, and I was the younger brother. (Pamela played the Harry character's wife, and Chris, who improvised every word of his dialogue, was our choreographer, basically a trial run for the Corky St. Clair character he would play in *Waiting for Guffman*.) I knew right away that I should play my part as Lawrence Orbach, my "Half-Wits" character from *SCTV*, because he made sense as this guy who idolized his older brother with such deep sincerity that, even though he couldn't swim, he would gamely go along with whatever his brother wanted him to do.

Lawrence was outfitted in swim trunks, a bathing cap (his elaborately contrived thinning hair would have dissolved on contact with the water), nose plugs, and, just to complete the effect, a child's life jacket. His spastic limitedness of motion, however, wasn't an act. A month earlier I'd suffered a serious bicycle accident in which I broke my collarbone, punctured a lung, and splintered three ribs. For the month of July, Nancy and I had rented a cottage up in Muskoka, the lake country three hours north of Toronto, with Andrea Martin and her husband, Bob Dolman, Nancy's brother. We had baby Katherine, and the Dolmans had their two little boys, Jack and Joe. It was going to be my last bit of family-time relaxation before I walked into the *SNL* buzz saw.

But then Andrea and I went for a bike ride in which, while speeding down a hill, I flipped over the front of the bike and landed with an ominous thud. I dusted myself off and stood up, but Andrea had this horrified look on her face and shouted, "Lie down! Just lie down!" Evidently a part of my collarbone was sticking out, and my skin was a sickly ashen gray. I was rushed to a hospital and spent the remainder of the month more or less immobilized.

And then? Straight down to New York and right into shooting "Synchronized Swimming," with me still in a sling when we weren't on-camera. The robotic arm motions that Harry and I did to the rousing strains of Frank Stallone's "Far from Over" were dictated by my handicap—which was, perversely, a great gift to the piece. Harry and I knew we had something strong.

We did another good piece together that August, "Lifestyles of the Relatives of the Rich and Famous." Harry was Robin Leach, and I was Katharine Hepburn's maternal third cousin, Nelson Hepburn, a hot-dog vendor in Central Park, who completed his Kate look—pinned-up frizzy hair—with a stained crop-top T-shirt and a pack of cigs rolled up in one sleeve. "We don't communicate at all," Nelson complained in his identical-to-Kate warble. "Never did. I tried—through letter, through phone calls, anonymous sometimes—and she'd hang up. One time, she stopped by here, and I said, 'Kate, don't you know me?' And she just looked at me and she said, 'More mustard, please!' "

A bit later, as we were starting to prep for the live shows, I remember going into Harry's office and saying, "You know what I want to do, Harry? I want to always hold back a piece that I'm writing, keep it in reserve—the kind of piece that you want your friends to respect. So that I can tinker with it, let it ferment." Harry heard me out and then immediately took to his typewriter, typed out what I had just told him, and said, "Sign this, won't you? I'm going to put it in my desk, so that when you come in every Tuesday evening without a fucking idea in your head, I'll be able to ask you how that 'fermenting' piece you're holding back for your friends is coming along." Harry was all too prescient.

Yet Billy Crystal always made me feel better about what we were getting into. He was prolific and kindhearted, with an adorable wife, Janice, and two young daughters. Like me, he was very driven to make something of this one-season opportunity— he'd been a late scratch from the original 1975 lineup of *Saturday Night Live*, and he wasn't going to let anything stop him this time. We had points of reference in common, too: a love of mid-century crooners and old-time showbiz. Billy, like me, did a Sammy Davis Jr., though he did Sammy as Sammy, not as a deranged albino.

Speaking of which, Jackie Rogers Jr. made the trip with me to *SNL*, as did Irving Cohen, as did Ed Grimley. Ed was a no-brainer—in every sense of the term. There was something intrinsic to him that made Ed perfect for the live format: manic energy. That, I learned as the season went on, was the key to success on *SNL*, and a big differentiator from *SCTV*: the need for insane, unexpected, can't-look-away energy. John Belushi had it. Gilda had it. Will Ferrell, when he did the show in the 1990s, had it. You can be incredibly talented comedically, but on the unforgiving stage of *Saturday Night Live*, if you don't bring that immediate energy, you just won't connect with the audience.

So it made sense to get Ed onto the show as soon as possible. For *SNL*, I gave him a new obsession. I loved the idea that Ed would be fixated upon a daytime game show; after all, what else could he possibly be doing with his days? Though I had never seen *Wheel of Fortune*, I knew that it was a big deal, and that the mere idea of Ed repeatedly, gushingly saying the name of its host, Pat Sajak, was inherently funny. So I wrote a sketch for the first show in which Ed applies to be a contestant on *Wheel of Fortune* and soliloquizes about the wonders of Sajak while waiting to be interviewed. It made the cut. I was starting to think this *SNL* thing might work out after all.

But then the dress rehearsal for Episode 1 was a disaster. At *Saturday Night Live*, you do the dress at 8:00 p.m. before a live audience, and it's not uncommon for pieces to get reshuffled, and for one or two to fall out completely, and for the feel of the show to change utterly for the better, because the bad energy of one piece is no longer hovering over the two pieces that follow it. I knew none of this then, however—nor did I yet understand the magic that can happen between dress and air. At the dress that night, the audience felt dead, and very little of our material seemed to be landing. We seemed, as Ed would say, as doomed as doomed can be.

Nancy arrived backstage at 11:10. I was freaking out. "You know what?" I told her. "They should put on a repeat tonight. And I'm not just saying that. None of it's working." Meanwhile Bob Tischler, Dick Ebersol's lieutenant on the show, had become convinced, along with Harry and me, that Dick should open the show with "Lifestyles of the Relatives of the Rich and Famous" rather than whatever opener we'd tried in dress—it was one of the few bits that had gotten laughs. Dick was concerned, though— and rightfully so—about starting a "live" show with a taped piece, and about abandoning the tradition of the cold open capped by someone shouting, "Live from New York, it's Saturday Night!" We argued to him that *SNL* tradition shouldn't get in the way of starting with our strongest material.

In retrospect, I think we should have adhered to the "Live from New York!" opening, simply because it's such a huge part of what *SNL* is. But we won the day, and the show opened with "Life-styles." In addition, Dick and Bob decided to run "Synchronized

Swimming," which was scheduled for the second episode, near the top of the first episode. This was robbing Peter to pay Paul, but again, the "strongest material" argument prevailed.

At 11:30 there was no going back, and the tenth season of *Saturday Night Live* began with "Lifestyles of the Relatives of the Rich and Famous," which not only didn't die a primetime death but was uproariously received by the studio audience. As was "Synchronized Swimming," as was Ed Grimley's *Wheel of Fortune* interview sketch, which Chris Guest and I did somewhere between the two pretaped bits. I was basically done by 12:10, and I had gone three for three in my very first show.

In other words, not only did my worst fears prove to be unfounded; I had just experienced, on October 6, 1984, one of the greatest nights of my career. Larry Brezner, one of my managers, came up to me at the end of the show, leaned in conspiratorially, and whispered, "Your stock just jumped *three-hundred-fold.*" Nan hugged me and said, "Okay, now you need to be institutionalized. You thought this was going to bomb?"

I could only say in reply, "I've done nothing wrong. If I had known this show could turn around like that, I swear, I never woulda . . ."

B ut Nan was totally right: I needed to settle down and keep my anxieties in check. I did the best I could, but the metabolism of that show was strangely punishing to me.

Sunday night, I'd start getting a sour feeling in the pit of my stomach. Monday morning, since I was a writer as well as a performer, I'd have to go in with the other writers to meet the upcoming show's host and start pitching ideas—"ideas," more like stuff I blurted out on the spot, just to get through the meeting. And if by the end of Monday I didn't believe in my ideas, and hadn't written anything that I felt I could actually work on the following day, I considered myself the biggest failure in the world. Never mind that forty-eight hours earlier I might have felt like the king of live television—that was irrelevant now. It was final exams every week.

I struggled through the second show, and for the third show, our host was the Reverend Jesse Jackson, who had run for the Democratic nomination for president that year—losing to Walter Mondale, but doing better than any of the pundits expected. Jackson was a big get for *SNL*, and the pressure was on to come up with material worthy of his newsmaking presence.

In those precomputer days, if you wanted a piece you'd written to make the Wednesday afternoon read-through at 1:00 p.m., you had to slide your notes under the producer's door so they could be typed up in script form, and you had to do so by 7:00 a.m.—no exceptions. It was 6:15 on Wednesday morning when one of my favorite writers on the show, Andy Breckman—who would later create the hit cable series *Monk*—said to me, "Do you realize that there will be nothing handed in for the read-through that Jesse will actually love? No one's done anything remotely political, related to what he actually does for a living. We've got forty-five minutes. Let's write something we know Jesse will adore."

Within a few minutes Andy and I had written an *SCTV*-ish sketch called "The Question Is Moot." Reverend Jackson was the host of a game show in which he would pose a question to three dim-witted contestants, but before they could fully answer, he would interrupt and say, "The question is moot!"—and launch into an anti-Reagan tirade. Later that afternoon Jackson gave the sketch his stamp of approval, and it made the show, where he was actually pretty funny.

I brought Ed Grimley back for that episode, too. The premise was that he'd won a trip to Hawaii on *Wheel of Fortune* and was now flying back home, and the passenger seated next to him was . . . Jesse Jackson. As an added twist, I borrowed from the plot of the famous *Twilight Zone* episode "Nightmare at 20,000 Feet," in which a young William Shatner is terrified by a gremlin that he, and only he, sees through the window of the plane. Ed would flip out when a monster appeared on the wing of the plane, grabbing Jesse aggressively, trying to convince the reverend that what he'd just seen was real, crawling over Jackson to get away. But I was told quite sternly by Jackson's handlers, "You cannot fall and crawl over the reverend in such an aggressive manner."

"Absolutely," I said. "I'll scale it back. Trust me on that." And that's exactly what I did—during dress. Live, however, I went bigger than ever, stepping and falling into Jesse, my head practically landing in his crotch. Jesse, a pro's pro, was totally cool with it—a trouper all the way.

I was no trouper, though. We had a week off after the Jackson show, during which Nancy, Katherine, and I went back home to Toronto for a few days, and I realized that I did not want to return. I wanted to quit *Saturday Night Live* immediately, three shows in. I simply wasn't having any fun, and I couldn't imagine continuing, given the pressure of the show and my (self-imposed) overwhelming sense of gloom and doom. That my contract was for only one season didn't help—it made me feel still more overwhelmed, because it meant that I could never coast, and that every show had to count.

So I sucked it up and flew back to New York. Michael McKean was the guest host that week, which was great for the show, since he was the third member of Chris and Harry's *Spinal Tap* triumvirate, and they were unveiling their new group alter ego the Folksmen, later to be seen in *A Mighty Wind*, the wonderful film that Chris wrote with Eugene Levy. But in my spiral of dread, I just felt excluded from the fun. That Tuesday I went into Dick Ebersol's office and announced I wanted to leave the show.

I intended for my departure to be completely honorable. I hadn't cashed or deposited a single paycheck I had received since joining *SNL*, in case of this very eventuality. My faultless Canadian financial savvy led me to reason that hanging on to the checks meant leaving wouldn't be a problem: I was giving the money back, so what's the big deal?

Dick handled the situation masterfully. He was apologetic ("Wow, this place must really be dysfunctional if a good guy like you is this unhappy") and complimentary ("But Marty, you have the highest Q rating!"—I still don't know, by the way, quite what a Q rating is). Above all, he was calm and reasonable. "Marty," he told me, "if you leave now, this will look bad for us. But I'm here to tell you, it will also look really bad for you, too." He offered a proposal: agree to stick around through Christmas, and if at that point I still wanted to leave, he would get me out of my *SNL* contract, no strings attached. Brilliant. The perfect thing to say. Since it was now almost November, I could already see the Christmas lights at the end of the tunnel.

Dick later told me that he was nearly certain what would happen next: I would get over the hump, figure out the show's rhythms, and complete the season. Indeed, I pulled myself through that fourth episode and figured it out: no matter what happens, Saturday night comes and there's a show to do. You can either plunge headlong into the process and, in a good week, see your stuff triumphantly realized on-air, or you can sit there petulantly like a spoiled, immature idiot and end up in one sketch at 12:50 if you're lucky, saying, "Yes, my liege" and handing someone a sword.

F or the remainder of the season I plunged in headlong. I was
never fully relaxed, because *Saturday Night Live* doesn't allow
you to be, but my perseverance paid off, and lo and behold, I actually started to have fun. In a few short months I saw myself elevated from cult comic beloved by the James Wolcotts and Conan
O'Briens of the world to a bona fide TV star. My repertory of
characters was known across America: Ed Grimley, Jackie Rogers
Jr., Irving Cohen, and Nathan Thurm.

Nathan was a new character, born on *SNL* and, like so many
of the characters I'd already created, based to a certain degree on
a real person. There was a long-serving, chain-smoking makeup
artist on the show—let's call her Isabel—who was without question the most defensive human being I'd ever met. You'd sit there
in her makeup chair and say, "Gee, Isabel, I look a little pale, don't
I?" And she'd say, "I know that! You don't think I know that? I'm
a makeup artist! I would know that."

Anyway, for the sixth show of the season (hosted by Edward
Asner), Harry, Chris, Billy, and I were writing a satire of *60 Minutes* in which Harry played Mike Wallace and Chris and Billy
played the Minkman brothers, whose venerable novelty business
was threatened by Chinese counterfeiters who were circulating
inferior whoopee cushions, dribble glasses, and plastic vomit. In
every Mike Wallace investigation on *60 Minutes*, he would inevitably conduct an adversarial interview with some stonewalling,
defensive corporate weasel. That was my role: Nathan Thurm, attorney for the Chinese counterfeit-novelty overlord, Ping E. Lee.

Billy said, "Why don't you do him as Isabel? You do her behind
her back all the time, anyway. She'd be perfect."

"Are you nuts?" I said. "I can't do that. She'd find out."

"C'mon, she'll never know," Billy said. "They never know when
you're doing them."

So when I did Nathan, I gave him Isabel's smoking and verbal mannerisms, a stock *60 Minutes* villain's defensiveness, and Richard Nixon's peculiar form of perspiration. You know how Nixon famously had that smear of sweat on his upper lip during his 1960 presidential debate with John F. Kennedy? We used glycerin to create that effect on my upper lip. I also gave Nathan a special cigarette, rigged with a thin metal wire, so the ash just grew longer and longer throughout his interview without ever falling off. And he had circular wire-rim glasses whose lenses were so thick that I could barely see out of them.

Harry and I did our little Wallace-and-Thurm pas de deux: him saying, "Pardon me for saying this, but you seem defensive," me saying, "I'm not being defensive, *you're* the one who's being defensive. Have you ever thought about that? Maybe you should think about that."

What I had forgotten was that Isabel would be there when we were taping the piece because, of course, she was the makeup artist. So at one point, as Nathan, I was saying, "I know that! You don't think I know that? I'm a lawyer, I would know that." And the director yelled, "Cut! He's sweating too much." And Isabel, none the wiser, just as Billy predicted, responded, "I know that! You don't think I know that? I'm a makeup artist, I know that!" It was insane.

The Minkman piece proved to be a big hit, and thereafter Nathan was a convenient figure to bring back whenever the show needed a defender-of-the-indefensible character. Like, when reports came out in the news that a circus was presenting surgically modified goats as unicorns, Nathan was called upon in a "Weekend Update" segment to represent the animal modification company, telling the interviewer (Chris), "Maybe the ASPCA should publicly condemn *you*. For being so uninteresting facially. Have you ever thought about that? Maybe you should think about that."

All this time, as Nathan recurred and re-recurred, Isabel never caught on. I was so relieved. But then, at the final after-party of my one season on *SNL*, one of her assistants got drunk and said to Isabel, "How stupid are you? Don't you realize that Nathan Thurm is *you*?"

Poor Isabel was so hurt. She stormed up to me at the party: "I thought you were my friend."

I felt so horrible: caught like a rat. "But I *am* your friend, Isabel," I said. "Don't you know that impersonation is the sincerest form of flattery?"

To which Isabel quickly replied, "I know that! You don't think I know that?"

I don't want to make my *SNL* season sound like an endurance test of unending anxiety. In the moment, onstage, I had some of the greatest fun of my life. Dick Ebersol did something really cool that year. In his zeal to revive the sagging fortunes of the show, he established a kind of rotating visiting professorship for veteran comic writers, wherein someone of great credentials—such as Alan Zweibel or Marilyn Suzanne Miller, both from *SNL*'s original 1975–'80 run—would join the staff writers for a week to give that Saturday's show some extra oomph. One week, to my delight, the invited writers were my *SCTV* buddies Dick Blasucci and Paul Flaherty. With them, I wrote a sketch that was one of the high-water marks of the season.

Well, first, I suppose, I should tell you about the sketch that, too *SCTV*-ish for the *SNL* audience, went down in flames in dress. The premise was that Lucille Ball (me) was coming back to do one last sitcom, playing Bess Truman in a show called *Look Who's Married Harry*. In the episode in question, Lucy and Eleanor Roosevelt (Mary Gross) wanted to wallpaper the Oval Office before "the boys" got home—with hilarious consequences! It was one of those curveball concepts that just might have worked in filmed form on *SCTV*, but boy, did it bomb before the live audience. I can still hear the crickets chirping. After the scene finished, I asked Chris Guest, "Why didn't they at least hit the Applause sign?" Chris replied, in all honesty, "They did."

But Dick, Paul, and I, this time abetted by Chris and Billy, made up for that clunker with a game-show sketch called "Jackie Rogers Jr.'s $100,000 Jackpot Wad," in which Jackie hosted a *Pyramid*-style program that paired civilian contestants with celebrities. It was nearly as absurd as "Look Who's Married Harry," but it was more palatably absurd, and, above all, everyone in the sketch was at the top of their game. Jim Belushi, as Captain Kangaroo, just wanted to know when he was going to be paid ("You are paying me in cash, right? No checks. That was the deal!"), and Mary Gross was his playing partner, a frightened schoolteacher from Harrisburg, Pennsylvania. Her challenger was Rajeev Vindaloo (Chris), a sexually ambiguous Indian private investigator, and his playing partner was none other than Sammy Davis Jr. (Billy). Chris and Billy were on fire in this one:

JACKIE: The category is . . . "Horn of Plenty." Sammy, describe these foods, if you will, sir.

(Popcorn.)

SAMMY: Okay, this is a thing at the movies, it comes in kernels, you heat them up in oil.
RAJEEV: Popcorn.

(Pickle.)

SAMMY: This is a little hot, spicy number.

RAJEEV: Rita Moreno.

SAMMY: No, babe. It comes from a cucumber; they let it sit in a barrel with its brothers so it becomes something else.

RAJEEV: A caterpillar.

SAMMY: Let's move on.

(Angel food cake.)

SAMMY: This is an après-dinner kind of thing, dessert, three layers, icing on top.

RAJEEV: Japuti.

SAMMY: No, babe. Say you're in heaven, you're flying around, you got a little halo, you're . . .

RAJEEV: Dead.

SAMMY: Yeah, but you did a lot of good stuff, you're . . .

RAJEEV: Blessed.

SAMMY: Yeah, but you got the wings, the halo, you're going from cloud to cloud . . .

RAJEEV: I don't know, what is it?

SAMMY: Next.

(Chocolate babies.)

SAMMY: Uh . . . This is, uh . . .

RAJEEV: Chocolate babies?

SAMMY: Right.

Another of Dick's big coups that season was to get Eddie Murphy to return as the host of the Christmas show. Eddie had been the savior of Dick's early days in charge of *SNL*, and now he was the biggest star in comedy. His first two movies, *48 Hours* and *Trading Places*, were hits, and he was coming on to promote his latest and biggest, *Beverly Hills Cop*. Well before the week of Eddie's episode, in fact, Dick was pestering all of us ringers, saying, "Are you writing stuff for Eddie? You've got to give me good stuff for Eddie. Eddie really wants to work with you guys."

The problem was that we four ringers—Billy, Chris, Harry, and me—considered ourselves the stars of that season of *SNL* and generally didn't care too much about writing material for the hosts. We were a little arrogant about our standing as *SNL*'s headliners; we basically thought that *we* were the hosts every week. But finally we yielded, devising a *Broadway Danny Rose*–like deli sketch in which Eddie revived his kvetchy, irritable, greenface Jewish version of Gumby ("I'm Gumby, dammit!"). Billy threw in a recurring old Jewish character that he did, the phlegmy Lew Goldman, while I, naturally, played Irving Cohen.

Eddie's show went fine, but it was another week in the *SNL* pressure cooker. Harry Shearer, increasingly discontented, lasted just one episode beyond the Christmas one—he, rather than I, became the cast member who quit before the season was up. In his view, he was writing quality material that wasn't making the show, while other writers' inferior work did. So he left, citing creative differences. Or, as Harry put it in his parting salvo, "I wanted to be creative, and they wanted something different."

Another guy who quit in a huff was Larry David. Larry was a writer for *SNL* that season, some years before his world domination as the mastermind of *Seinfeld* and *Curb Your Enthusiasm*. He's now one of my closest friends, but back then we were merely coworkers who didn't know each other that well. Larry was in a constant state of aggravation that season, because only one of his sketches ever made it to air. I do remember going to precisely one lunch with him. I can't forget it, because all he did was vent: "Can you *believe* this place? Nothing is done the way it should be!"

I actually witnessed Larry's famous row with Dick Ebersol, in which he quit on the spot, a few minutes before airtime one Saturday night. It's a famous TV moment because it later became the inspiration for a *Seinfeld* episode, "The Revenge," in which George Costanza angrily quits his job but immediately regrets it, and decides to show up at work the next week as if nothing has happened. That's exactly how it went down. Larry walked right up to Dick and simply unloaded: "You don't know what the fuck you're talking about! You're totally incapable! You have no comedy background, no artistry!" And out he walked, into the freezing Manhattan night—realizing, suddenly, that he'd made a horrible mistake and needed every penny he could earn. So Larry just showed up the next Monday morning, pretending he hadn't quit and greeting people with perky geniality: "Hey, guys, how's it going?" His job remained secure, as if nothing had happened.

I t says a lot about the volatile nature of *Saturday Night Live*, at least in that era, that a writer could curse out the executive producer more or less without consequence—that it was, on some level, an acceptable part of getting the show to air. But good lord, it wasn't my thing. I'd spent two and a half years in Television Oz at *SCTV*, and I knew I would be strictly a one-year baby at *SNL*.

Not that I don't appreciate that season. It changed my life and opened the door to friendships and opportunities I'd never have experienced otherwise. I still know no greater high than what I felt when I walked offstage from an *SNL* episode that had gone well. And because I was still relatively young and impressionable, this high was extended by going to the after-party and having someone like Warren Beatty walk up to me and say, "Love your work"—or by going to the manager Jack Rollins's seventieth birthday party and being told, "Woody really wants to meet you." (As it turned out, Woody offered me little more than a cursory nod, but I knew that going in.)

In our final show of the season, I experienced the exquisite joy of watching our guest host, Howard Cosell, play Ed Grimley's Uncle Basil, complete with the hair-horn and plaid shirt, and hearing him ward off an intruder by saying, in That Cosell Voice, "Unhand my nephew, I must say."

Cosell was actually pretty apprehensive about doing the sketch. After the dress rehearsal, I had one note to give him about his performance as Uncle Basil. His mere entrance triggered huge laughs, what with his face matched with the pointy hair. But, I told Cosell, it would be even better if he entered with the signature wincing Grimley facial expression, the upper lip raised to expose the top teeth. I demonstrated this for him, and there was a surreal moment in which I was standing there, my face two feet from Howard Cosell's, contorted in the Ed expression, while he stared back in stony contempt. Just before the show I heard Cosell talking to Chris outside my dressing room: "Okay, I'll do that piece-of-shit scene—but I'm not doing the fucking teeth!"

And when it was all over—that episode, that season—I exhaled. Nancy and I started thinking about the Pacific Palisades again. And I was getting feelers about the movies. What a lovely place to be after twelve months of frayed nerves. My inner Grimley was filled with excitement: *L.A., the movies, no weekly pressure . . . oh, I'm going mental, GIVE ME A BREAK!*

EIGHTIES-HOT

'␣ve always loved this story about Hollywood. In 1981, the legendary costume designer Edith Head passed away. A few days later,
the great actor William Holden died tragically from a fall. In the
same time period, Allen Ludden, the host of the game show *Pass-
word* and the husband of Betty White, died as well. Now, according
to Hollywood folklore, celebrities *always die in threes*, and nothing
thrills Hollywood more than seeing its bogus folklore realized. So
newscasters on all the L.A. television stations were proclaiming left
and right, "You see, it's true—*they die in threes.*" And then suddenly
Natalie Wood died, and the newscasters dropped Allen Ludden.
Even in death, his heat was fleeting.

In Hollywood, you're hottest at the point when you're all
about anticipation: when everyone in the business knows you
have product pending, but none of it is out yet. You're busy, in
demand, hectically jumping from one job to the next, energized
by a sustained industry murmur of *MartyShortMartyShort* . . .
Couldbebigcouldbebig . . . *Ihearhe'ssomethingIhearhe'ssomething* . . .
DoyouhaveaMartyShortthing'causeIhaveaMartyShortthing.

My own professional hot streak started in May 1985, when I flew back to New York—*SNL's* season had wrapped mere weeks earlier, but Nan and I wasted no time resettling into our Pacific Palisades rental—to do *Late Night with David Letterman.* It wouldn't be my first appearance, by a long shot. Paul Shaffer, Dave's bandleader since the show launched in 1982, was, of course, a good friend. And Dave had been a fan of my work on *SCTV* and *SNL,* a fandom more than reciprocated by me; like everyone else on the 1980s comedy scene, I was in awe of Dave and the clever, anarchic ways he had revolutionized the late-night format. So this appearance on Dave's show wasn't in itself a big turning point. By now I was such a regular guest that Paul had his own entrance music for me, Julian Lennon's "Valotte," the title song from Julian's one mega-hit album—and an inside joke between Paul and me, one of approximately twelve million we've shared since *Godspell.* It goes like this: In December 1984, the guest host of *SNL* was Ringo Starr, and the whole week I was working with Ringo on the show, he kept remarking to a friend he'd brought along, the producer Allan McKeown, "Don't 'ee look like Julian? The spittin' image of Julian!" I told Paul this, and—boom!—"Valotte" became "Marty's theme."

(FYI, after Dave moved to CBS in 1993, Paul changed my tune to the theme from *Hollywood and the Stars,* an early 1960s NBC program about Hollywood's golden age, hosted by Joseph Cotten, that Paul and I were both obsessed with as kids. The theme, written by the great movie composer Elmer Bernstein, has a swelling, Oscars-ceremony sentimentality to it, the sort of music that would herald the slow, minder-assisted entrance onstage of some frail human legend slated to receive that year's Irving G. Thalberg Memorial Award.)

What really kicked off my season of Hollywood hotness was

the meeting I had with Lorne Michaels during this New York trip. He'd gotten in touch with me beforehand, wanting to discuss a movie he was doing, *¡Three Amigos!* I was excited about this—no one had ever wanted me for a movie before—so I went to Lorne's apartment straight after the *Letterman* taping. The first thing he asked was surprising to me: Was I at all interested in returning for another year on *Saturday Night Live?* It wasn't yet official, but Lorne was poised to take over the show again, having recovered from the burnout that had driven him away five years earlier. Perhaps, Lorne said, I could be persuaded to reenlist.

"But I thought you wanted to talk to me about *¡Three Amigos!*" I said. "How would I be able to do both?"

"Well, you *know*, Marty," Lorne said, in that wry tone I would come to know well, "I've heard tell that *occasionally* schedules can, in fact, actually be sorted out in show business."

In retrospect, I think I could have managed it. My career might have benefitted from pulling double duty and doing Lorne's rebooted *SNL* and *¡Three Amigos!* at the same time. But it probably would have been at the expense of my sanity. So I told Lorne, "I'm not sure *SNL* is in my future. But you say you're producing a Western-type movie?"

¡Three Amigos! is an anomaly in Lorne's long and illustrious résumé: his only screenwriting credit on a feature film, shared with Steve Martin and Randy Newman. It was your basic Old West bandito musical comedy of mistaken identity, featuring three dopey silent-film stars who happen to perform in mariachi costumes and get themselves mixed up in a Mexican turf war with the villagers in a small, gangster-besieged town, who mistake them for real crime fighters.

I think that at one point it was going to be Danny Aykroyd and John Belushi as the other two amigos alongside Steve. At another point, it was going to be Bill Murray and Robin Williams. Then it became Chevy Chase and John Candy, but Candy was too busy by the time the production schedule finally snapped into place, and that's when it became Chevy Chase and Martin Short, with John Landis slated to direct.

The very day after the meeting with Lorne, I was back in L.A., headed to Steve Martin's house in Beverly Hills to meet him and pick up the script. I have this philosophy around people I don't know but am excited to meet that I call "immediate intimacy": I do an impersonation of someone who is relaxed, loose, and not at all intimidated, in the hope that this impersonation will ultimately become reality. Because I *was* intimidated by Steve. We're the best of friends now, but at that point I was this mere sketch-comedy guy and he was *Steve Martin*, the most innovative stand-up comic of the 1970s, who had done so many great comedy films. The latest to date, *All of Me*, had blown me away, not to mention *The Jerk* and the ambitious musical *Pennies from Heaven* and all the TV specials, and then there was his groundbreaking "white suit" era.

I was immediately overwhelmed upon arriving at Steve's house. I'm pretty certain that everyone who has ever visited his home for the first time and gone from room to room has been struck by the very same thought: How many portraits can one man possibly sit for? In all seriousness, I was astounded by what I saw. In one direction, there was a Picasso. In another direction, there was an Edward Hopper. And in a third direction, there was . . . Steve himself. That's when I blurted out, "How did you get so rich? Because I've seen the work."

Steve burst out laughing. Wow, I thought, I just made Steve Martin laugh. Pretty damn cool. My heart jumped an extra beat of joy. As it turned out, my icebreaker was more perfect than I could have known. Steve, I would soon learn, is an inherently shy and unrelentingly self-critical person. A joke that is both at his expense *and* makes him laugh is the ideal combination.

Still, it took a while for me to feel like I belonged in his and Chevy's world. Nancy and I were invited that autumn to the premiere of *Spies Like Us*, the movie John Landis did before *¡Three Amigos!*, which starred Chevy and Danny Aykroyd. It was my first Hollywood premiere, and the first time I underwent the experience of walking a red carpet, having my name announced, and hearing a crowd of strangers on the street cheer for me. I'd been in such a bubble while doing *SCTV* and *Saturday Night Live* that this was the first moment when it became real that I had connected with the public, and not just people in entertainment. The following day, I joined Chevy and Steve for lunch at the Grill, the consummate Beverly Hills industry lunch spot. Chevy was smarting from the reviews for *Spies Like Us*, yet still voicing his confidence in Landis. Steve was fretting about his level of preparedness and telling me, "It's different for you, because you have *real* talent." I couldn't help but step out of myself for a moment. *You're sitting here with Chevy Chase and Steve Martin, and you're one of the Three Amigos. Gee, I hope you don't blow this! Just pretend you're someone who wouldn't.*

In fact, in this period, when I had agreed to do the movie but we hadn't yet begun shooting it, I suggested to John Landis that I do my amigo, Ned Nederlander, as another one of my bizarre and dim-witted creations, in the same world as Ed and Jackie and Lawrence Orbach. I just didn't believe that my own face could be as comedically rewarding as the tic-laden, makeup-heavy characters of my last four years on television.

But when I pitched this to Landis, he shot it down immediately. "Absolutely not," he declared. "Do you know the problem with you people from *SCTV*? You overanalyze. You're cute, and you're going to look cute. *Period!*"

I don't know about John's macro point about us people from *SCTV*, but he was right in one important regard. If I was going to make it in the movies, I'd have to be brave enough to be me, and to find the comedy in the character's sweet-faced innocence, without hiding behind prosthetics, bald pates, and the like.

A nd was I ever an innocent. On the first day, on the film's first set, I went into my first trailer. I went to the sink, filled a glass with water, drank the water, and nearly retched. Nobody had told me that you don't drink the trailer water, because trailer water is just for washing your hands. Then I opened the toilet, and there was a giant turd in it. I was never certain if it belonged to Chevy or some teamster who was trying to break me in—I didn't have it sent to the lab. Knowing how his mind works, though, my money's still on Chevy.

But I adapted quickly. It was my "immediate intimacy" philosophy put into practice: I needed to feel as if my two established-movie-star costars were my real buddies, so mentally, I fast-forwarded three years ahead in our relationship. When we first started filming *¡Three Amigos!* on a Hollywood backlot, Nancy came by the set, and Chevy was completely discombobulated by her; "I feel like I'm cheating on my wife by just looking at your wife," he told me. (Nancy had this effect on men. She underestimated her own beauty, and therefore carried herself nonchalantly, which only made her more attractive.) In our downtime Chevy loved nothing more than to play Scrabble. To my frustration, he and Steve were much better at it than me. I got sick of losing. So during one game, while Steve was deliberating on his next move, to make Chevy laugh, I very classily passed Steve a handwritten note that read, "I will let you ball my wife Nancy for an E or a Q."

My first experience shooting a movie was a relatively happy one, even though Chevy and John Landis had a testy, somewhat combative relationship, a carryover from their collaboration on *Spies Like Us*. I saw them butt heads more than a few times. But in a way, I think, my presence helped defuse the tension. I'd had a similar effect as the new guy in the cast of *SCTV*. Though the *SCTV*-ers were all old friends, by 1982 they were getting on each other's nerves more frequently. (What's that old expression about what familiarity breeds?) Yet all it took was the presence of a new person—"Mr. Litmus Paper," Andrea Martin called me—to put them on their best behavior. Same deal with Chevy and John— neither guy wanted to be seen as the jerk in front of Impressionable Li'l Marty on his first picture.

And I have to give John credit for fighting for me when the studio behind the film, Orion, resisted some of my more unusual flights of unscripted fancy. Whereas Steve and Chevy's characters, Lucky Day and Dusty Bottoms, were confident in their stardom, my former child star character, Little Neddie Nederlander, was still stumbling on his adult legs like a wobbly foal. I improvised a scene in which, in a misguided attempt to impress the village children, Ned tells how, as a boy, he met the great silent-screen actress Dorothy Gish: "And she looked me in the eyes, and she said, 'Young man, you have *got it!*' *Dorothy Gish!* It's a true story!"

The Orion people definitely didn't want this scene in the movie. They felt it was too improvisational and too far over people's heads—and granted, there *was* some deliberate *SCTV*-style insider silliness going on. Ned wouldn't have been big enough to meet the more famous Gish sister, Lillian, I thought; he'd only have met Dorothy. But John put his foot down, and the scene stayed. Another of my favorite lines in that movie was "Sew, very old one! Sew like the wind!"—Ned's rallying cry to an elderly Mexican woman in the movie's climactic scene, where the whole town uses its sewing skills to vanquish the villain, El Guapo.

Chevy was someone who loved to push his comedy as far as he could. Three years after ¡Three Amigos!, he and I were seated next to each other at an American Film Institute tribute to Gregory Peck. At one point Charlton Heston stood up at his table and delivered a characteristically windy, bombastic toast that concluded with the words, "I guess you could say, Greg, that I've been one lucky guy." To which Chevy boomed out at high volume, still looking down and cutting his steak, "I'll say!"

No one knew where the crack had come from, including Heston, who glanced around the room, rattled, while Chevy calmly went on cutting his meat. That same evening, Chevy spotted Mary Hart of Entertainment Tonight way off in a corner of the room interviewing Zsa Zsa Gabor. Palming a roll in his hand like a baseball, he asked me sincerely, "I wonder how far a human can actually hurl a baguette?" He then stood up, threw it with all his might, and, with jaw-dropping accuracy, beaned Hart square on the noggin. Even the generally unflappable Chevy was stunned. He quickly lowered himself back into his seat like a naughty schoolkid hoping not to be caught by the teacher.

I was the target of Chevy's penchant for mischief on the night of the ¡Three Amigos! premiere in December 1986, with Steve complicit in his scheme. Chevy told me that the studio wanted us to show up for the big gala in our complete mariachi costumes: a great red-carpet visual, to be sure. So, that night, Nancy was all dolled up, looking fantastic, and I was compliantly dressed in my amigo outfit, my bedazzled sombrero tucked under my arm. The limo had just arrived at our house, and we were about to get in, when I heard the phone in our house ring. It was Chevy: "Marty! Don't wear the costume! Wear a tuxedo! I'm so sorry, it was a joke." I hung up, and a second later the phone rang again. It was Steve: "Marty, thank *God* you're home! *Please* don't wear the mariachi outfit. Get into a tux. I'm so sorry. Chevy and I . . ."

Well before that premiere, I'd already wrapped movie number two, *Innerspace*. That's where I met another person with whom I would develop a lasting and close friendship, Steven Spielberg, the picture's executive producer. He paid me a sort of gestural compliment right off the bat. Though I was something of a hot property at the time, Warner Brothers still wanted me to read for the part. Some actors take this as an affront, believing that once they reach a certain phase of their careers, they should never have to read again. I never saw it that way and still don't. No matter who you are, you should read for a role, because maybe you're not right for the material, or maybe the material is not right for you. It's a pragmatic thing, not a personal one.

Anyway, I went to Amblin, Steven's production company, to audition for Steven, Joe Dante, the movie's director, and Mike Finnell, its producer. Shortly after we were introduced, and before I read, Steven got up and said, "We're good here, I was just leaving," making it clear he didn't need to see me audition.

I got the part, and then I got a phone call from Dennis Quaid. He was playing the macho navy pilot who volunteers for a secret government miniaturization project and ends up getting injected into the body of my nerdy grocery-clerk character, Jack Putter. "Hey, dude," Dennis said, "this is going to be a blast!" It was

1986, and it is embossed upon my brain: the first time anyone had ever called me "dude." As a Texan, Dennis was way ahead of his time.

Dennis was so right: *Innerspace* was a blast to make, and it's also where he met Meg Ryan, who was gangly and nervous and heartbreakingly adorable. She called everyone "Mister": Mister Spielberg, Mister Dante. And though she was playing Dennis's love interest, Dennis's character was stuck inside my body, so *I* got to kiss her.

When we started that film, Dennis was going out with Lea Thompson and Meg was with Anthony Edwards, but from the very beginning you could tell that Meg and Dennis were infatuated with each other. Then again, *every* guy on the set was infatuated with Meg, so irresistibly cute was she. Thank heavens for Nan's wise words, which forever echoed in my head: "If I ever find out that you've cheated on me, I won't say anything during the day, but at night, when you are asleep, so help me God, I will take an empty wine bottle and smash it over your head." That certainly can get a fella thinking.

S o, as of December 1986, I'd completed two major motion pictures in which I had a leading role. Chevy, Steve, and I flew together to New York to triple-host *Saturday Night Live*, with Randy Newman as the musical guest. (This is what Lorne would call synergy.)

It was far preferable to be on *SNL* as a conquering hero than as a beleaguered cast member, though it seemed that things had definitely stabilized on the show that season, with Lorne having recruited the talented likes of Dana Carvey, Jan Hooks, and Phil Hartman for the cast. I reprised Ed Grimley and got a huge cheer just making my entrance, in a strong sketch in which Jon Lovitz, as the devil, tries to steal Ed's soul.

I wasn't just hot, I was *'80s hot*: always welcome on Dave Letterman's couch, my calendar chockablock with movie work, my hair tousled and poufy, my wardrobe a succession of boxy, big-shouldered blazers and dress shirts worn with the top button buttoned—what scholars of '80s fashion call the "air tie." (See also Winwood, Steve, and Bolton, Michael.) And in my next movie, I was playing the *handsome romantic lead*!

The year 1987 began with me filming *Cross My Heart*, a romantic comedy centered around a third date, the one in which, if all goes well, a couple is supposed to have sex. JoBeth Williams was originally supposed to play opposite me, but she got pregnant, so Annette O'Toole was recast in the role. Talk about '80s hot: Annette was ravishingly beautiful, and the script called for nude scenes. I was determined to get in shape for my role, so I enlisted the services of Dan Isaacson, the Hollywood trainer who had whipped John Travolta into glisteningly chiseled perfection for *Staying Alive*, the sequel to *Saturday Night Fever*.

I was still filming *Innerspace* when I started training for *Cross My Heart*. Nancy would walk into the living room at night to find me working up a sweat on the exercise bike I'd installed there. "God forbid you'd have done this for me!" she joked. "All these years I've had to live with a shell-less turtle, and *they* get Buffed Boy."

Cross My Heart marked the only time I had the articulated abs and sexily hollowed cheeks of the truly pumped up. Dennis Miller ran into me and said, "Heeey, Marty, I hear you've gone all Piscopo on us!" I wouldn't go that far, but I got as buff as this particular five-foot-seven frame will ever allow.

Cross My Heart was also the closest I would ever get to knowing what it is like to shoot a porno. There were days when I would literally wake up, shower, have my coffee, kiss my wife and kids good-bye, drive to the set, and then take off all of my clothes to spend hours naked in bed with Annette. Then I'd come home and want to talk about work. I'd say, "Jesus, Nan, it was so weird, I had to tweak Annette's nipples in a scene today, and then—"

Nancy would cut me off. "Okay. You know what?" she'd say, hands up in front of her face. "We're not doing this. I can't hear about your workday and the hardships of you having to tweak Annette's nipples."

"But baby . . . ," I'd plead as she got up and stormed out of the room. Point taken.

Believe it or not, I had a nudity clause in my contract. In my Canadian modesty, I did not want the world to see the Marty member. Lawrence Kasdan, who wrote and directed *Body Heat* and *The Big Chill*, was the producer of *Cross My Heart*, and there came a point when he and I got into a heated discussion in my trailer, because they'd added a scene in which my butt would be shown. That I didn't mind, but I minded that, of necessity, the crew positioned on the other side of me would get an unobstructed view of my penis.

Larry tried to reason with me. "We have no intention of showing your penis. After all, we'd like the film to make money," he said.

"Yeah," I said, "but people like Jan, my hairdresser—she's gonna see my dick."

"Fine," Larry said. "We can rig it."

And we amicably reached a compromise wherein they rigged up some kind of sock that kept my genitalia covered while the rest of me was exposed. A big sock, I might add. *Really big*, as the late

Ed Sullivan used to say. Like, the kind you hang on the mantel on Christmas Eve.

Filmmaking is a strange kind of work, in that for two or three months, you're very intensively and intimately working with a group of people over long, long hours, and you get to know everything about everybody—and then, once the filming's over, you never see most of these people again. This serves the libidinous and affair-minded well, but it's hard on friendships. After working with Larry Kasdan, and successfully navigating this ridiculous situation with him, I made a mental note to myself that I never wanted to lose this guy from my life. Happily, he and I have been close friends ever since. And he has still never seen my penis.

M y awesome '80s hotness did not, alas, translate into boffo box office. None of those three films, *¡Three Amigos!*, *Innerspace*, and *Cross My Heart*, did particularly well financially. I think *Innerspace* was the biggest surprise in this regard. It had tested through the roof, as they say in the trades, and it got strong advance reviews. For heaven's sake, Gene Shalit declared unequivocally on *Today* that "*Inner* . . . is a winner!"

On the eve of *Innerspace*'s release, I was called in on short notice to appear in a video with Rod Stewart for his cover of Sam Cooke's "Twistin' the Night Away," which appeared on the movie's sound track. It was then—on the set of that video, flanked by Rod and some beautiful models, in as '80s a tableau as I'd ever inhabit—that I allowed myself a little moment of excitement: *This is going to be fun, to be in a colossal hit.*

But the movies didn't open big, and my days as a leading man were numbered. I was disappointed, of course, but I can't honestly say I was devastated. This was partly a matter of my innate Canadian suspicion of massive success—*Oh, it's probably not gonna work out anyway, eh?*—and partly because the takeaway from these experiences was never "Marty can't act." I mean, Janet Maslin, in her *New York Times* review of *Cross My Heart*, came right out and said, "Martin Short makes a delightful leading man even when there's little for him to do." Critics were if anything overly generous toward me. What I came to understand is that critical favor, talent, and tenacity are only part of the formula for a hit. You also need luck and good timing. Today, *¡Three Amigos!* is on several "100 Funniest Movies of All Time" lists, and young adults accost me all the time to tell me how much they love *Innerspace*. I say to them, "Where were you when these movies opened?" And then it occurs to me: *Oh, that's right. You were lying on your back in a crib.* It wasn't until these pictures took on a second life on cable and DVD that they became quote-unquote classics.

As it happened, the fourth of my leading-man movies of the '80s, *Three Fugitives*, did decently at the box office, although the critical reaction was mixed. Personally, I have warm feelings about that picture, and I adored working with its French writer-director, Francis Veber, who is a master of cinematic physical comedy. The movie was an adaptation of a French-language film that Veber had done with Gérard Depardieu.

Three Fugitives was especially memorable for me in that it gave me the chance to work with that lovable, crazy lug of a nutball named Nick Nolte. With a voice that sounded like a rusted hinge on a heavy old door, Nick played a just-sprung convict who is taken hostage at a bank by a bumbling, desperate schlemiel—you guessed it, me—who has resorted to crime to raise money for the medical care of his mute little daughter.

I had never before met Nick. It was my understanding that, while he'd had his struggles with booze and other substances, he was currently on the wagon, and had been for many months. We were introduced at a dinner party held by Lauren Shuler Donner, the executive producer of the film, and her director husband, Dick Donner. Jeffrey Katzenberg, the studio head of Disney, whose Touchstone division was producing the film, was also there with his wife, Marilyn. It was all a little nerve-racking: we two leads, having never met, sitting there on display for the powers that be. A butler came over and said, "Would you like something to drink, Mr. Short?"

Because of the weird pressure of the night, I really wanted a drink. But, mindful of Nick, I said, "A Perrier, please." Then the butler said, "Mr. Nolte?" And Nick said, "I'll have a triple vodka and Seven." Well, that night, Nick proceeded to triple, or maybe more than triple, his triple vodka and Seven. He fell right off the wagon; he too was a bundle of nerves over this dinner. At one point he went silent at the table for a long stretch before suddenly turning to Nancy and proclaiming in a loud voice, "I like to salt my food. Do you like to salt your food? A lot of people start judging you when you start salting your food—like the manipulative assholes they are. Do you ever find that?"

He proceeded to pour about half a shaker's worth of salt on his branzino before again falling into a prolonged silence—a silence that, this time, everyone else at the table, momentarily stunned, joined him in. About fifteen minutes later, by which time everyone but Nick was back in convivial conversation, he abruptly stood up, rising to his full height, and loudly inquired to no one in particular, "Do you ever find that, like, you get the feeling that, like, you walk in a room—or you're in a moment, and—*aaaah*, fuck it!" And down he sat again. I could see the concern on Jeffrey

Katzenberg's face: *We've got $60 million going into this one. Good lord...*

Somehow the movie did get made. We shot it up in Tacoma. I grew really fond of Nick, who was wild but dear. He'd always want me to have a drink with him after we'd wrapped for the day. The first time he asked, I said, "Absolutely!" and hurried back to my trailer to get changed. Suddenly Nick was pounding on my trailer door, saying, "What are you doing? Don't get changed. Be an *actor*. Actors drink in their wardrobe."

"But Nick, the wardrobe people want to go home," I protested.

"What are you talking about? They're in my trailer, drinking."

Nick also had great stories about working with Katharine Hepburn on *Grace Quigley*, one of the last films she ever made. He was frank about having been strung out on cocaine at the time, and he remembered a moment in which he sat, whacked out and glazed, while Hepburn turned to the movie's director, Anthony Harvey, and said, "Look at him, Tony! Look at him! There's *no one fucking there!*"

Hepburn, Nick told me, took pity upon him, saying, "Nick, I think I can help you. Spencer would get like this, too. He'd go on these tirades, but at least he had the decency to wait until he'd finished working. But *I can get you some Thorazine!*"

Nick politely declined her offer. "That's very kind of you, Katie," he told her, "but I'll be fine." When Hepburn left, someone in the trailer declared, "Nick, I can get you some black beauties," the preferred pick-me-up of long-haul truckers, a combo of speed and dextroamphetamine. Quickly perking up, Nick said, "*Those* I'll take."

The most poignant thing about Nick during *Three Fugitives* was that he set a bedtime for himself of 8:00 p.m. I found this astonishing. "When do you get up?" I asked.

"Around three thirty in the morning," he said.

"And what do you do at that hour, Nick?"

"I take a long bath."

"And then what?"

"Well, I try to read, but I get kinda tired."

"So why do you go to bed at eight, then, Nick?"

"To avoid those dangerous hours, buddy."

There was a scene in *Three Fugitives* in which Nick had to wear hospital scrubs, and that became his basic look, I think, for years thereafter. Circa 2005, more than fifteen years after we'd worked together, I was at the Toronto Film Festival, staying at the Four Seasons, when who should walk into the elevator but Nick Nolte—in hospital scrubs. Not having noticed me, he took his place at the front. I had, during our time on *Three Fugitives*, developed a dead-on impression of him. In my most ravaged, guttural Nolte voice, I croaked, "I hear Nick Nolte's a fuckin' asshole."

Nick didn't know it was me, and in hindsight, he might very well have turned around and punched me in the face. Arguably, he *should* have. But he merely pivoted partway, not even bothering to look back, and said resignedly in *his* most ravaged, guttural Nolte voice, "I don't disagree."

crammed one other movie into the 1980s, Chris Guest's first as a director, *The Big Picture*. More conventional than his later mockumentaries, it was about a young screenwriter, played by Kevin Bacon, whose promising script and life get mangled by the Hollywood machine. I played a small part as his character's agent, Neil Sussman. I took no salary and no billing. The salary part I don't regret, because Chris's movies are tiny-budget labors of love. But it was foolish of me not to take billing. It just happened to be a cool thing to do in movies at the time: the unbilled cameo.

Chris loves the idea of characters who are sexually ambiguous, or whose sexuality is ambiguous only to them. So Neil was developed as this in-between figure, neither gay nor straight but definitely vain, full of himself, and also full of show business bullpoo. Here's how Neil pitched his agenty woo to Kevin's character:

This is the thing: If you decide to sign with me, you're gonna get more than an agent. You're gonna get (holding up four fingers) *three people. You're gonna get an agent, a mother, a father, a shoulder to cry on, someone who knows this business inside and out. And if anyone ever tries to cross you? I'll grab them by the balls, and squeeze till they're dead.*

Chris is very loose in granting his actors leeway to mess with the dialogue, but very detail-oriented in developing his characters' looks. My hair was longish then, so we had it curled and tinted orange. Chris really wanted Neil to look like someone who had obviously undergone a really bad face-lift, so the makeup people taped my face back as far as they could, fastening the tape at my temples and covering it with my tufted hair. It was far from comfortable, and by the end of each shooting day, after several takes, I had huge welts on the sides of my face, like I'd been in a fight.

A while afterward, Chris and I were discussing Neil, and he was mad at himself for having blown an opportunity to work in an extra joke. He should have had me appear in my first scene with conspicuous bags under my eyes, he explained. And then, the next time

I appeared, the eye bags would be gone. And here's the key Chris Guest part: *none of this would ever be explained.* Like the *SCTV* cast, Chris loves subtlety—layers upon layers of texture and micro-jokes that people will either pick up on or not. This is why, over several films, Eugene Levy and Catherine O'Hara have worked so well and so instinctively with him.

A fringe benefit of working with and becoming friends with Chris was getting to know his extended family, which included not only his very cool wife, Jamie Lee Curtis, but also her father, Tony Curtis, another big figure from my youth—*Some Like It Hot, Spartacus, Sweet Smell of Success*—and therefore an exciting person to see in the flesh.

I met Tony at a birthday party that Chris and Jamie were having for one of their kids. I was impressed by the sheer Tony Curtis–ness of him: he still had the dark hair then, not the Jor-El pompadour he would later adopt, and he just looked so exactly like himself, if you know what I mean.

But the person most impressed by Tony was my five-year-old daughter, Katherine. She had no idea who he was, but he fussed over her at the party and even got out his paints to do a quick sketch of her, which he presented to Katherine as a gift. (Like the other big Tony of my youth, Bennett, Curtis had a major side-line as a painter.) Tony clearly made quite the impression on my little girl. As we were leaving the party and saying our good-byes, Katherine loudly asked him, "Mr. Curtis—would you like to have my phone number?"

On cue, a dozen voices at the party cried out, "Boy, Tony, you still got it!"

And the next day, upon returning from some outing, we saw the light flashing on our answering machine. Nancy pressed play: "Hello, Katherine, this is Tony Curtis, calling to say what a plea-

sure it was to meet you yesterday." Needless to say, we kept that
one for a while.

S peaking of people with whom I was obsessed as a youth:
in this same period, I finally met Sammy Davis Jr. He was
playing a concert at the Hollywood Bowl with Frank Sinatra,
so Nancy and I made a date with the Crystals, Billy and Janice,
to see the show. It was the Shorts' responsibility to provide the
champagne for the limo ride, and the Crystals' to provide the
caviar. I can still see a beaming Billy emerging from their house
with an elaborate platter weighted down by a huge tin and all
the accoutrements: toast points, hard-boiled eggs, capers, and
so forth.

Sammy did the first set, Frank did the second, and at the
end they teamed up to perform a few songs together. At in-
termission, after Sammy's set, Billy went backstage to visit
Sammy, who he'd gotten to know in his pre-*SNL* days, when
he opened for Sammy in Las Vegas. (It was during that period,
working up close to the legend, that Billy mastered his im-
peccable Davis impersonation.) As Sinatra was about to begin
his set, Billy rejoined us and excitedly whispered, "Sammy and
Altovise are having a party at their house tonight, and they've
invited us!" My heart skipped a beat. I couldn't believe that the
same man I'd seen at fifteen in the Broadway show *Golden Boy*
(and whose mannerisms I'd appropriated in albino whiteface
for Jackie Rogers Jr.) would soon be welcoming me into his
home.

When we arrived at Sammy's house on Summit Drive in
Beverly Hills—which was immediately next door to Pickfair,
the legendary fifty-six-acre estate once owned by Douglas Fair-

banks Sr. and Mary Pickford—the first thing that struck me
was that every square inch of every wall was covered in show-
business memorabilia: Dorothy's slippers from *The Wizard of
Oz*, sheet music from Fred Astaire musicals, and framed pic-
tures of everyone from Frank and Dino to JFK and Richard
Nixon. By the swimming pool was a giant statue of Maurice
Evans as Dr. Zaius from the original *Planet of the Apes* movie.
And the fireplace had been glassed-in and turned into an aquar-
ium, with tropical fish swimming in it. How strange, I thought.
Also, Sammy had seemingly invited all the Bobbys from 1970s
Hollywood: Bobby Culp, Bobby Blake, and I want to say Bobby
Vaughn.

Sammy was a magnanimous host and tour guide, leading us
around while clutching an unlit cigarette in one hand and an
empty cognac glass in the other. He explained to us that the cigs
and booze had been his traditional rewards after a performance,
but that he needed to avoid them now. "But the props still make
me feel comfortable, man," he said. In retrospect, I think Sammy
might have known that he was not long for the world. He died
within a year of our visit, and that night he told us that he'd been
nervous before the concert because he had recently undergone
hip-replacement surgery; a lifelong dancer, he was new to relying
solely on his singing voice in performance.

At one point Sammy led us to his upstairs study, away from
the rest of the party. There were just the Shorts, the Crystals,
Sammy, and Heinrich Himmler's elaborately engraved waist gun
on the wall above us in a glass case. (I guess Sammy, famously a
proud Jewish convert, cherished the idea of disarming Hitler's pit
bull.) I took the opportunity to tell Sammy about how I'd seen
him on Broadway in *Golden Boy* as a teen, and how formative an
experience it had been for me.

His expression turned quizzical at this confession. "I have mixed feelings about that time, man," he said, "because that was the *old* me, the me that I'm not necessarily proud of." Billy and I discussed these words afterward and deduced that Sammy was alluding to his well-documented substance-abuse issues. A few days later I related this story of our heart-to-heart with Sammy to Paul Shaffer. That night I turned on the *Letterman* show, and there was Paul on TV saying, "Dave, hey, I'm so sorry about my past behavior. I feel terrible about the *old* me, the me that I'm not necessarily proud of." I made a mental note: *Never share anything with Paul.*

One more thing about Sammy. As we two couples were taking our leave, I somehow ended up alone with Sammy in the hallway leading to his front door: just the two of us in a narrow corridor. "Lay a little of the dance on me," he said. I didn't know what he meant, and told him so.

"You know, man," he said, "the *Grimley* thing."

And I, demonstrating the presence of those balls of steel that John Candy long ago ascribed to me, replied, "I'll do the dance if you sing that soaring passage from that Leslie Bricusse song"—"Tomorrow," an amazing song written by Bricusse and Anthony Newley that I had never heard until the concert that night. The thing about Sammy was that, to my generation, he became such a joke for a while, but then you'd go see him perform and realize, *Oh, yeah, he's massively talented—that's how he got famous in the first place.* Sammy obligingly broke into song—"Tomorrow is the looong and lonely moment . . . when I look the future in the eye!"—and I simultaneously went into my ecstatic Ed dance.

It was at this moment that Billy, wondering what the hell was taking me so long, appeared in the doorway. "Boy," he said to

TOP Eric Fischl's painting of our 2009 vacation in St. Barth's, with Nancy in the foreground and *(from L–R)* April Gornik, Anne Stringfield, Steve Martin, me, and friends Mary Jane Marcasiano and Ralph Gibson.
(Courtesy of Eric Fischl)

BOTTOM At least Nan thinks I'm funny. Opening night of *Little Me*, 1998.

Photos are courtesy of the author unless otherwise noted.
Interlude photos are courtesy of The Second City Entertainment, Inc., NBC Television, Comedy Central/Viacom Media, and Buena Vista Pictures/Disney/Everett Collection.

TOP Chevy, Steve, and me riding high in the fake saddle on the set of *iThree Amigos!* *(HBO Films)*

BOTTOM Evil little sweet-faced Clifford. What better role for a forty-year-old? *(Orion Pictures)*

TOP A typically shy me makes a surprise visit during a Steve Martin appearance on *Letterman*, October 2009. *(Getty/CBS)*

MIDDLE Playing it straight as lawyer Leonard Winstone (with Len Cariou) in the FX series *Damages*. *(Craig Blankenhorn/Fx/ Everett Collection)*

BOTTOM With Jason Alexander in the L.A. production of *The Producers*.

TOP Four slices of ham: Robin Williams, me, Jerry Lewis, and Steve Martin at the Aspen Comedy Festival, 2000.

ABOVE LEFT AND OPPOSITE LEFT In heavy prosthetics to play Larry David and Tom Hanks's Forrest Gump in TV sketches.

OPPOSITE RIGHT Jiminy Glick gets carnal with Kathie Lee Gifford on *Prime Time Glick*, 2002. *(Comedy Central/Everett Collection)*

TOP Nan and me with bearded Tom on the accordion at our annual Christmas party, 2000.

MIDDLE In Sun Valley at the top of 2010, (*from L–R*) Tom Hanks, Rita Wilson, me, Nan, Patti Scialfa, Bruce Springsteen, Jann Wenner (holding son Noah) Matt Nye, Debra and Bing Gordon.

BOTTOM With the fabulous Nora Ephron, 2008.

TOP The Short family Christmas card (with Buster the dog), 1994.

BOTTOM Thanksgiving at New York's Tavern on the Green, 2006 *(from L–R)* Henry, Oliver, Katherine, me, and Nancy.

ABOVE The Mountie: my beloved Nan, Central Park, 1999.

Sammy and me, "it's hard to get you people to do what you do, isn't it?"

B ut truly, my ultimate childhood-fantasy realization came when I did *The Tonight Show* while Johnny Carson was still hosting it. Moronically, I had resisted going on the Carson show for a while, despite being offered opportunities. There was a feeling in the air during the 1980s that maybe it wasn't hip to do Johnny anymore, especially with Dave Letterman catching fire. Besides, Dave and I had developed such an easy rapport, and Paul Shaffer was my good buddy. And finally, if I was being honest with myself, the idea of sitting in the chair next to Johnny Carson scared the hell out of me.

However, by the later part of the decade, the rumors were growing stronger that Johnny was soon to retire, and I realized how absurd my resistance was. What's more, I didn't have to go the hard-knock route that comedians from Drew Carey to Jerry Seinfeld had taken, where you did your five minutes of stand-up, and if Johnny liked you, he *might* wave you over to take a seat on the couch. I was invited on in mid-career as a successful actor, prebooked in couch class, with extra legroom.

So on January 7, 1988, I finally did Carson, ready for my moment with the great man. What I didn't anticipate was that I would be following, and therefore sitting next to, one of the true legends of the Hollywood screen, Bette Davis. Bette was visibly unwell at that point—she'd suffered strokes and been ill with breast cancer, and would live only a year and a half further. She couldn't have weighed more than ninety pounds. And yet she was totally styling, decked out in a bold, nautically striped skirt suit, white gloves, and a wide-brimmed white hat.

And she was completely tough: fiery, witty, on the ball, and, her deteriorating health notwithstanding, smoking like a chimney. At one point, before I went out, I was watching from the green room as they came back from a commercial. Johnny, a smoker himself, was adept at sneaking a last-minute puff before the show resumed, but this time the camera caught him hurriedly stubbing out his cigarette while Bette sat there eyeballing him, proudly puffing away. "One thing about you and me, Johnny," she said, "we both *love* to smoke!"

"Oh, I know, Bette," Johnny guiltily responded. "But . . . but it's so *bad* for you."

"Oh, I suppose," Bette responded. "But to be told not to! As if we were *little* children." No one was going to bully that old dame.

The day before the taping, when I received word that I would be following Bette, I told my friend Rob Reiner about the situation. Rob said, "I'll give you a hundred dollars if you do Bette Davis *to* Bette Davis." So the very first thing I did after walking out and taking my seat was to turn to Bette and say, "And what a *pleaszh-ah* to meet *you!*"

Johnny and Ed McMahon immediately broke up, and Johnny even said, "You had the nerve to come out and do her right away!" But clearly, Bette didn't "get" my impression. She had no idea who I was. As far as she knew, I was some weirdo talking in his normal speaking voice.

The good news is that Johnny took to me immediately. He had the same insane Jerry Lewis obsession that I do, and he loved my Jerry—it got genuine, eyes-watering laughs out of him, which was tremendously gratifying in the moment and tremendously moving to consider now. As I got looser and looser, emboldened by Johnny's goading and enthusiasm, I turned to Bette and did a Jerry-style startle-take: "Yeah, John, howyadoin', and—*BETTE!*"

More big laughs from Johnny, Ed, and the studio audience. But nothing from the impassive Miss Davis.

A little later in my segment, I tried a different tack, going Ed Grimley on her: "If I had known you were going to be here—you are *so* decent. I suppose your movies aren't the best in the world? Give me a break! Pleasure to meet you." I extended my hand. Very reluctantly and limply—as if I had extended a line-caught fluke in her direction—she shook it.

Johnny kept encouraging me to do impressions, so I ran through David Steinberg, Paul Simon, Robin Williams, Doug Henning (Johnny, incredulously: "Doug *Henning*? Is there a big call for that?"), and Gary Cooper. Finally, from my other side, I heard Bette pipe up, "Do you do *me*?"

Well, I'd already done her, so to speak, minutes ago, and she hadn't picked up on it. So I replied, once again in my most de-clamatory, high-volume, *All About Eve* voice, "Well, I mean, you *ahn't* that easy to *do*!"

Bette still had no clue that I was doing her. "Then we'll *skip it*!" she said.

Or maybe Bette was slyer than any of us realized, and she was pulling the legs of us all. She was still unbelievably sharp, and I wouldn't put it past her. A lot of people commented to me afterward that they didn't think Bette should have been out in public, looking as emaciated as she did. But you know what? She did a full three segments on the show, killed in each one, and proba-bly went out to the Ivy afterward for a couple of margaritas and a great dinner. Good for her! I hope I'm in such fine fettle for Conan, Colbert, Kimmel, and Fallon when I'm eighty. Hell, I'll even wear Bette's outfit from that night, provided JCPenney is still in business.

I made up for lost time with Johnny, appearing six more times on *The Tonight Show* before his 1992 retirement. The final appear-ance was five shows before Bette Midler sat on the piano and sang "One for My Baby (And One More for the Road)" as he teared up. (Carson's very last show was a guestless farewell in which he showed old clips.) At the end of one of my later appearances, after the show was over, Johnny leaned in and said, "Next time you come, Alex and I would love to take you to dinner." (Alexis was his fourth and final wife.) That was a bit of a *whoa*, but the dinner never happened, which is probably just as well, because Johnny, away from his NBC throne, was known to be a different person socially, very reserved, and Nancy and I would have been knotted up with anxiety the whole time.

I did see Johnny once, though, in a supposedly more relaxed set-ting: a stag poker night. In L.A. in the 1980s, the movie pro-ducer Dan Melnick convened a monthly poker game at his house with some pretty heavy regulars, among them Johnny, Chevy, Steve, Barry Diller, Neil Simon, and Carl Reiner. Steve got me in for one of the nights. I was the poorest and least accomplished person there, but Steve reassured me, "The most anyone has ever lost is six hundred dollars, and you just might *win* six hundred."

Within fifteen minutes at the table, I had lost $1,800. I pan-icked and basically gave up at that point. I figured that if I merely lost the ante, I wouldn't have to go home and announce to the family that the house was for sale. Even with four aces, I'd fold.

We took a break for dinner, an elaborate spread prepared by Melnick's cook. I got to sit next to Johnny. At one point, Steve said something funny, I can't remember what, and it cracked me up. As I laughed, a little lump of mashed potatoes flew out of my mouth. But I had no idea where it had landed. My eyes quickly scanned the table in desperation to see where the spuds had gone, finally locating them . . . on top of Johnny Carson's hand.

I didn't know what to say or do. Fortunately, Johnny didn't seem to notice. I looked away for a moment and then looked back. The potatoes on his hand were gone. Had he eaten them himself? If so, it was an honor and privilege to pre-chew Johnny Carson's food for him.

MARTY THROWS A PARTY
JUST TO SING

When Nancy and I were sitcom actors in the late 1970s, I always thought of L.A. as boarding school, a place where I'd spend a few seasons of adventure and mischief before snuggling back into the bosom of Mother Canada. But by 1987, with a growing family, Nan and I had to make a decision on living in one place or the other, and we realized we were ready to put down roots in southern California. Little Katherine and Oliver would have dual citizenship—I'm way too Canadian for them not to—but they, along with young Henry Short, who came along in 1989, would grow up in a pretty house that Nan and I found at the end of a quiet street in Pacific Palisades. It was the perfect house for us—not ridiculously large or grand (the boys always shared the same bedroom), but airy and cozy, with a big living room anchored by a fireplace and an elegant, curved staircase straight out of one of my favorite childhood sitcoms from the 1950s, *Father Knows Best*. The location was beautiful, too: walking distance from the bluffs that overlook the Pacific. The master bedroom opened onto a balcony where the water sparkled blue in the distance. We can't afford this, I thought every time I looked out at the ocean from my new bedroom. How could I possibly deserve this view?

We bought the house on the basis of the income I was about to make from two pending movies. You can guess what happened next. Practically the second that Nancy and I signed the mortgage, one of the two movies, a David Lynch film with Steve Martin entitled *One Saliva Bubble*, fell through. I was in a panic. I anxiously said to Nan, "What if we can't afford this place? What if we have to sell it?"

"Well, I guess we'd move somewhere," she calmly replied. "But that's not going to happen, goofy. You know that." Twenty-seven years later, I'm still here.

There are those who make a hobby of real estate, forever buying and flipping houses, getting bored with a residence after a year or two. I'm totally different; keep in mind I spent the first twenty years of my life in the same house. I like to make a house a home and stay put; Nancy, too. So we did. I think this became part of the appeal of the family Short as we settled into the Palisades. We were show folk, with all the deviancy and egocentrism that such a description assumes, but we lived like a normal American nuclear family—or perhaps like a family on a long-running sitcom: going through the journey of life together on the same comfortingly familiar stage.

The most concrete manifestation of our traditional Short-family values was our annual Christmas party. It started out modestly, as a dinner for my extended family in which my brother Michael (an excellent blues piano player who used to tour with Ronnie Hawkins) would sit at the piano as we all gathered around and sang carols. But by 1988 the party began to evolve into a bigger deal: a carefully planned event held in mid-December (before people went off on their holiday vacations) that featured not only Nan's superbly potent French punch, but performances by my performing friends. Tom Hanks has described it as "like a Mormon Family Home Evening—a lot of participation, a lot of 'Everybody, come on up!'" Except with amazing, generally non-Mormon personnel. Basically, over the course of the 1990s and 2000s, our party became a private, camera-free, celebrity-studded holiday TV special like the ones Perry Como, Andy Williams, and Bing Crosby used to put on.

The party started at 7:00 p.m., with dinner served at 8:15. Then, at 9:30, the show began. I served as emcee, while the Broadway and movie composer Marc Shaiman served as my accompanist and musical maestro. Marc is a dear friend who goes way back with me, to when he served as *Saturday Night Live*'s rehearsal pianist in my time there. He and his longtime professional and personal partner, Scott Wittman, have done the songs for everything from *Hairspray* to the Academy Awards. They were also my co-conspirators on my 2006 Broadway show, *Fame Becomes Me*. However, this impressive résumé did not absolve Marc of his duties as my designated piano mover.

In my house, there's a little piano room between my office and the living room where we keep an old Yamaha upright. As 9:30 approached, it would always be Marc's duty to position himself behind one end of the piano and, with a great show of groaning and hypochondriacal expressions of imminent vertebrae slippage, push until the piano arrived at its destination, against the wall that rises under the curved staircase. As Marc pushed, I would carry the lightweight piano stool over, just so I'd feel a part of things. Marc would routinely complain, "How did this ridiculous tradition start, where *I* have to push the piano in to begin the show?"

"I can't remember, Marc," I'd say, "but it's *tradition*. Keep pushing."

We'd have a ten-foot Christmas tree standing in the crook of the staircase's curve, and Marc and his piano would be stationed to the tree's right: a natural stage set for our holiday pageant, visible to all of the sixty or so revelers squeezed into our living and dining rooms. Bernie Brillstein was always the first guest to nab a seat, loading up a plate with food around 8:00 p.m. and parking himself on the couch nearest the stage, lest anyone obstruct his view. It was that unmissable a show to Bernie, who had managed everyone from Jim Henson to Belushi, Lorne, and Gilda.

At 9:30, with a flourish, I would bound onto the piano's top, pretend-crushing Marc's fingers in the process, and open the show with a song whose lyrics varied from year to year, but this version will give you the idea.

{ IT'S THE MOST WONDERFUL SHOW OF THE YEAR }

(to the tune "It's the Most Wonderful Time of the Year")

Lyrics by Shaiman/Wittman/Short

It's the most wonderful time of the year
Tom Hanks is a-tuning
While Nancy is crooning
Arianna Huffington IS HERE!
It's the most wonderful time of the year

It's the hap, happiest season of all
Now the party's just startin'

'Cause here comes Steve Martin
He'll juggle a ball!
It's the hap, happiest season of all.

They'll be no hymns or pews here
There's just showbiz Jews here.
My agent's dead drunk in the john.
Goldie Hawn and Kurt Russell
Are doing the hustle
"Aren't you glad that we made Captain Ron*?"*

It's the most wonderful show of the year.
(Marc) Celebrity butt you'll be kissing
While high notes you're missing
(Marty) And this . . . from a queer!

It's the most wonderful time
It's the hap, happiest time
It's the most wonderful show . . . OF THE YEAR!

Nancy performed, too. Though she had long ago given up her show-business career, she loved to sing and was totally uninhibited about performing for this crowd. Often we'd duet—on the Pogues' Christmas song "Fairytale of New York," say, or "Hurry Home for Christmas," a number made famous by Steve Lawrence and Eydie Gormé.

In the early years the show was a more spontaneous thing, a "Who's going next?" kind of deal where you'd simply get up and do your bit. Catherine O'Hara would sing the old hymn "Count Your Blessings," a remnant of her Irish-Canadian upbringing. One year Nathan Lane got up and did a Danny Kaye homage in which he spluttered in rapid-fire fake Russian and ended with a huge pratfall. Another year, Phil Hartman and Billy Crystal joined me in a suitably cheeseball medley as, respectively, Frank Sinatra, Sammy Davis Jr., and Liza Minnelli. Bernadette Peters, when she was in town, offered us a moving version of "Have Yourself a Merry Little Christmas." (A year later, I spotted a similarly luxuriant head of curly hair in the crowd and shouted, "Oh, look, Bernadette is back!" When the head turned to face the guests, it was Kenny G. Hey, I was just sayin' what everyone was thinking!)

But given the wattage of the guest list and the quality of performances, the Christmas party took on a slightly more polished look as the years advanced, with no one wanting to half-ass it in front of this crowd. I think it might have been the moment when I saw Tom Hanks, Walter Parkes, and Glenn Frey intently rehearsing a tune in the piano room, guitars in hand—while Marc, who flew in from New York each year just for this party, was feverishly going over some sheet music on the piano—that I thought, Jeez, this looks like backstage at Carnegie Hall.

People would start e-mailing sheet music to Marc and Scott in advance, and asking if they could come ahead of time to rehearse, compelling Marc and Scott to arrive at our house earlier and earlier. "Look at all this stuff I'm being given," Marc kvetched as he sat at the piano, before the party decorations had even gone up. "Thank God I'm a genius, or I'd be in a tizzy!" Steve Martin spent something like four months mastering how to play "Auld Lang Syne" on the banjo. Victor Garber, one of the most accomplished actors and singers in modern theater, spent thousands of dollars on vocal coaching to prepare for his party performances. In that soft, lilting voice of his, he did a beautiful version of "I'll Be Home for Christmas," and, another year, "Peace" by Michael McDonald and Beth Nielsen Chapman. Steven Spielberg nervously joined the fray one time, playing clarinet alongside his wife, Kate Capshaw, as she joined Rita Wilson and Nancy to sing "Kung Fu Christmas," a soul-song takeoff that Bill Murray used to do in the *National Lampoon Radio Hour.*

Probably the award for most elaborate preparation should go to Tom Hanks. He had seen a Christmas rerun of Judy Garland's 1963 Christmas special on PBS, where Judy welcomed fake guests into her fake living room while she was making merry with her real children, Liza Minnelli and Lorna and Joey Luft. Tom particularly loved the part where the handsome young pop singer Jack Jones made a terrific entrance, old-style corny in the best way. The doorbell rang—*ding-dong!*—and Jones barreled across the threshold with a pile of wrapped presents, launching straight into a swing version of "Wouldn't It Be Loverly?" from *My Fair Lady*, distributing the presents to the kids as he sang.

Tom was determined to re-create this scene more or less shot-for-shot. He worked out a cue with Marc and me so that his appearance would be as sudden and straight-into-the-routine as Jones's was. Then Tom waited patiently outside for a period as other people performed.

It worked perfectly. As I went into my cue—"Now we have so many people"—I was interrupted by the doorbell: *ding-dong!*

"Well, who the heck could *that* be on this most wintry of winter nights?" I asked. Then I went over to answer the door, and Tom, wearing a replica of the slick sharkskin suit Jack Jones wore in 1963, strode in, singing "All I want is a room somewhere, far away from the cold night air . . ." And instead of handing out presents to the gathered children, he handed out $20 bills from a stack in his palm. He brought the house down—and, more important, won the kids over with the cash.

My family members were encouraged to become a part of the

show as well. Oliver, a drummer, would set up his drum kit to accompany his sister Katherine on piano and Andrea Martin's boy Joe (my nephew) on saxophone, along with Uncle Bobby Dolman (Joe's father, Nancy's brother, and Andrea's then husband) on harmonica. Together, they'd launch into an instrumental version of "Santa Claus Is Coming to Town." And then my brother Michael, per Short family tradition, would perform the R&B Christmas standard "Merry Christmas Baby" on piano and vocals.

There was no requirement that every guest had to perform, or that, if you did, your performance had to be musical. One of the most original nonmusical moments came courtesy of Jan Hooks, who was not only a star of *Saturday Night Live* but also played Jiminy Glick's wife, Dixie Glick, in various TV shows with me, as well as the movie *Jiminy Glick in Lalawood*. Jan is a southerner, from Georgia. I asked her if she was going to do anything, and she casually replied, "Oh, I don't know. I might do something from *To Kill a Mockingbird*. But if I do, and if, at one point, I run away, catch me."

More than a little puzzled, I said, "Very good then." At the next opportunity, I stood before the crowd and announced, "Ladies and gentlemen, Jan Hooks!"

Jan stood before the crowd, slowly eyeballed the gathered attendees with a surly face, and then began ranting at high volume.

"I got something to say! And then I ain't gonna say no more!" she shouted. "He took advantage of me! And if you fine, *fancy* gentlemen ain't gonna do nothin' about it, then you're just a bunch of lousy, yella, stinkin' cowards! The whole bunch of ya! And your fancy airs don't come to nothin'! Your 'Ma'am'-in'! And your 'Miss Mayella'-in'! It don't come to *nothin'*, Mr. Finch!"

At that, fully committed, she ran tearfully into my arms. It was Mayella Ewell's angry courtroom tirade from *To Kill a Mockingbird*, after the attorney Atticus Finch has ripped holes in the young woman's testimony that his black client, Tom Robinson, raped her. Such a deeply bizarre, borderline sick choice of something to do at a Christmas party, yet it was brilliant.

Jan's *SNL* castmate Jon Lovitz didn't have the same innate understanding of the party's family spirit. He worked too blue too early in the evening. It started with some celebrity-roast-style potty humor about Bernie Brillstein—"I remember one time Bernie was in a stall beside me, and he came into my stall and said, 'Am I clean, kid?' "—and just devolved from there. I could see the terror rising in my kids' faces. Marc did, too. He pulled an oversize candy cane off the Christmas tree and gave Lovitz the hook.

Scott Wittman had a fabulous tradition to end the show. Marc would start playing "Let It Snow," joined in by everyone at the party, while Scott went with my three children up to the top of the staircase, where they would sprinkle snowflakes they'd made with scissors and paper onto my head as I sang. And then I'd wish everyone a very Merry Christmas from the bottom of where my heart should be.

There was only one year where Marc and Scott and I got into any sort of disagreement creatively concerning the Christmas program. In 2003, they were flying in from New York for the party on the Friday before, and because they had a six-hour flight, they had lots of time to write a new song for the party. So to the tune of "On the Atchison, Topeka and the Santa Fe," a 1940s song by Harry Warren and Johnny Mercer, they wrote new lyrics about the party and its noted guests and entitled their creation

"Picture-Perfect Christmas in the Palisades." Unfortunately—from my gracious-host view, anyway—the lyrics also roasted nearly everyone who would be attending. For example:

See the stars walking up the drive
It's good to see that Bernie Brillstein's still alive.
He's been in the biz since the Crusades
It's the picture-perfect Christmas in the Palisades.

Diane Keaton's here, she's one brave chick
I hear she flashes titty in that Meyers flick

The damned thing went on and on, taking a swipe at virtually every friend I'd invited. After reading all their lyrics, I told Marc and Scott, "Absolutely not."

They were stunned and truly irritated by my apprehension and protectiveness. "Remember when you used to have an edge?" Marc said, meaning it.

"I am not going to potentially offend guests who I have welcomed into my home," I replied. In the end, we worked out a compromise. After the main show, when it got late and the party got smaller—and most of those named in Marc and Scott's lyrics had departed—I told Marc, "Okay, now we should do it, at the *second* show."

"You mean it's fine as long as it's behind people's backs," Marc said.

"What can I say?" I said. "I'm guided by the spirit of Saint Nick."

The second show, if I may clarify, was for the faithful and intrepid In Crowd, a smaller group that numbered somewhere between fifteen and twenty people. Just like in the *SNL* days, there was an after-party to the big party, a group including such people as Steve; Tom and Rita; Kurt Russell and Goldie Hawn; Paul Shaffer, if he was in town; and Victor Garber, ditto. The after-party began around 12:30 a.m. The kids were asleep by then, so you could and would work blue. (It was the Christmas season, after all.) One year I opened with my own bawdy composition, "Christmas Is a Lady," set to the tune of the late-period Sinatra song "L.A. Is My Lady."

> *You've got to treat Lady Christmas kindly*
> *You've got to sprinkle her with myrrh*
> *Then she'll light your tree and warm your Christmas balls*

One year Richard Belzer got up to talk about his close friendship with Jerry Lewis and how our party reminded him of a story Jerry had told him about an event at Ira Gershwin's house back in the 1950s. Seemingly all of old Hollywood was there, said Jerry, who was still a fresh face on the scene and excited to meet two of his comic idols, Jack Benny and George Burns, for the first time. Jerry had listened to Benny for years on the radio, but he had never heard him saying anything racy or off-color. So Jerry was standing there, hanging on every word uttered by the two older men, when Benny turned to Burns and said, "You see Gina Lollobrigida over there, George? Do you know what I would love to do? I'd love to get my cock out, put it in her mouth . . . and just have her say her name over and over again."

I was standing between Kate Hudson and Larry David when Belzer's line landed—with such force that it literally sent Kate to the ground, writhing in hysterics.

It wasn't lost on my Christmas-party guests that a big component of the joy I took in throwing these annual shindigs was that I got to sing before a captive audience. I seized the occasion to let loose on my most heartfelt versions of such standards as "It Happened in Sun Valley" (apt, given that many of us ski there at Christmastime) and "You're Just Too Marvelous." Marc, clever chap that he is, and knowing me far too well, had figured out my ulterior motive for throwing these bashes, and composed a song whose lyrics are reproduced here. It's sung from Marc's point of view.

{ "A MARTY SHORT WINTER WONDERLAND" }

Every year, mid–December
Comes a night to remember
With me at his side
We'll watch the guests hide
'Cause Marty throws a party just to sing

See his eyes, how they're glistening
He don't care if you're listening
You think that we're guests
But nobody rests
'Cause Marty throws a party just to sing

Now his house is bright and lookin' fancy
All the guests are here and looking chic
But though the dress is worn by his wife, Nancy
He thinks he's Judy Garland at her peak . . .

INTERLUDE

A MOMENT
WITH
FRANCK

Franck was a character I played in **Father of the Bride**, a 1991 movie cowritten by Charles Shyer and Nancy Meyers, and directed by Charles.

Franck is a wedding planner of indeterminate nationality, indeterminate gender, and indeterminate vowel-pronunciation choices. A wedding is a "wahdding" and a cake is a "keck." For some reason, in the filmgoing public's memory, Franck pronounces the latter word as "cock." I get people in airports all the time coming up to me and saying, "We just had a wedding cock, too!" Now, don't get me wrong; I'm all in favor of honeymoon sex. But I swear, Franck never said "cock." I'm just too subtle a performer for such a choice.

The concept of Franck in the movie was that he and his "Where would that accent be from, exactly?" otherness symbolized the alienation of the father (Steve Martin) from the process of planning the wedding of his daughter (Kimberly Williams). The daughter and the mother (Diane Keaton) could understand Franck perfectly, while Steve's character struggled to decipher every word.

In the first scene that I shot in the movie, set in Franck's office-atelier, we did take after take, ratcheting up or down how broadly I played Franck, and how unintelligible his accent was. At one point the accent had become so subtle that Steve said, "Well, now the scene doesn't make any sense, because I understand him completely." But Nancy and Charles were apprehensive, and rightfully so, about the idea of me playing Franck super big; nothing else in the movie was remotely heightened. In the end, though, they ran with the broader takes. As long as my portrayal seemed true to Franck's fastidious and strange little wedding-planner world, he could get away with just about any idea we came up with.

I could never figure out a way to incorporate Franck into my touring stage show, in which I unleash many of my characters. Unlike Ed Grimley and Irving Cohen, he wasn't the product of years of improv and TV work, and I didn't know what in the name of God he could talk about; he couldn't just talk about "vahdding keck." (Or, for that matter, "cock.")

Then, one night in 2008, I was at a dinner party, holding forth on why I thought Barack Obama was unbeatable in that year's election. It wasn't so much because of what Obama had to say, I said, but because he had an undeniable star quality. Someone responded, "What a shallow take on politics!" And then the lightbulb went on. That's it! I thought. Who's shallower than Franck? He should talk about who in the public eye does and does not have style. From that moment on, Franck found a place in my concerts.

FRANCK

Hellooo, how are you, lovely to see you! Don't you all look fabuous. Very chic. Oh, look at you in da front-row-type place. I love your outfit! I loved it when it was in style . . . eighteen years ago. It's amazing what they sell in thrift shops. The frontage is very low-cut. (**Starts barking like a dog.**) One suggestion: Why don't you put those together and make one good one?

To me, it's all about how you look. Because if you don't have style, people don't want to know you. They run from you like a straight man from a Celine Dion concert.

Chris Christie? I wish he would run for president. Just to see him run. He'd be the first oval in the Oval Office. When he goes to a casino buffet, the cook yells, "I need backup."

Kim Kardashian? Not so bright. She thinks "soy milk" is Spanish for "I am milk." Because let's face it, some people are born great, and other people have greatness thrust into them. You know, **kardashian** is an ancient Armenian word. It means "fame whore."

Donald Trump? He looks like a bouncer in a lesbian bar. That's not just hair, you see, it's a way to see if there is a wind advisory.

So remember, style is like a condo in Detroit; once you own it, it's yours forever.

And when in doubt, the little black cocktail dress is always in style . . . especially for women.

WHEN LIFE HANDS YOU LEMONS, PUT ON A FAT SUIT AND SQUASH THEM BETWEEN YOUR THIGHS

P laying Franck in *Father of the Bride* and its 1995 sequel was a riot—who wouldn't want to be paid to spend time hanging around with Steve Martin and Diane Keaton while they do most of the work? During the shooting of the first *Father*, in 1991, the three of us would scurry off to Diane's trailer between setups to play cards. I hadn't known Diane before, and quickly discovered that being around her was exactly how I'd hoped it would be when I first fell for her in *Annie Hall*. No, actually, it was better—Diane is smarter and more captivating company than Annie. When she was called to the set, leaving Steve and me behind, we looked at each other, simultaneously placed our hands over our hearts, and went, "Ahhhh." Now, perhaps Steve was having trouble digesting the corned beef sandwich he'd just eaten, but me? I was smitten.

That's the effect that Diane has on the fellas. And she's so guilelessly funny, which only makes her more endearing. At the time we were making *Father of the Bride Part II* together, the O. J. Simpson trial was in full swing on television, replete with its ridiculous cast of characters—Johnnie Cochran, Kato Kaelin, Chris Darden, Marcia Clark—and Diane was riveted. In a typically noisy makeup trailer, she was straining to hear every word of the trial on TV above the din of hair dryers, idle gossip, and me doing comic bits for Steve's amusement. Unable, due to my chronic loudness and these other factors, to hear the proceedings in Judge Lance Ito's courtroom, Diane turned to me in exasperation and said, "Hey, man, if you don't shut your mouth, I'm gonna suck your dick!"

Steve and I went completely hysterical. Then Steve calmly said, "Diane, just to be clear: When you threaten someone with the words 'I'm gonna suck your dick,' it's not as strong a threat as you think it is. In many countries, sucking a dick is considered a *reward*."

The first time I saw Diane in person was in 1983, when Nancy and I were dining in a beautiful restaurant in Toronto called Fenton's. She and Mel Gibson, who were in town filming the movie *Mrs. Soffel*, were seated right next to us. We were so excited that Nan and I barely spoke a word to each other for fear that we might miss a second of their conversation. After about fifteen minutes of us pretending not to be eavesdropping, I asked Nan to pass the rolls, only to be met with a stern "Shhhh!" Years later, I told Diane this story and kidded her that, while I was listening in, I heard her say to Mel, "What are we going to do about all those Jews?"

As fun as the *Father of the Bride* movies were to make, an uncomfortable reality was setting in: While those two movies were hits, my role in them was secondary. As for movies in which I was the lead or co-lead, my hitless streak from the late 1980s continued right into the '90s, with *Pure Luck*, costarring Danny Glover, and *Captain Ron*, costarring Kurt Russell.

Another picture I did, *Clifford*, fell victim to the whims of the industry: we made it in 1990, with my friend and frequent *SCTV* co-conspirator Paul Flaherty directing, but the studio behind it, Orion, folded, and the movie didn't receive a theatrical release until 1994 (and even then a pathetically halfhearted one). Also, critics, apart from a few hip ones, hated it. Now granted, its central premise—me, at the age of forty, playing a prepubescent ten-year-old boy with an otherworldly affect—made *Clifford* a very strange beast indeed. Clifford—the boy in question—was obsessed with dinosaurs and desperate to visit a theme park called Dinosaur World; he carried on his person at all times a plastic dinosaur action figure that he called Stephan, to which he confided his innermost thoughts.

To achieve a suitably creepy man-boy look, the makeup people lightened my hair a few shades and gave me a prep-school side parting, while wardrobe dressed me like a little Etonian, in a dark blazer accented by a series of rep ties and tennis sweaters. Also, because I was wearing shorts throughout the movie, I was told to apply Nair, the hair-removal product, to my legs the night before the first day of shooting, so that they would be optimally little-boy hairless. Of course I forgot to do that, so when I arrived in the makeup and hair trailer that first day, I suggested to the movie's hairdresser, Christine Lee, and her young female assistant, who I had never before met, that they Nair my legs while I was getting into makeup—just to save time and keep everyone on the set from waiting.

I quickly took off my pants, stripping down to my boxers, and propped my legs up on the counter. As I chatted away with my makeup-artist friend John Elliot, the two women spread Nair lotion all over my legs, from thigh to ankle, and started method-ically rubbing and rubbing and rubbing the hair off. Ten min-utes later, when they had finished and left the trailer to wash out the towels, I looked down to realize, to my mortification, that my penis had been out and exposed the whole time, staring the poor ladies in the face. It took me weeks to have enough nerve to broach the subject with Christine.

"Hey, so, uh," I said. "You know . . . uh, regarding that first day when you were Nairing my legs: Were you aware that my penis was out of my underwear?"

Christine didn't flinch. "I sure was," she said. "And if I had known you then like I know you now, I would've shoved that thing back in."

I spent the bulk of *Clifford* tormenting one of the funniest actors I've worked with, Charles Grodin, who played the boy's uncle, and smaller amounts of time tormenting the other tal-ented members of the cast, Mary Steenburgen, Richard Kind, and Dabney Coleman. I'm quite fond of this daring, adventurous little picture, and it always makes me laugh when I'm flipping TV channels and there it is. But at the time no one would give *Clifford* a fair hearing. Roger Ebert memorably wrote of it, "I'd love to hear a symposium of veteran producers, marketing guys, and exhibitors discuss this film. It's not bad in any usual way. It's bad in a new way all its own. There is something extraterrestrial about it, as if it's based on the sense of humor of an alien race with a completely different relationship to the physical universe. The movie is so odd, it's almost worth seeing just because we'll never see anything like it again. I hope."

Even the act of publicizing the film proved tortuous and un-precedentedly weird. While I was in a limo in New York City, en route to do the *Letterman* show to promote *Clifford*, I received a phone call from the actor Tony Randall on the car's phone (this was before everyone had a cell phone). First of all, I'd never met Tony, so how on earth did he have the car's phone number? Anyway, the reason he was calling was that he had reached out to me a few weeks earlier about starring in the Georges Feydeau play *A Flea in Her Ear*, which he was hoping to mount with the theater company he'd founded, the National Actors Theatre. I wasn't interested, and politely told Tony I would have to pass on his kind offer.

Tony went quiet for a second. I could tell that he wasn't pleased. "Martin, may I tell you something?" he said in that officious Tony Randall way, sounding very much like the characters he'd played in *The Odd Couple* and those old Rock Hudson–Doris Day movies.

"Sure, Tony, what is it?"

"You mustn't make silly movies," Tony declared. "That's what I did, and it cost me dearly." Great, I thought, now I'm being lectured.

"For you to have come to Broad-*way*," he continued, "would not have hurt you at all. And I suppose your management tells you you're hot. But let me tell you something, dear boy. *That's how we lost Marlon.* And we never got him back."

(Now, which Marlon could he have meant: Brando, or Marlin Perkins from *Mutual of Omaha's Wild Kingdom*?)

"Well, thanks for the advice, Tony," I said, somewhat coldly. "So great chatting with you, it really was." I then hit the END button on the phone and, while looking at it, said, "Go fuck yourself, you hot bag of gas!" Then I decided to call Nancy to see if she had any idea how Tony had found me in the limo. As I was jabbing at buttons, trying to reach Nan, I suddenly heard Tony's voice booming through the receiver with alarm: "Martin! *Martin!*" To my shock and horror, I realized that I hadn't hit the END button; I'd hit the

SEND button by mistake, and Tony had heard every word. That night, to Dave Letterman, before his studio and viewing audiences, I told the Tony Randall Anecdote verbatim. Months later I finally met Tony in person—at the Tony Awards, funnily enough—and with a big grin on his face he said, "I saw you on *Letterman* trying to blame the movie *Clifford* on me." The "hot bag of gas" got the last laugh, as well he should have.

A h, *Clifford*—what to make of it? Let's see: poor box office, bad studio karma, critical excoriation . . . all the prerequisites for a *cult hit*. Which is indeed what *Clifford* has become. My first inkling of this came on an American Airlines flight from Los Angeles to New York a couple of years after the movie's release. I was sitting in first class, and so was Nicolas Cage, about three rows up from me. I'd never met the man, and I didn't want to bug him while we were settling into our seats. But he had recently won an Academy Award for his harrowing performance in *Leaving Las Vegas*. At the right moment, I'll get up, introduce myself, and congratulate him, I thought.

Half an hour into the flight, I was lost in the *New York Times* when I noticed a figure hovering in the periphery of my vision: Nic Cage, crouched in the aisle beside me, his eyes locked on mine. "Can I just say something to you?" he said, a very Nic Cage-y intensity to his voice. "The dining room scene in *Clifford*, with you and Charles Grodin, where he's confronting you and you keep lying to him"—a sustained battle of wits, much of it improvised, in which Clifford drives Grodin's character to the edge (Look at me like a human boy!)—"well, I broke my VCR watching it. I watched that scene twenty-five times in a row, and I rewound it so much that the machine jammed and the tape broke."

On and on Cage went—and *he* had just won the Oscar two nights before. When I finally got to speak, replying, "And congratulations on your Oscar, great performance!" it seemed like I was merely returning his compliment—though, Nic, if you're reading this, I swear, it was always my intention to compliment you first.

In any event, Mr. Cage was not alone. On the one occasion I ever had to meet Elizabeth Taylor, she pronounced herself, to my astonishment, "a total *Clifford* freak." And *Clifford* took on a vigorous afterlife in the heyday of Blockbuster Video stores and repeat movie viewings on premium cable. Today, anyone twenty-five and under who approaches me in public only wants to talk about *Clifford*. Some of them tell me that when they and their friends get nostalgic for their early years of childhood, they get stoned and watch *Clifford* in their dorms.

I take a measure of satisfaction in *Clifford*'s belated discovery of its audience, but it was no consolation in the early 1990s. Between that movie's disappearance and the disappointing box office of *Captain Ron*, my feeling was, and I actually heard these words in my head: *Fuck the movies! I'm tired of the movies! Too much caprice, too many random factors, too much disappointment!* Of course, one factor that made it so easy to say "Fuck the movies" was that no one was offering me any. It's amazing how something like that can strengthen your resolve.

However, the beauty of my career and my diverse skill set was that I knew I had options. One of which was, as Tony Randall would put it, Broad-*way*. I had always felt in my heart that the theater was my first love, followed by the movies, then television, and then, perhaps, my family. In May of 1992 I auditioned for Marvin Hamlisch and Neil Simon to play the male lead, the so-called Richard Dreyfuss role, in the new musical version of Neil's script *The Goodbye Girl*. As I was leaving the audition, the casting director, Jay Binder, came running out, grabbed me by the shoulder, and turned me around, exclaiming, "You are a Broadway star! Do you hear me? You are a Broadway *star*! *And* your sweater matches your eyes!"

I got the part, and on March 4, 1993, opposite the beautiful and exquisitely talented Bernadette Peters, I fulfilled Jay Binder's declaration (although I was wearing a different colored sweater). The critical reaction to the show was wildly mixed, but I won the Outer Critics Circle and Theatre World awards for Best Actor in a Musical and was nominated for a Tony Award. Not only that, but I also got my caricature up on the wall at Sardi's, the fabled restaurant I'd visited with my brother Brian in 1965, on our first trip to New York. It was the ultimate Broadway honor, although I was forced to acknowledge that the restaurant's first attempt to capture my likeness didn't quite work out. The portrait was unveiled live on CNN, which would have been much more exciting had it looked remotely like me; instead, it was of a cross-eyed guy who apparently had a severe thyroid condition. Grasping for something to say on TV, I commented, "Well, what's interesting about this is, if Karen Black ever did a Broadway show, they could save on the framing."

Afterward Vincent Sardi Jr., the restaurant's owner, came up to me and sweetly inquired, "Mr. Short, you don't like the picture?"

"Oh, no, no, it's a great honor!" I protested. "It's just that . . . I'm not quite convinced that it looks much like me."

"This new guy we're using," Mr. Sardi said ruefully, "he just isn't as good as the old guy."

"How long have you been using him?" I asked.

"Twenty-eight years," Mr. Sardi said.

In any event, *The Goodbye Girl* ran for 188 performances, and I reinvented myself in midlife as the singing, stage-loving ham that I've secretly always been anyway.

W ell, hang on. I shouldn't make it sound quite so tidy. In the mid-1990s I had another of my periodic moments of self-doubt, akin to Breakdown Corner in 1977 and my pre-*SCTV* doldrums. It might have begun one day when I was sitting on my porch in the Palisades with Chris Guest. "Martin," he said to me, "have you ever felt that our style of comedy is already a little antiquated?"

It was ten years on from *Spinal Tap* and *Saturday Night Live*, but it had never occurred to me that I had a particular style of comedy that could be pegged to a specific time period. I'd never pondered that. Then again, the very reason I was with Chris at that moment was because he was appearing as a guest on an NBC show I was doing, *The Martin Short Show*, that was, if I may again borrow from Ed Grimley phraseology, as doomed as doomed can be. It was a sitvar—a hybrid of a sitcom and a variety program—in which Jan Hooks played my wife and I played a guy named Marty Short. We had some really inventive, funny premises, like one in which we found a lost white poodle with a tracking device on it. It was determined that the dog belonged to Elizabeth Taylor. We returned the dog, but Jan's character rigged the animal's tracking system so that we had a live audio feed and could listen in on Taylor and her then-husband, Larry Fortensky. Smash-cut to me as Taylor, shouting "Larry! *Gladiator* is on!" Jan and I also did a lot of character sketches in a variety of costumes and guises, not a world away from what Carrie Brownstein and Fred Armisen now do so successfully on *Portlandia*.

Whatever. The show didn't take. NBC wanted something

more traditional like *Home Improvement*, I wanted to include more sketch work, and the thing was yanked after three episodes. My kids were still young, so while I'd had success on Broadway, it wasn't viable for me to commit full-time to that life, away in New York for months at a stretch—not when Nancy and I had made a commitment to being an un-nomadic family. Another round of roles in unsuccessful movies followed—the kid-oriented pictures *Jungle 2 Jungle* and *A Simple Wish*, Tim Burton's *Mars Attacks!*— and suddenly it was the summer of 1997, and I was at our summer place on Lake Rosseau in Canada. My profile was strong, but none of my post-*SNL* projects had turned into anything remotely raging hot. I had nothing new lined up.

I'd always pressed my agents and managers to be brutally honest with me, in good times and bad: *Don't sugarcoat anything. Be honest. This is a business.* So around that time, I checked in with one of my agents to get the lay of the land. Here's what the guy said: "Do you know what it is, Marty? Everyone loves you. Everyone admires you. Everybody thinks you're talented. They're just not talking about you these days."

Oh.

I gathered myself and replied, "Boy, I—wow! I appreciate the clarity of that statement. Thank you!"

I was staring at the water and thinking, I'm forty-seven years old. Maybe I'm done. Maybe I've hit a wall that has no intention of giving. Not just thinking these things, but saying them to Nancy: "I think we're in trouble, Nan. I think it might be over."

Another reason to love my wife: she didn't buy it for a second. She saw the bigger picture. She said, "Mart, cream rises to the top. You'll never go away. People just wouldn't have it." Me, I wasn't so sure.

In that moment, Nancy was more mindful of the flawless logic

of my Nine Categories system than I was. We had three beautiful kids. We had each other. And look at where we were sitting:
this beautiful summer retreat, a stone-columned lakefront estate
built early in the twentieth century by a Toronto department-store
magnate and his wife.

In 1992, in the dead of winter, while I was in Puerto Rico with
Kurt Russell making *Captain Ron*, Nan had trudged through
four-foot snowdrifts down to the edge of a lake, looked back at
the seventy-year-old cottage that overlooked it, surrounded by
ten acres of wooded lakefront property, and said, "We'll take it."
She never checked with me, nor would she have needed to. I'd
have just said, "Whatever you think, baby," trusting her wisdom
about such things. (For years, my private name for our new estate
was Yes, Dear.) Tucked into an area of Lake Rosseau called Snug
Harbour, Snug, as I've come to call the property, became our family's favorite place, with spectacular vistas, pine-scented northern
woods, and loons that greeted us with their cries each evening—
our own Golden Pond, with money. Kurt was so taken with our
Rosseau place when he visited us—he and I had become great
friends during the filming of *Captain Ron*—that he and Goldie
Hawn bought land and built their own compound just across the
lake.

Nancy was also aware that I, more than she, am susceptible to
that condition sometimes ascribed to actors known as neediness.
I was driving once, late at night on a quiet road, and the solitude
and darkness sent me into a torrent of thought about how small
we are in the infinite scheme of the cosmos, how fleeting our time
is, and how mortal we are. I started contemplating the fact that
someday I will die and be no more. I started thinking of the sadness that would overcome my family and friends at the news of
my death. And I actually started tearing up. When I got home,

I reported this experience to Nancy. She said, "That's the sickest thing I've ever heard."

"Wait a second. You've never imagined your own death and teared up?"

"Of course not! I've imagined *your* death and teared up!"

"Well," I said, "that's my point."

S uffice it to say, Nancy was right: My career wasn't over, and good things did come up. That fall, I flew to London to play eight different characters in *Merlin*, an NBC miniseries with a wonderful cast that included Helena Bonham Carter, Sam Neill, and John Gielgud. Sir John Gielgud! I had a blast filming that project, which stretched into winter, and, with Nancy and the kids, enjoyed a magical Christmas break at Brown's Hotel in London, where a Boxing Day snowstorm lent the whole city a Victorian storybook feel. Sam, Helena, and I were nominated for Emmys, and my faith in the working actor's life was once again restored.

Concurrent with *Merlin*, I was collaborating with Rob Marshall, who had just codirected (with Sam Mendes) and choreographed the Roundabout Theatre's hit revival of *Cabaret*, on an updated adaptation of Neil Simon's musical *Little Me*. Simon and the songwriter Cy Coleman had originally created the show in the early 1960s as a vehicle for the high-energy comedian and TV pioneer Sid Caesar. Rob and I just clicked; he and I had adored working together in March of '97 doing the limited-run *Encores!* production of Simon's *Promises, Promises* at New York City Center, and we were looking for something else to do together. Like *Merlin*, *Little Me* would require me to play multiple roles—though in this case I would get comically killed in each one. Plus, I'd get to sing!

Rob and I found a week of time to put together an idealized draft of *Little Me* that lifted bits from different productions of the show over the years while adding in new concepts all our own. Yet at the end of the week I was overcome with uncertainty. If there was one thing I had learned from working with Neil Simon on *The Goodbye Girl*, it's that you don't rewrite a word of Neil Simon, the dean of American theater. "Why are we doing this, Rob?" I asked my collaborator. "We're wasting our time."

Still, Rob and I arranged a meeting with Simon and Coleman at Coleman's office in Manhattan. We sent over our script in advance. As we walked to the meeting, I started fearing the worst, getting increasingly worked up: "You know what, Robby? To hell with them and their closed, ancient minds! They think we're a pair of twenty-one-year-olds! Let me tell you something. They won't know what they'll be missing out on when they pass on this!"

Then we went into the meeting, where a relaxed, smiling Neil Simon greeted us and cut to the chase. "We love it, guys," he said. "Great job. Let's do it."

Moments later Rob and I were at the bar of the Four Seasons hotel, drinking martinis in rapid succession, half in celebration, half in panic: *Oh my god, now we have to actually do this.*

We opened in November 1998, with the delightful Faith Prince as my romantic foil, to the kind of notices an actor dreams about—"the stage loves him the way the camera loved Garbo," wrote the *New York Times*'s Ben Brantley. I won a second Outer Critics Circle Award, and, the following spring, the Tony for Best Actor in a Musical. When I reached the stage to accept the award, I instructed the audience to please be seated, even though they already were. I went on to say that there were so many people I could thank, but the reality was, I'd done it all myself.

The big takeaway from this for me was that, while such troughs of despair as I'd experienced in the summer of '97 were valid and important, and maybe even necessary, they did not need to be repeated. That lakeside moment of reckoning and anxiety would only be valuable to me if it was instructive—if I squeezed every bit of wisdom out of it so that I would not repeat it.

What I'd learned—and the lesson seemed to stick this time— was that I could and would survive quite handsomely in show business because I had the versatility to just keep moving. You don't want me in movies? Fine, I'll do TV. You don't want me in TV? Fine, I'll do theater. Just in the last year, for example, as I've been writing this book, I've had as full and eclectic a schedule as I could ever have hoped for: working on the sitcom *Mulaney*, playing a supporting role in Paul Thomas Anderson's film *In-herent Vice*, and continuing to do concerts all over the country, sometimes on my own and other times as part of a two-man team with Steve Martin.

The summer after *Little Me* ended its run, I launched my own syndicated talk show, which ran for one season (1999–2000) and was a good test of my resilience. Like my sitvar, it was called *The Martin Short Show*, and it was another attempt to find a niche by crossbreeding one TV genre with another—in this case, the agreeable daytime chat show crossed with *SCTV*-style sketch comedy. If I have any one regret about the talk show, it's that we should have waited a little longer to bring it to air, because the syndicator, King World, had not finished selling it to the local affiliates when we launched. Consequently, as time went on and more stations picked up the show, it was airing in a wild variety of time slots in different cities—early morning, late morning, afternoon, late night—and it became difficult to know what kind of audience to play to.

In San Francisco, for example, we were on at 1:00 a.m. In Boca Raton, 7:00 a.m. So, somewhere in south Florida, some poor ninety-year-old was sitting in an assisted-living home, saying, "What the hell is this guy doin' pullin' wacky faces this early when I'm trying to figure out if I'm still alive?" Even though the reviews for the show were terrific (the *New York Times* said, "At its hilarious best, which it often was during its premiere yesterday, Martin Short's new comedy-talk show is like a fresh edition of *Saturday Night Live* with interviews"), by Christmas the ratings were tanking, and not even six Emmy nominations could help. Once again, a show called *The Martin Short Show* was as doomed as doomed can be.

And yet something lasting and good came out of the project. One thing we did was a series of remote segments in which, playing a character, I would interact with real people. For the first one we tried, I spent about two hours in makeup, getting a bad prosthetic nose, a goofy wig, and pockmarked skin. I wanted to be unrecognizable, and the premise was that I would be this cheerily eccentric fishmonger at the L.A. Farmers Market who offered whole fishes to people, unwrapped, with his bare hands. Yet people immediately recognized me and asked for my autograph. The footage was unusable, which was frustrating, because I really liked the concept of getting lost in a character.

And then I remembered a scene I'd done in the movie *Pure Luck* in which my character was stung by a bee. He had an allergic reaction and his whole body swelled up, head to toe. I was getting made up for that scene, completely swathed in prosthetic blubber, when Danny Glover walked in, did a double take, and said, "Marty, I literally cannot see you in there."

Oh, that's what I want, I thought: to be totally unrecognizable. So that's why celebrity interviewer Jiminy Glick, of whom I now speak, was conceived as a fat guy. Jiminy was a product of my desire to do dispatches from press junkets, awards shows, and movie premieres not as myself but in character as a vapid entertainment reporter. He was also a symptom of my growing disenchantment with daytime television. I'd never watched much of it, but since I was getting into it, I wanted to familiarize myself with the terrain. Some of it, like *The View* and Rosie O'Donnell's show, was cool. (And this, mind you, was before the time of Ellen DeGeneres's show.) But boy, most of what was on was profoundly moronic. I came to realize that there was a whole daytime-TV ecosystem of morons who had large staffs at their beck and call: multiple assistants, segment producers, and so forth. I decided to make Jiminy a product of this ecosystem—a moron with power. The power of his TV platform!

As has been the case with all my characters, Jiminy took shape as an amalgam of various influences. There was a neighbor of ours back on Whitton Road in Hamilton named Mr. Braden whose speaking voice slalomed unpredictably from the very top of his range to the very bottom. Mr. Braden was the owner of the Kenmore Theatre, where we kids went to the movies. He didn't like us running across his lawn—he was older, and all his kids were grown—and he told us that if we stayed off his lawn for an entire year, we'd each get free passes for one Saturday matinee and one box of popcorn. (By the way: bad deal.)

There was also a soupçon of Merv Griffin's fawning in Jiminy, plus a vapid intensity borrowed from an old physics teacher at my high school, Mr. Devot. From the superagent Swifty Lazar, I borrowed the heavy black eyeglasses that were his visual trademark. And—unconsciously, I later realized—I borrowed my father's penchant for the unforeseen put-down. By the time the hair, makeup, and wardrobe people were finished with me—what with the fat suit, the latex goiter, the pompadour wig, and the huge glasses—the Jiminy look was complete, and the character took on a life of his own.

One of my first outings as Jiminy was at the Emmy Awards, where game actors who knew it was me, people like Jane Krakowski, totally embraced the concept and went along with it. "Jesus, Jiminy," Jane said, "it's been ages!" But Jack Lemmon didn't seem to understand that Jiminy was a character—more than likely he'd never heard of Martin Short, either—and when he gave me sincere answers to Jiminy's questions (referring to the abrasive old-time head of Columbia Pictures, I asked him, "Harry Cohn—was he mean?" and Lemmon sincerely replied, "He was never mean to me"), I decided not to use the footage. I wasn't out to dupe people, least of all national treasures like him.

At the American Comedy Awards, though, we had a little tent set up, and Goldie Hawn, one of my close friends, played it like Jiminy was a totally entrenched pillar of the Hollywood media. "Oh, Jiminy," she said, "you're so full of wisdom—you always have been." Since the Jiminy bits were improvised, I'd use these little snippets of commentary from his interviewees as information, to supply him with a backstory. Tom Hanks told Jiminy, "During the actors' strike in 1980, I watched that morning show of yours every day," and I instantly replied, "Well, we did it from the Beverly Garland Motel in Studio City"—and just like that, I had another piece of Jiminy's history: a teatime program from somewhere in his semi-distinguished past.

Daytime talk's loss was Comedy Central's gain. The cable channel was gung-ho about letting me devote a full program to the Jiminy character. Furthermore, after a year of walking onstage every day as myself, in a talk show bearing my name, I was downright sick of performing as me.

For the three wonderful seasons that we did *Primetime Glick* (2001–'3), my real face never once showed up on-screen. I'd do one-on-one Jiminy interviews with a celebrity, either before a studio audience or as a pretaped remote. I'd do sequences in which the celebrity joined Jiminy in a steam room. I did sketches showing Jiminy reading sordid Hollywood tales to schoolchildren (the story of how Sal Mineo was murdered, for example, or how Eddie Murphy was caught helping a transgender prostitute get home safely in a sketch entitled "The Damsel in Dis Dress"), and we'd have marionettes reenact the stories as Jiminy read. We would also see Jiminy at home with his beloved wife, Dixie (again enlisting the great Jan Hooks), as well as his four robust sons: Morgan, Mason, Matthew, and Modine. And we did some *SCTV*-type commercial parodies in which I played other characters and impersonated such figures as John Malkovich, who was promoting his new sitcom, *Malkovich in the Middle*. For the studio-audience sequences, Jiminy was joined by the brilliant Michael McKean as Adrian Van Voorhees, his harp-playing bandleader, who masked his chronic skin condition with a tragically orangey foundation.

The interview segments were my favorite. Not since Second City Toronto had I been given a chance to improvise so anarchically. I was as surprised as anyone at some of the bizarre things that came out of my mouth. I'd use expressions that I never, ever used in my daily life, such as "I take great umbrage." I made a knowing reference to a 1940s actor named John Hodiak and later had to look up who he was—where the hell had that come from? It was as if Jiminy was some sort of *Altered States* exercise in recovered memory and primordial regression.

More to the point, Dave Foley, of *Kids in the Hall* fame, said,

"Marty, you've finally created a character who is as mean as you really are."

I wouldn't go that far, but Jiminy, a man of appetites, had an unfettered id that was both fun and scary to watch in playback. He cut off an answer from Edie Falco with an abrupt, cruelly sibilant "*Shhhh!*" that truly startled her, followed by his admonition, "Just because I ask you a question doesn't mean that I need to know the answer. If you keep interrupting me when I have more questions, how can I possibly double-task!" (And when Edie said that she never watches her own work, Jiminy reasoned, "You can't look at yourself, because you see the *limited range*.") Jiminy scandalmongered without restraint, answering Conan O'Brien's complaint that he wasn't making eye contact by saying, "I'm looking right into your peepers—*which is what Wally Cox used to say to Marlon at night*."

Jiminy showed himself to be an improbably horny bastard, too—ever in need, he'd say, of his "nightly pop." He unabashedly molested Ellen DeGeneres and Catherine O'Hara, forcing himself upon them in fits of lust. Ellen rolled with it, literally, as we carnally tumbled over the studio set—the host and guest chairs and the big platter of doughnuts on the table between them. One nice discovery I made about the fat suit, which is filled with foam, is that it was a real gift to a physical comedian—I could do flips, rolls, and pratfalls with abandon because I was fully padded.

One of my favorite hallmarks of Jiminy was his utter lack of preparation. He always had a sheaf of research that his staff had compiled for him, but he clearly never read it, or merely cherry-picked it for a couple of factoids—which he still got wrong. To Steven Spielberg, he said, "I loved this film you did, *Schindler's Express*, with Goldie Hawn," and demonstrated his willingness to ask the tough questions by inquiring of the esteemed director,

"You've made so many films—when are you gonna do the big one?"

Steven was apprehensive about doing *Primetime Glick* because he hadn't been on a talk show since Dinah Shore's in the 1970s, and because he is not a performer. But he was a terrific straight man. The one cue I gave him in advance was that, when I asked him a question about his process and his craft, he should ramble on at length, and get so wrapped up in his answer that he looks away from Jiminy, his eyes focused on the middle distance. Steven handled this assignment expertly, earnestly enumerating his influences: Howard Hawks, Preston Sturges, and so on. Jiminy, bored to stultification by this answer and distracted by his ever-present hunger, slowly and stealthily slid out of his chair like a melting wheel of brie left out too long in the sun, commando-crawling over to the craft-services table to binge on food—and then slithering back just in time to pop back into place and offer a banal reply, his mouth full of pretzels and crudités: "Well, that sounds, like, really good!"

Jiminy was, in essence, the polar opposite of a character I'd done on *SCTV* named Brock Linehan. Brock was a straight-up parody of a well-regarded Canadian television interviewer named Brian Linehan (really subtle name-change detail on my part), a thinking man's host of the 1970s and '80s akin to Dick Cavett or Charlie Rose. Brian Linehan was known for his meticulous preparation for interviews—all the more impressive in the pre-Internet age—and his cerebral manner and turtlenecks. I'd been on his show in 1977, when I was first attracting notice at Second City Toronto, and he was gracious and solicitous.

But my *SCTV* homage to Linehan became so popular in

Canada that Linehan reported back to me that he was increasingly having a hard time being taken seriously in public. A waiter, he told me, had broken up with laughter when he, Brian Linehan, was simply trying to place his order. So, he asked me, could I please stop doing my Brock Linehan character? I said of course, and did stop—though I withheld from him that we already had three more Brock segments in the can.

Anyway, back to Jiminy: he was a wild, liberating character to do, and, when paired with an accommodating guest, was prone to embark upon dark, dangerous journeys deep into the comedic unknown. Alec Baldwin and Jiminy got to discussing Alec's left-wing politics, and Jiminy went straight to the Communist place: "A lot of people speak ill of the Blacklist, and I don't get it . . . Tim Robbins and Susan Sarandon. Personally, I'd like to see them isolated in Catalina!"

Alec ran with it, indignantly: "A United States penal colony in Catalina?"

Jiminy: "I would have Tim Robbins in a cell!"

Alec: "But Susan on a boat!"

Jiminy: "Yes!"

Alec: "So would I."

We took a break, and Alec was excited, clearly getting into the Glick spirit. "Ask me about women," he said. So we rolled tape, and every woman Jiminy mentioned, Alec acknowledged having had sex with. Meg Ryan? "She couldn't get enough of it." Sarah Jessica Parker? "What do you do, she comes to your apartment at three o'clock in the morning after she wraps the friggin' TV show." Dame Maggie Smith? "It was just a thing in the back of a car with an overcoat over my lap." Dianne Feinstein? "She liked to watch. I was with Barbara Boxer. Feinstein came up to me, she'd had a few, and she said, 'Would you, um . . . would you like to do

Barbara? And would you mind if I watched?' And I said 'Whatever blows your dress up, let's go.' "

Over the course of the program's run, Jiminy had his way with Jerry Seinfeld, Julia Louis-Dreyfus, Jon Stewart, Steve Martin, Mel Brooks, John McEnroe, Goldie Hawn, Ben Stiller, and Ice Cube (Jiminy: "I love Rex Harrison, he was one of the first rappers"), among many others. All of this with me now in my fifties. It was welcome reassurance that the well of comic invention had not run dry.

Eugene Levy has said that Jiminy is my greatest creation, which, coming from my oldest and dearest friend, is an especially moving compliment. Not that Jiminy was particularly reverent toward Eugene. He pronounced his last name incorrectly on *Primetime Glick* (as "LEE-vy" rather than "LEH-vy") and greeted him by declaring with an accusatory pointed finger, "You're not exactly who I assumed you'd be." The interview carried on for a couple more minutes, with Eugene holding forth on some subject, when Jiminy brusquely interjected, "Gabe Kaplan! From *Welcome Back, Kotter*! *That's* who I was hoping you would be!"

INTERLUDE

A MOMENT WITH WITH JIMINY GLICK

Jiminy is the most interactive of my characters. He is, by definition, an interviewer, and therefore needs an interview subject once he has finished puffing himself up in his introductory remarks. And speaking of puffing himself up: when I was doing **Primetime Glick**, I wore carefully applied latex makeup to appear Jiminy-obese, along with a very convincing and elaborately conceived fat suit. But in my live stage show, since I have to do a lot of quick costume changes, there isn't time to re-create Jiminy's look as thoroughly.

Instead, I have a special Jiminy mask that is split at the back and quickly Velcros together, and a wonderful, custom-built, easy-in, easy-out fat suit that I simply step into and zip up the back, as if it were a store-bought child's Halloween costume. The fat-suit costume is filled with foam and includes a blazer, striped shirt, necktie, and matching trousers. When it's drooping unused on a hanger, it looks like a carefully deboned Halliburton executive.

I first started doing live Jiminy interviews during the 2006 run of **Fame Becomes Me** on Broadway. Originally, we had famous ringers in the audience that I pulled onstage—Jerry Seinfeld, Nathan Lane, and so on—but we soon realized that it was just as funny with a civilian. A dentist, say. Because Jiminy is the egotist and the anarchist who sucks up all the oxygen, all the interviewee has to do is play it straight.

That said, I do try to have my office book a local luminary to join Jiminy, simply because it's good promotion; if the popular deejay or weatherman in your city knows he's going to be onstage with Jiminy, he'll plug the upcoming Martin Short concert all week. I also like having mayors on, because they're good straight men and women, inherently self-conscious about their images. Occasionally Jiminy will get aroused by a lady mayor and will jump her and start pumping her. But all in good fun; she merely feels the soft impact of foam padding for two or three seconds, whereupon Jiminy collapses back into his seat and lights up a cigarette.

Before I let Jiminy speak for himself, permit me to provide you with an abridged version of the bio I wrote for him back when **Primetime Glick** was heading to air.

Jiminy Glick was born in 1948, in Akron, Ohio, the youngest of eleven children born to Omar and Isabella Glickman. After graduating from Gale Gordon High School, he enrolled at the prestigious DeVry Institute of Technology, but left after the first semester when he won the role of Onlooker #2 in a bus and truck theater production of **Forty Carats**, starring Miss Lana Turner.

By the time he was thirty, Jiminy had grown confident enough to move out of his parents' house and pursue a career in acting. Sure enough, he landed a job as a busboy at Chasen's, where he stayed for the next eight years. He worked only occasionally as an actor, most notably as Buddy Ebsen's kleptomaniac nephew in a **Barnaby Jones** two-parter.

Jiminy found acting jobs few and far between and was ultimately forced to take a position as a personal assistant to the legendary Charles (**Death Wish**) Bronson. He remained in that lofty capacity for five turbulent years. Then, in 1991, while moonlighting as a bartender's assistant at Roddy

McDowall's People's Choice Awards after-party, he befriended former **Laugh-In** producer George Schlatter. As luck would have it, Schlatter was looking for a host for his new syndicated celebrity interview show, **LaLaWood**. Glick got the nod, and after two short years, **LaLaWood** rocketed to the top 100.

Jiminy now lives in Tarzana with his wife of twenty-two years, Dixie, and their four sons. When he's not hosting his current show, **Primetime Glick**, you'll most likely find Jiminy coaching his sons' Little League team, rebuilding the engine of one of his classic steam-engine cars, or browsing for antiques.

"Thank God he's a man and he's so fat, or I'd be worried about my job. He's **that good!**"
—Diane Sawyer

JIMINY GLICK

I believe celebrities are the most persecuted minority in America. A celebrity walks into a room, and people have already made up their minds as to whether or not they like him. We, and by "we" I mean me, are victimized by prejudice. And I think there is no room for prejudice, unless you're talking about Samoans. Because we all know what **they're** like.

I recently interviewed the wonderful Pope Francis. He's a celibate who loves the tango. So apparently it only takes **one** to tango.

Also, unlike his predecessor, he's a humble

man. He's not wearing the fur-lined cape. Except, of course, when he has Lady Gaga tickets.

I also recently interviewed the wonderful Elton John. I'll let you all in on a little showbiz secret. (**Whispering.**) Gay.

I also interviewed the late James Brown—well, I didn't interview him as much as we carpooled together to the women's shelter to pick up our wives.

Let's be honest, celebrities are our touchstones to "Where was I and when." I think we all remember where we were when the Queen had Diana killed. I certainly know where I was. I was getting some polyps removed from my duodenum. And the doctor had just berated me because I'd forgotten to fast. Suddenly the head nurse came running in and announced that the princess was gone. It felt like somebody had taken a knife and plunged it deep into my gut. Then I realized that the doctor was still in mid-procedure.

Aren't you in wonderful shape, for someone who's let himself go? And whatever cosmetic surgery you've had, I'd say twenty percent more and then I'd stop! You know, I used to be quite heavy myself, but now I'm doing Atkins. Not the diet, his widow. I've been on Jenny Craig more times than Mister Craig.

But enough about me. I want to know about your journey. But not too much detail, 'cause I don't really care. Let me ask you this . . .

If Lincoln were alive today, would he be pleased with his tunnel?

Am I crazy, or is Italy shaped like a young man filling out a police report after a rugby team has had its way with him?

Why did God give men nipples if we're not supposed to breast-feed our pets?

Do you feel badly for the **g** in **benign**?

Why did they put an **s** in the word **lisp**? It seems cruel, no?

Those toilets that flush automatically—do they see when you're finished, or are they guessing?

LOVE, LOSS, AND BUMPKISS

Tom Hanks had this habit with Nancy. We'd all be gathered somewhere, being loud and boisterous—at a dinner party, say, or on vacation—and he would ask her, "Don't you ever get tired of laughing at Marty's jokes?"

And Nancy would always say, "No, I actually don't." And it was true. Nancy was the opposite of the stereotypically obeisant show-business wife, but she loved to laugh, and she never wearied of hearing the same jokes (and I mean the *same* jokes) time after time. Laughter was central to our relationship. And here's the other really important point: Nan was hysterically funny herself. Way back in 1974, when we first hung out together at the jazz club with Paul Shaffer and Mary Ann McDonald, we were amazed to discover how similar our senses of humor were. By the time we were parents and longtime marrieds, we'd become comfortably complementary.

Nan and I could tell a million stories of our adventures together, some of them pretty embarrassing, but nearly all of them uplifting in some way, or at least worth a chuckle. The first time we ever took a getaway trip on our own, without the children, we went to Hawaii for five days. We were, like all exhausted parents of young kids, psyched to grab a literal moment in the sun. I called Carlos, the driver we always used, to take us to the airport. He told me that unfortunately he would not be available when we needed to leave, but he would send someone else from his car service.

I looked out the window and saw a big limo pull into our driveway. And out of it stepped a six-foot-four African American man, beautifully dressed in chauffeur's livery—much more proper than Carlos, and very elegant and poised, like a character in a Wes Anderson movie. Right as he was pulling up, Nancy called out to me from the bedroom, asking if Carlos was picking us up. I shouted back to her, "No, he's sending someone else." That is all I said.

I ran upstairs to bring our bags down, and by the time I did, Nancy was outside with the driver, introducing him to the children and the nanny, and kissing the kids good-bye. We got in the car and hit the road. As we were moving along, Nancy leaned forward and said to the driver, "Oh, Bumpkiss, you know we're going to American Airlines, right?" And he said, "Yes, I know."

Nancy wasn't done. "Bumpkiss," she said, "are you gonna take the Marina or the 405? What do you think is the best route?"

The driver looked at her a little longer this time through the rearview mirror before announcing, "The 405 is clear."

I, meanwhile, hadn't even been officially introduced to him, so I'm thinking, Wow, what a name—I've got to use that name. So I said, "Oh, Bumpkiss, you know that we've arranged to have a greeter meet us at the terminal, right?"

He stared at me through the rearview mirror for a beat longer than he just had with Nan, his eyes a little deader than before. "Yeah," he replied.

Something seemed off. I stage-whispered to Nancy, "How do you know his name is Bumpkiss?"

She stage-whispered back, "Because *you* told me!"

Whaaat? "What are you talking about?" I hissed. "When did *I* tell you his name is Bumpkiss?"

Nancy whispered, "I asked you, 'Is Carlos picking us up?' and you said, 'No, Bumpkiss is.' "

"I did *not* say that!"

"You certainly did!"

Fantastic. Not only were we calling the driver by the wrong name, but we had also assigned him some vaguely racist name straight out of Margaret Mitchell or *Show Boat*.

Flushed with embarrassment and liberal guilt, I whispered to Nancy, "What are you talking about? I said, 'He's sending someone else.' That doesn't sound anything like 'Bumpkiss'! "

Bumpkiss—er, the driver—delivered us to LAX's American terminal in prompt fashion. After he and I finished unloading the bags onto the skycap's cart, I pulled out a wad of hundreds and gave them to him as fair recompense for our unintentional psychological abuse. "Thanks, and I'm so sorry," I said. "There might have been some, uh . . . some confusion about—well, I'm sorry, what is your name?"

"My name is Larry," he replied with a tight smile.

Once we landed upon the beautiful island of Kauai, though, the tension went away, and Nancy and I had the most romantic, Zen vacation of our lives. Apart from one harrowing experience, that is. We paid a visit to Brennecke's Beach, a place famous for its bodysurfing, and couldn't resist testing its waters. We quickly paid for our curiosity—the two us were pummeled by a giant wave that we didn't see coming. It threw us high into the air, and we each landed with a heavy thud, facedown in the sand. The beach was pretty crowded, and when I stood up to see if Nan was okay, I saw her getting to her feet, unaware that the top of her two-piece was now missing. "Can you believe how *big* they are?" she shouted over to me. She was referring to the waves. But all the guys on the beach who were now smiling and doing double takes didn't necessarily see it that way.

E ven though Nancy and I had a lot of fabulous show-business friends because I happen to be in show business, the truth of our social world was that Nancy was very often the greater engine of our social life. She and Rita Wilson, for example, became very close very fast—playing tennis together, recognizing in each other kindred competitive-jock spirits, and sharing thousands of laughs—and their friendship accelerated the development of my own with Rita's husband, Tom Hanks. Nancy and Nora Ephron bonded over being voracious readers and witty, tart conversationalists—trading books, articles, and poison-dart commentary about how insane everyone but they were—and that's how Nancy and I became a frequent dinner quartet with Nora and her husband, the author and screenwriter Nick Pileggi.

As acclimated as Nancy and I became to the Hollywood scene, a few figures still froze us in our tracks, neutralizing our normal gregariousness with their megawatt presence. One was George Harrison. You never get over the fact that a Beatle is a Beatle, even after he has stopped being a Beatle. Nancy and I met George in 1990, at an L.A. dinner party hosted by Dick Donner and Lauren Shuler Donner. I'd met Ringo Starr when he was on *SNL*, and later would work with Paul McCartney, but George seemed the most mysterious and reclusive of the surviving Beatles. To Nancy and me, there was something otherworldly about him.

We knew in advance that George was going to be at the Donners' party. On the drive over, we played *Rubber Soul* over and over again, and Nan kept saying, "Wouldn't you love to just corner him and ask him every Beatle question you've ever wondered about?" We both laughed, and I said, "Yeah, boy, he'd sure love that, wouldn't he?" And then we went silent and just listened for a while to the genius music that George made with the three other guys in his old band.

There were ten other guests there that night, and when George walked through the door all I could think was, *My god, he looks* exactly *like George Harrison.* George was perfectly friendly throughout the dinner—in fact, he brought along a tape of the still-unreleased second Traveling Wilburys album, which he eagerly played for all of us on the Donners' stereo like a proud teen showing off his garage band. I found that sweet. But Nan and I maintained a cordial, deferential distance from him, fearful that the word "Beatle" would come out of our mouths in an involuntary, Tourette's-like outburst.

After dinner, we all retired to the Donners' screening room, where Dick had arranged for us to view an advance reel of *The Hunt for Red October.* I ended up sitting right next to George on the couch, with Nancy on my other side. Dick Donner, an outgoing, no-B.S. guy with a thick thatch of white hair, announced, "Does anyone mind if I smoke a doobie?" Then he pulled out a large joint, which he proceeded to light, his plans clearly not contingent upon anyone's answer to the question.

As we watched *The Hunt for Red October,* the joint was passed around until it landed with Nan. My wife, who could never really handle any kind of smoke, took one puff just for the sake of sociability. She immediately started coughing and, as fast as she could, passed the Donner doobie to me.

I took a hit, and then it was my turn to pass the joint to George on my right. But all of a sudden I started to panic, wondering about the etiquette of it all: *Do I pass this to a Beatle? Maybe I shouldn't. Am I going to offend him? Gee, I wouldn't want to offend him. Would the Maharishi Mahesh Yogi be pissed or elated? Or maybe it would be rude if I didn't pass him the joint. Oh, what the hell. Probably best to just pass George Harrison the joint.*

I gently nudged George, who was engrossed in the movie, and offered him the spliff. He looked at it, smiled, and in his best documentary-narrator's voice said, "Ah, the *sixties!*" He happily accepted the funny cigarette and took several drags on it.

I looked back at Nan, and she was already fast asleep, her head bent back, her nose in the air. George, on the other hand, became totally amped, very gregarious and chatty, talking right over the movie. "I have a hard time watching Sean Connery in a movie, a hard time accepting him in the part he's playing," George said, his voice now rising to lecture-hall volume. "Because he's too bloody famous, too iconic—it's like watching a *Beatle.*"

At that—George's fortissimo pronouncement of the word "Beatle"—Nancy's head shot up with a start. Not even quite sure where she was, she muttered, "Who said that?"

Meanwhile Lauren Shuler Donner had been contemplating for the last minute or so whether or not it was okay to shush a Beatle. Now she concluded that it was. "Guys," she whispered, "*shhhhh!*"

George and I both went quiet like reprimanded kids in the fourth grade. After a moment, I turned to him and whispered, "Way to go, asshole!" The two of us burst out laughing, eliciting, now from the entire group, a new round of shushing.

For the remainder of the evening—away from the screening room—George and I enjoyed a rich, funny, fast-moving conversation. He was even familiar with some of the work I'd done, which I found incredibly flattering—but then he was a comedy aficionado, close to Lorne and Eric Idle of Monty Python. As we said our good-byes at the end of the night, George and I exchanged numbers, and we made a plan to have lunch the next day.

Nancy, having benefitted from a refreshing, head-clearing nap, said to me as we buckled into our car seats, "Out of curiosity, how do you intend to have lunch with your new best friend George Harrison tomorrow, given that you're flying to Boston first thing in the morning?"

Mother's balls! I'd forgotten that I had a gig in Boston!

The next day, as early as I could without being rude, I telephoned George and told him I'd forgotten about my trip. He was gracious and told me that we'd make it happen another time.

Sadly, that other time never came. Our paths never crossed again, and George passed away in 2001.

Just a few months after his death, I was in Bungalow 8, a New York club that Paul Shaffer had dragged me to, when I noticed a skinny fellow who was the spitting image of George, only *young* George, coming right toward me. Before I could say anything, this young man embraced me in a tender hug. And then pulled back to explain himself.

"I'm Dhani Harrison," he said. "One of the last things my father told me was that if I ever come across people who were important to him, I should give them a hug."

E arly in 2007 Nancy and I returned to our home in the Palisades after a nice stretch in New York, where I'd spent the latter half of '06 on Broadway, doing *Martin Short: Fame Becomes Me*. That show was the ultimate in ego gratification and attic-fantasy realization: a musical expressly built for me, with my name in the title, and with original songs written for the show by Marc Shaiman and Scott Wittman. (Marc also joined me as a performer onstage, while Scott directed the show, along with Kathleen Marshall, the polymathically talented sister of Rob.) *Fame Becomes Me* was loosely autobiographical in the loosest sense of "loosely autobiographical": vaguely based on my life and career, yet filled with patent untruths. (I was not raised as a gypsy, did not go through a twelve-step program, and never starred in an all-nude, tribal-rock musical version of the second-greatest story ever told, *Stepbrother to Jesus*.)

As spring began, we were in a good place, familywise: Katherine had graduated from New York University and was contemplating grad school, Oliver was doing a semester abroad in London while enrolled at Notre Dame, and Henry was still with us at home, though soon to follow his brother to South Bend. Somewhere in the period leading up to Easter, Nancy felt a lump in her groin and thought she might have a hernia. She'd had one when she was twenty-four and thought it might be an avocational hazard of being a jock who hiked and played tennis all the time.

The Wednesday before Good Friday, Nancy went into Cedars-Sinai Medical Center for outpatient hernia surgery, and I accompanied her. Neither of us thought much of it; while I waited, I jotted down jokes for the speech I was going to deliver the following Monday in New York, at the Film Society of Lincoln Center's Gala Tribute, whose honoree that year was our friend Diane Keaton.

But the doctor had an ashen face as he addressed the two of us after Nancy's procedure. He had discovered not a hernia, he said, but a mass. He put the likelihood at 90 percent that it was cancerous—a diagnosis that the biopsy confirmed the next day.

This was not Nancy's first go-round with the terrifying word *cancer*. Ten years earlier, in 1997, she'd had a double mastectomy after her doctor discovered carcinoma in situ, an early-stage form of cancer, in both breasts. It was obviously traumatic to us, but because Nancy didn't have to go through chemotherapy and radiation, she charged through the unpleasantness with her typical unshakable Mountie spirit, and that was that—cancer gone. Unfortunately, at that time, they hadn't yet developed what is known as the BRCA gene test, in which a patient's blood is analyzed for mutations in her BRCA1 and BRCA2 genes, which naturally suppress tumors. Mutations to these genes indicate a higher susceptibility to ovarian cancer as well as breast cancer. Had the test existed then, Nancy might have undergone a preventive hysterectomy as well.

All of that was moot when we got the bad news that Thursday. The big question was, how widespread was Nancy's cancer? We wanted to know right away, but the only way to get clear information was via PET scan, and it wasn't possible to schedule one for the next day, Good Friday, in Los Angeles. But our internist, Dr. David Kipper, arranged for his brother, Dr. Michael Kipper, a radiologist and one of the pioneers of the PET scan, who was based in San Diego, to open up his clinic just for us. We drove down that Friday in dreary, overcast weather, wordless and tense.

The scan didn't reveal any cancer beyond her pelvic region; no spreading, as far as they could tell. Though this news was not definitive, we received it ecstatically, in tears. We drove home and toasted Nancy's good health with cosmopolitans. And the truth of it was, Nancy looked and felt great. This was just something to be gotten through. The main thing that concerned us was keeping her medical ordeal under wraps, out of the press. Nancy was private to begin with, and the last thing she wanted was for her friends and family to be worried about her, or, worse, to learn of her condition by reading about it.

Nan was supposed to accompany Henry and me to New York. Monday was the Diane Keaton gala. Tuesday I was taping Conan O'Brien's show, then *Late Night*, on NBC. Wednesday, there was a release party for the original cast recording of *Fame Becomes Me*. And then that night we would all fly to London to visit Oliver while the boys were both on spring break. Nancy, though, wasn't up to flying, given what she'd just been through. As for me, the thought of leaving Nan's side and fake-exuberantly bulldozing my way through a series of functions and talk shows seemed utterly incomprehensible. But Nancy would have none of my protestations. She urged Henry and me to carry on. Henry, she said, shouldn't be cheated out of the London trip, and any abrupt cancellation of my scheduled appearances might raise some eyebrows that she was not ready to have raised.

So off to New York I went with my adorable seventeen-year-old son. Henry had a great night at the Lincoln Center event, with Meryl Streep sweetly heaping loads of attention upon him at the dinner after the ceremony. At one point I interrupted their conversation to ask Henry, "Are you aware of all the brilliant films Meryl has been in?"

Henry smiled nervously; he couldn't actually think of any of her movies at that moment.

"You can't name one?" boomed Meryl in mock indignation.

I offered, "*Sophie's Choice*, you know that one?"

Hen just shook his head no.

"*The Devil Wears Prada*?" asked Meryl.

"Didn't see that one either, sorry," Henry said, shaking his head in embarrassed laughter.

Meryl suddenly stood up and declared, "You know nothing of my work! How *dare* you!" And then she threw down her napkin and circled the table dramatically, as if to exit—before finally swooping back to Henry to give him a big hug. So fantastic and loving. But then, she has a son named Henry too.

Earlier in the evening I had delivered my typical defamatory roast speech in Diane's honor.

> *To say being here tonight for Diane is a thrill . . . would be something I've just read off the teleprompter.*
>
> *Actually, it's more than a thrill. It's an obligation.*
>
> *Diane Hussein Keaton has been responsible for some of the most memorable performances of the past thirty-five years. Although, right now, I'm drawing a blank.*
>
> *On the cab ride here tonight—'cause they wouldn't send a car—I was thinking about the first time I ever saw Diane in person. It was on Broadway, in the musical* Hair. *I re-member sitting there in the second row. Just me and my bin-oculars. And I remember being disappointed because Diane had refused to accept the fifty-dollar bonus given to any per-former willing to get naked. Times change. Now, for fifty bucks, Diane will give you a massage with a happy ending.*
>
> *I don't think I'm being indelicate here when I say that when you work with Diane, you fall madly in love with her. And I'll be honest: I once made a move on Diane, and she was very responsive. But unfortunately, at the last minute, she was able to chew through the duct tape.*
>
> *And when we watch Diane with her children—those of us who know Diane, who love Diane—we are all struck with the same thought: What's with all the hitting?*

The speech went over well with the audience that night, and working on it all day had been a welcome, cathartic diversion from the unsettling news I had received earlier that afternoon. Around two p.m. my cell phone rang, with the name of Bernie Brillstein, my sainted, salty manager, on the caller ID. I picked up, and Bernie began the call with the words "Confirm or deny: the *National Enquirer* has a report ready to go that Martin Short and his wife, Nancy, had been to Cedars-Sinai on Wednesday, cancerous mass discovered, the full extent of her illness is not known, blah blah blah." In all likelihood, someone at or affiliated with Cedars had leaked the information the second we'd walked out the door.

"I'm assuming this is bullshit," Bernie said.

"It's not," I told him.

Bernie sighed. "Fuckin' life, huh?" he said. "I'm sorry, kid. It's all going to be all good, you know that. Well, what do you want me to do?"

"Let's not do anything, Bernie," I said. "Maybe they'll have a bit of soul and not print it."

"Very unlikely," he said. "Remember, they're all cunts."

At the party after the Lincoln Center event, I pulled Steve Martin aside. Earlier I had told him about Nan's cancer, but now I wanted his advice on what to do re the *National Enquirer*. "Steve, the *Enquirer* has a story ready to run on Nan, and—"

At those words alone, Steve went completely white—whiter than normal, which is really saying something. "Those fucking bastards! Those fucking *bastards*!" he said. "How dare they?" Then, softening, he asked, "How are you?"

I was honest: "I'm hanging on by a thread." This hit Steve harder than the *Enquirer* news, because I never say things like that. Everyone's accustomed to me being the smiley Mr. Positivity of our group. Steve began sobbing in full view of many of the guests, then grabbed his wife's hand and said, "We've gotta go." He turned to me: "Can I tell Anne?" I told him he could.

Nancy Meyers, who was also at our table, had observed this scene, and walked over to ask what it had been all about. I manufactured an excuse. "Oh, we got to talking about John Candy," I said. John had died in 1994. "Wow," she said, understandably confused. "It's been thirteen years. You're both still that affected?"

"Well, you know," I said, "we take it day by day."

I didn't know what else to say, but I knew that I had to get back home to Nan as soon as possible. I sent baby Henry on to London alone to see his brother. As I was waiting to board a plane back to L.A., Bernie called. "Well," he said, "The bad news is, it's in. The good news is, it's a nice picture."

Fuck. I put on a cap and sunglasses like a spy and walked into a magazine shop at JFK to pick up a copy of the *Enquirer* and peek inside. They didn't have the full details, but what they did have was accurate.

I didn't tell Nancy until I was home in person. I'm glad I waited, because she was really upset—first, a major health ordeal, and now this violation.

The good news was that the story kind of went away, an evanescent tabloid nuisance that made an impact upon the Short household but not upon the *Enquirer* readership. More important, if any friends of ours read or heard of the report, all of them had the decency to pretend that they hadn't.

Well, actually, the really good news was that Nancy was enjoying a good quality of life even though she was ill with ovarian cancer. Despite the hopeful PET scan in San Diego, the cancer had indeed spread. She underwent two more surgical procedures that spring, performed at Cedars-Sinai by Dr. Ronald Leuchter, one of the best gynecologic oncologists in the business. By coincidence, he too grew up in Hamilton, Ontario, and had known my brothers as a boy. In a further coincidence, he had been Gilda's surgeon when *she* had ovarian cancer. I chose not to share that particular tidbit with Nan.

Nancy rallied remarkably well from the debilitated state in which she found herself after the surgeries. Then we entered the realm of chemotherapy, hair loss, and regular trips to the doctor to get the latest blood numbers. We learned all about CA-125, the protein used as a biomarker for ovarian cancer detection; an elevated CA-125 level means trouble.

Nancy had all manner of wigs made—short, medium, some of them to be worn with a bandana, so it looked like she was going through different cycles of getting her hair cut and having it grow out. She was careful about which friends she told about her illness; as Nora Ephron, a true student of the gossip's nature, told her, "You tell one, you tell twenty."

Nancy's reticence wasn't about stigma; she wasn't ashamed of having cancer. It was mostly a matter of her fundamentally private nature and her wish not to be drawn into heart-to-heart conversations on the subject, for which she had no tolerance. She knew that all manner of acquaintances, no doubt well-intentioned, would queue up to "look after" her, and she wanted no part of it. "Deb," she told Deb Divine, Eugene Levy's wife and one of her oldest friends (and one of the few whose help she accepted), "you've got to keep the candy-stripe brigade away."

In staggered stages, Nancy let friends know she was sick. That summer we went as usual to our cottage on Lake Rosseau, for there was no place that she loved better. She powered through her usual routine of kayaking, hiking, bicycling, and tennis. She even decided to take up golf, studying it and practicing her swing obsessively, so that the months of chemo wouldn't be chalked up as wasted time—a true "Nine Categories Girl" after my own heart.

At one point during that summer we had Marc Shaiman and Scott Wittman come up to stay with us for a few days. Nancy, not wanting to worry about keeping a wig on at all times, decided before their arrival that she would let them in on her condition. Now Marc and Scott, as much as we adore them, had put us through a certain degree of strain and agita during *Fame Becomes Me*. They'd been a couple for thirty years, but in the course of mounting the show, they broke up—and then got back together as soon as the show was finished.

So when Marc and Scott arrived at our place, and Nancy, a serious look on her face, told them, "We have to talk," Marc was braced for a stern lecture. Marc's joke is that he was so relieved that Nancy wasn't angry with him and Scott that he said, "*Cancer?* Oh, thank god! I was afraid you were mad at me!"

N an finished her round of six chemotherapies that September at Princess Margaret Hospital in Toronto, to which we'd commuted from the cottage all summer for the treatments. Now it was simply time to wait, and pray for the strength to stay positive. In November, by which time we'd returned to Los Angeles, we went in for a CT/PET scan, and, miracle of miracles, everything was perfect. The scan showed nothing bad, and her CA-125 was down to 15, a healthily low count. Our family had the happiest Christmas 2007 imaginable.

But three months later Nan went in for another CA-125 test, and her number had jumped to 48, which naturally threw our entire family into panic. Why had the number spiked like this? Was it just a fluke, or was it possibly a sign of what her Los Angeles oncologist ominously suggested was "early resistance" to the chemo? *Early Resistance*, I kept thinking. What a great name for a movie, and what a horrible thing to have to hear your wife's doctor say.

Yet Nan remained strong, even as I struggled to. She sent me an e-mail during this period:

> Hi darling . . . I'm going to my golf tournament
> today and forgetting about all this. There is
> nothing we can do anyway. As long as I feel
> this good I'm going to have fun and enjoy life.
> If, God forbid, I have to start chemo again
> in the future, I won't feel like doing all my
> sports and I won't have my energy. In my heart
> I don't believe anything is there, but we have
> to be realistic. The PET scan will tell in April.
> Keep in mind . . . Sarah Ferguson [her Toronto
> oncologist] wasn't alarmed. I feel like she is the
> only person I want to talk to about all this.
>
> Let's try to forget about all this until we have
> to.
>
> I love you baby.
>
> Have faith in me and my amazing ability to
> persevere!
>
> xx Nan

I was dumbfounded by my wife's gift for compartmentalization. We were now told to sit tight and wait for another six weeks, at which point they would retest her to see where her CA-125 number was. Had it been me with her condition, having to just wait things out, I would have been paralyzed with anxiety and fear. But not Nan. When David Geffen invited us to join him in early 2008 for a trip to Bora-Bora in the South Pacific, on his boat, *Rising Sun*, my first thought was, it's too risky for Nancy to travel all that way. Nancy's was, who on earth would turn down a private yacht trip to Bora-Bora? So we went, as did Steve and Anne, and had a magnificent time. Nancy laughed and played cards and swam without an apparent care in the world.

When we returned to Los Angeles and she was retested in April, though, the news wasn't good: her CA-125 number was now 94. The cancer wars were once again the headline on our front page, and a new game plan had to be formulated. We were told definitively that Nancy would never be cured of cancer but that the doctors would attempt to keep it at bay through a series of maintenance chemo infusions to be administered every six weeks.

By early 2009, almost two years after her initial ovarian cancer diagnosis, we found ourselves, amazingly, in a pretty good place. Nancy's CA-125 number was hovering around a very pleasing-sounding 15; the drugs were doing their job. We went to Steve and Anne's home in St. Barth's, in the Caribbean, right after New Year's, and Nancy was as active as ever. The Martins' house was a happy place for Nan and me. Usually when we went down, there was a group: not just Steve and Anne, but also Walter Parkes and Laurie MacDonald, or the artists Eric Fischl and April Gornik (yet another married couple). The days unfolded at a leisurely pace. We'd get up to find April already doing her yoga, Eric working on a watercolor, and Steve checking his e-mail with earbuds in his ears (bluegrass, probably). Sometimes Steve and I would play cribbage over our coffee. Or maybe we'd all take a little hike to the beach and back, returning in time for midmorning massages from the masseuse that Steve had brought in. Then there was a big lunch. By three p.m., when the sun wasn't so strong, we'd go down to Saline Beach for some swimming and bodysurfing. It was a great respite from the grind of real life: a way for the 1 percent to finally have a chance to pamper itself.

Eric created a beautiful painting during that 2009 trip of us all in our bathing suits on the beach: April, Anne, Steve, me, and a couple of others, with Nan perched on a towel in the foreground. We had settled into what seemed like a pleasant remission routine, if that's not an oxymoron: every six weeks Nancy got an infusion of her maintenance drug, Doxil, got her blood checked, and life went on. This was workable.

I was reminded a lot of how my mother handled her illness, defying the grimmest of prognoses and forging onward, stubbornly unwilling to accept death at the very first moment it came knocking. Nancy was aware of the parallels, too; I had become adept early at keeping loved ones alive by telling their stories. I had regaled her and the kids with so many tales of Olive and C. P. Short, and they had all heard the audiotapes from my childhood so often, that they felt intimately acquainted with my parents, despite never having met them. Even now my middle child, Ollie, will sometimes call me out on my more cutting remarks by saying, "Oh, how typical Chuck is that?" And then break into a perfect Chuck impersonation himself.

Nancy, though she was the antithesis of a spiritual person, found it useful to talk to my mother—to sit on the porch or the balcony off our bedroom and internally converse with Olive. It brought her serenity. But one day in April 2009, I found Nancy crying on the porch. I asked her what was wrong, and she said, "I've been talking to your mother and asking her for strength, because I'm scared right now."

Nothing was physically amiss. Nan said she felt fine, with

no new symptoms, and she looked great. But she had a sense of unease. Her body *knew* something and was tipping her off: she was coming out of remission.

When we went every six weeks to get Nancy's blood work done, I was always the one who received the CA-125 number. That was the system we had worked out: she was the patient, and I was the information coordinator. Right after Nancy's outburst—which I call an outburst because Nancy rarely betrayed emotion about her sickness—I received the results of her latest test. The number was 20: a significant uptick from the 14.8 six weeks earlier, but still not necessarily terrible news. The doctors said it needed monitoring, but it could be just a fluctuation.

At that point, for the first time on our cancer journey, I made the decision that I was not going to share the CA-125 number with Nancy. So I told her that things were holding steady—a white lie not unlike the one my mother had used to keep me from falling apart as a little boy. I was influenced by that period a year earlier when Nancy's CA-125 number had shot up to 48. Though I was impressed then by her activeness and sangfroid, she confided to me now that she had hated the six weeks of dreadful anticipation that followed the high reading. "I wish I could have those six weeks back," she told me, "because if I can't do anything but wait, why tell me? Why burden me?"

Over the spring and summer of 2009, Nancy's CA-125 number kept going up, though not precipitously; more like 22, 24, 28. But I never told her. When she asked, I would say, "Everything's perfect, Nan. Everything's fine." But we were now also consulting with a specialist in New York, and we had an October appointment to see him. I knew, since we would be sitting down with him to discuss possible courses of action, we would have to be out in the open about the way Nan's numbers were trending.

Nora Ephron and Nick Pileggi generously lent us their guest apartment on the Upper East Side, which Nick used as his writing studio. My plan was to tell Nancy the truth about her numbers the night before the appointment. Then I remembered that Nora and Nick had invited us to a dinner party at their place that night, and I didn't want to ruin the party for Nancy. So the next day, the morning of the appointment, as we were getting ready to go to the doctor, I asked Nancy to sit down. She did.

"Nan," I said, "I've been lying to you about the numbers."

For a moment, she was stricken and let out a bruised "Awww."

Then I explained it all: the incremental upticks, my decision to shield her from them, the fact that now we'd have to talk about all this with the doctor.

She took my hands in hers and said, "Thank you, baby." The choice I'd made, she told me, was the right one.

The New York doctor's news, alas, was not good: her CA-125 number was now at 52, and radiation was the next step. A whole new phase of debilitation. Nonetheless, Nancy wasn't going to let something like metastasizing cancer and radiation treatments get in the way of living her life. We had plans to spend our Christmas vacation skiing with the kids at our home in Sun Valley, Idaho, followed by a few days in January at the Martin residence in St. Barth's. And off we went.

I had signed on that year to be a regular in the third season of Glenn Close's FX series *Damages*, playing Leonard Winstone, the sad-sack lawyer for a Bernie Madoff–esque Ponzi schemer. *Damages*'s creators, Daniel Zelman and the brothers Todd and Glenn Kessler, liked using comic actors in serious roles, trusting them to be looser and more inventive with dialogue, and they had already enlisted Lily Tomlin and Ted Danson to great effect.

The filming took place over the winter of 2009–'10, and honestly, to this day, I don't know how the hell I pulled it off, given what my family was going through. I'm no Method actor, but in that case, my state of mind informed my performance. There was a day in December 2009 when I received devastating news from Nancy's doctors, that her CA-125 number had skyrocketed to 160. She and the kids were already in Sun Valley. I was no longer going to withhold information from her, but I decided that I would wait to tell her the bad news in person rather than over the phone. That night we shot a scene where Leonard goes to a nursing home to visit his frail old mother, only to be informed that she has died. I can see it on my face in that scene: the conflation of a character who's just received news of his mother's death with an actor who's just received news that his wife's cancer is aggressively taking over her body. I'm quite good in that episode, but I wouldn't recommend my process.

Terminal illness is so deceptive. There are wonderful days when the sick person rallies and it seems like there is genuine reason for hope, and rough days when the illusions come crashing down. I have a photo of a group of us gathered that winter in Sun Valley: Nan and me, Tom and Rita, Bruce and Patti Springsteen, and Jann Wenner and his partner, Matt Nye. Nancy is the only one in a white ski jacket, so she stands out, and she appears radiant, the picture of health. But I also remember a night in St. Barth's, the last time we went there together, where we went to bed early, around nine, because Nan felt utterly drained of life force. We lay there side by side, wordlessly holding hands, both of us looking up at the ceiling, both of us knowing that we were at the beginning of something very bad.

By February Nancy was sicker than ever, and she wasn't expected to make it through March. I abruptly pulled out of two big things I was supposed to do over a ten-day period, one of them being the opening number at the 2010 Academy Awards. Steve Martin and Alec Baldwin were cohosting that year (they'd just done Nancy Meyers's *It's Complicated*), and I was meant to duet with Neil Patrick Harris on the curtain-raising song—a number that, ironically, was about teaming up and not doing things alone. Neil valiantly carried on solo. The second big thing was the closing ceremonies of the Vancouver Olympics, in which I'd have appeared alongside such Canadian luminaries as Catherine O'Hara and Michael J. Fox.

Whether or not the closing ceremonies were a fitting tribute to my homeland is arguable, but Nancy's opinion was clear. Watching the gaudy spectacle at our home in the Palisades, she turned to me and said, "It's the only upside of my cancer."

"What is?" I said.

"You didn't have to be in that."

The oncologists at Cedars-Sinai told me that there was no longer any point in putting Nancy through further chemo unless she wanted to give it a try. I put the proposition to Nancy. She said without hesitation, "Let's go. Let's do it."

I've learned that there are two worlds in the land of terminal illness. The first is the one where you hold out hope of a shot at getting better: *I've got to get the furs to the cleaners for summer storage, because I'll need them to be ready for next winter!* The second is the world where you graciously accept death as an inevitability: *Bring me paper and a pen so that I may write letters to be read posthumously at our daughter's wedding.* You can't really live in both worlds; they're mutually exclusive.

Nancy was emphatically of that first world, not that there's anything wrong with the second. And somehow the next round of chemo, though it didn't bring her all the way back, put her upright and out among the living again. She resumed driving herself to tennis, and in July I found myself flying with Nan back to our summer cottage in Canada—a scenario that, in the privacy of my own mind, I had never in a million years envisioned coming true.

As late as the end of July, Nancy was still lowering herself into a kayak to go for a paddle in the lake, her never-say-die Kate Hepburn instincts overpowering cancer and common sense. But by August she was losing steam. We left Snug Harbour on the sixth day of the month. Kurt Russell and Goldie Hawn were among the few who knew how seriously ill Nancy was, but they'd kept the news from Kate Hudson, their daughter, until a few days before our departure. Kate, Goldie reported to me over the phone, was inconsolable: she adored Nancy. And she and Rita Wilson insisted upon sending a private plane to deliver us back to L.A.

We returned to our house in the Palisades, and Dr. Kipper, our internist, visited a day or two later, just to check in. After I walked him to his car, I returned to Nancy, who sat propped up in our bed. "You know, Mart," she said, "I don't want you to think this is the beginning of the end."

"I don't!" I said.

"Well, you sure *look* like you do."

Even at that point, Nancy still believed she might rally—and not entirely without reason, for she had before. She wasn't mournful or mopey. She was pissed off at the situation. Those were oft-spoken Nancy words: "Marty, tell me this wouldn't *piss you off*!" She refused to treat her final days like a weepy, valedictory send-off.

But no further rally was in the offing. Nancy only weakened further, slipping gently into unconsciousness within a matter of days. She finally passed away on August 21, 2010. Before she lost consciousness, as, struggling for breath, she saw nine paramedics hurry into our bedroom after I'd placed a frantic 911 call, she calmly turned to me, took my hand, and said, "Marty, let me go."

And so we did. With me and all three kids in our bed, holding her hand, we let her go.

Nancy's death was awful, by far the most awful thing I've ever been through. Yet life had given me valuable experience to draw upon—not just for my own benefit, but for my kids'. And so I put it to use. The night before Nan died, when we knew it was just a matter of time, I took a moment with Henry, our youngest, to soak in our backyard Jacuzzi. He needed loving and calming. Katherine and Oliver were in the house, keeping vigil.

"Henry, I know it seems unimaginable, but you are being empowered tonight," I told him. "You are being given something that is horrible, but is also a life lesson. This will make you stronger. This will make you more determined. You'll be in your office somewhere, someday, and some pompous asshole will say something to you. And you'll supposedly be upset, and you'll supposedly be fearful of your boss's reaction. But then you'll think, 'This is gravy. This is fine. I couldn't care less about this prick. I'm not upset *now*. I was upset the night my mother died.' "

KATHIE LEE
WASN'T WRONG

Nora Ephron took over. Just hours after we lost Nan, she and Nick were at our door, bearing platters of food. So were Eugene and Deb Levy: four kind, familiar faces, a tremendous comfort to me and my kids. The first thing Nora said when she presented herself was, "We loved Nancy, and we love you." She really turned it on that night, regaling us all with tales of interning in the JFK White House, and how knock-kneed she'd been by the sexy president: "I'm telling you, even the amount of *shirt cuff* he showed wearing a suit jacket was sexy!" Nora and company took our minds out of the moment in the most considerate, compassionate way.

The next day, the condolence calls started coming in, and the Palisades moms were telling me that I needed to open the house and let people express their grief. I'd been put off by the whole concept of the wake-style open house ever since my brother David's death, when, to my dismay, I saw people laughing and drinking in our living room in my family's deepest moment of sorrow.

But Nora advised me to let it happen. She planned all the food for that day and made sure our house was ready for the onslaught.

The day after our Short-family shivah, Nora came by with a huge platter of chicken at dinnertime, even though there was a ton of leftover food in the house. "Nora," I said, "it's just us tonight. We already have so much food."

Nora replied, "And now you have more food. This is the way Jews do it. I don't like everything about being Jewish, but I like how we do this."

For a day after the visitor stampede, there was a pleasant lull—a merciful period of quiet. Then, on day three after Nancy's death, I took a call from Paul Shaffer. He said, "Dave wants to reach out to you. That okay?"

I said, "Of course. Why, did you just tell him?"

"Marty," Paul said, "it's on the Internet."

And almost on cue, as he said the words "on the Internet," my buzzer started going, my phone started ringing nonstop, and there were flower deliveries and paparazzi massed at my gate. And all I could think was, Jesus, I've gotta get out of here.

Fortunately, the kids and I had scheduled a trip the next morning to our Canadian refuge in Snug Harbour. We'd already had Nancy's body cremated so that we could spread the ashes up there. We flew from L.A. to Toronto, and then, from Toronto, took a seaplane that touched down right by our dock.

What the kids and I witnessed as the plane floated into the harbor brought tears: all of my siblings, their spouses, and my beloved nephews and nieces lined up on the dock. And flowers everywhere. Kurt Russell, I later found out, had gone to the florist in the next town and bought out the whole store. Then he went to an antiques store and bought flowerpots. Goldie offered to help, but he told her, "It's okay, honey, I gotta do this myself."

He planted all the flowers in the pots and lined the dock and the pathways leading up to the main house with them.

Paul Shaffer came up, as did Eugene and Deb, and Walter and Laurie, and we turned it into a celebration. Nancy was adamant that there not be any kind of formal memorial or big fuss, so we honored that. We sprinkled some of her ashes by the tree near her beloved tennis court, and the rest in the lake. The plan was for the kids and me to jump *into* the ashes as they dissipated into the water. Oliver was the last to jump, and as he did so, he shouted out, "MOTHER!"

It was cathartic. There was laughter instead of crying, and that night, we had a bonfire and a big dinner for the twenty-five or so people gathered. Songs were sung a capella outside, and then we went inside, where Paul played the piano and we kept on singing. The evening was not unlike our Christmas parties—and just how I imagine Nan would have wanted the night to go.

When everyone had gone off to bed, I sneaked back outside to the still-burning fire in the fire pit, overlooking the lake. I stared into the fire, as if looking into Nan's eyes, and said out loud, with no one else around, "Nan . . . losing you is losing half my soul. I'm not sure if I'll ever get over this, but I know that I'll love you forever. And I promise you, I'll keep our children safe. Love you, baby."

I couldn't sleep, so I sat there till dawn. And why not? It was a wondrous night, clear and unseasonably warm, stars everywhere in the sky. When she was alive, with me, there was no place Nan loved to sit more.

t was now late August. Katherine and Ollie had to go back to their jobs in L.A., and Henry back to Notre Dame for his junior year. Before Ollie departed, he gave me a hug and whispered in my ear, "Dad, next year, I want this place *filled*." His meaning was obvious: filled with the energy and laughter and the joy of living that Snug Harbour had always represented to our family.

I think everyone was a little apprehensive of leaving ol' widower Marty alone in his big house in the woods, but it felt completely right to me. I was very clear to everyone: if being here all alone gave me the heebie-jeebies, I'd bail and return to L.A. in a heartbeat.

But I'll tell you, I felt at peace up on the lake. I spent a further three weeks in Canada, and I enjoyed the solitude. I kept a journal to scribble down my jangled thoughts. At one point Mel Brooks phoned me. He had lost his wife, Anne Bancroft, five years earlier, and he gave me what he felt was the most important advice he could impart: "Don't go out with any fucking couples. They'll just piss you off." Mike Nichols also called, urging me to "just keep the conversation going." This was valuable wisdom, because the constant banter I maintained with Nancy was like oxygen to me, and to suddenly no longer have it in my life seemed incomprehensible—and, in bad moments, suffocating. In a funny way, I was kind of rooting for something weird to happen, for a sign from my wife. I'd had only that one quasi-paranormal experience as a boy: the profound sadness I felt at summer camp the morning I learned of my brother David's death.

So there I was, sitting in my kitchen in Snug Harbour, staring at a coffee cup for ten minutes: *Move, for Christ's sake! Nan . . . where the hell did you go?*

And indeed something odd did happen while I was alone. I'm not saying that it means anything, but it was a little strange. The first night I got to the lake, as night fell, I got up from my armchair to turn on the lights. I went to switch the stairway light on: *pop*, it flickered out. Next, the upstairs hallway light: *pop*, it flickered out. Next, our bedroom light: *pop*, it flickered out. Then the boys' room: *pop*, it flickered out.

I told Goldie and Kurt about this the following day. Goldie totally believed it *was* some kind of sign, saying, "Babe! Oh, babe! This is classic. Read any book on the paranormal. It's the first thing that happens."

Kurt, on the other hand, responded in his typical man's man way. "Y'know what I'd do?" he said. "I'd phone Gord. I think you got a short."

Gord Gallagher, our caretaker, came over. He checked things out and said, "I'll replace the bulbs, but Marty—there's no short."

A damant as Nancy was that there not be a memorial, Rita Wilson called me when I returned to L.A. that September and said, "Marty, Nan's birthday is coming up on the twenty-sixth and I have to do something. All of her girlfriends are walking around and have no closure. Some of them didn't even know how sick she was." Rita was, needless to say, totally right. So the Hankses hosted a warm, beautiful, low-key daytime thing at their home, mostly women. Rita put no pressure on me to come, but I did—for part of it, anyway, as did two of my children, Katherine and Oliver. A smattering of guys, too: Tom, Kurt Russell, Victor Garber and his partner, Rainer Andreesen. And of course Marc Shaiman, who was there to play piano for old time's sake.

Some people got up and read tributes. Others sang. Victor was too overcome with emotion to do so, but Bette Midler got up and did "The Rose," which was as powerful and moving as you can imagine.

The assumption at the gathering, understandably, was that I

wouldn't sing. But when Tom, who was acting as an emcee of sorts, suggested as much, I put my hand up and said, "Well, if I'm not going to sing, then *why do I have these lyrics in my pocket?*" And out of my pocket I pulled a sheet containing the lyrics to "Nancy (with the Laughing Face)," a song made famous by my idol, Frank Sinatra. With Marc at the keyboard as ever, I launched into the song, whose words so aptly and uncannily described my wife.

> *She takes the winter and makes it summer*
> *Summer could take some lessons from her*
> *Picture a tomboy in lace*
> *That's Nancy with the laughing face*

I've kept a collection of the tributes to Nancy that were read on that day, and that flowed into my computer's in-box in the weeks and months that followed Nancy's death. Katherine, my daughter, wrote a letter to her mother that she read at the memorial at the lake, and it still melts me. I won't quote from it at length, but she alluded to our sprinkling of her mom's ashes in the lake, and wrote, "Whenever I swim in the lake, I'll be swimming all around your spirit. I will feel the waters rush over me and I'll feel you."

Laurie MacDonald was particularly cogent about how Nancy handled her illness. "I don't think she was completely in denial, particularly in those last heartbreaking months," Laurie wrote. "My sense was that she had reached a state of grace, or, to be careful not to slip into spiritual cliché, a state of Nan: treasuring every moment with her family, but with a clear and fearless eye toward the mountain in the distance that she would have to cross alone."

Catherine O'Hara wrote to Nancy, "You'd refuse to suffer fools. Little fools, big fools: 'You know what? Bye!' You'd rather turn away from a boring dinner companion than misuse one precious moment. You wouldn't stand for bullshit. You'd be awestruck at ignorance. You'd take the time to help those truly in need and fearlessly foil the self-indulgent, the self-conscious, and the self-pitying."

Rita Wilson wrote, "Nancy taught me how to notice if a snake had crossed a trail by pointing out the *S*-shaped rut left in the dry dust. . . . In the mountains, where Nancy cross-country-skied, snowshoed, and hiked, it was hard to keep up with her. If you were Nancy's friend, you were 'walking the walk.' Literally."

My brother Michael wrote, "If there's a heaven, Nancy is up there getting things ready for us. I imagine there's some redecorating going on. She'll tell God he has nice shoulders, and he'll make the changes. And sure enough, by the time the rest of us get there, it'll be perfect."

Eugene Levy wrote to me, "I miss being able to say 'Marty and Nancy.' I miss the sound of her name rolling off of Ed Grimley's lips whenever you had an apology to make for some petty domestic offense. I miss seeing her at the kitchen island juggling five side dishes to a meal she dismissed as 'Oh, this is nothing.' I miss her coming to my defense at your dining-room table every time you attacked the size of my portions."

One of the most touching tributes came from Steve Martin, who composed a song in memory of Nancy for his 2011 banjo album with the Steep Canyon Rangers, *Rare Bird Alert*. The song, an instrumental, is called "The Great Remember." In his liner notes to the album, Steve writes, "I almost wrote lyrics for this tune, but realized that lyrics were somehow, mysteriously, implied. It is dedicated to the memory of Nancy Short, whose vitality and love of laughter made elegies easy but grief doubly hard."

Steve, as polished and poised a stage presence as he is, had a hard time performing "The Great Remember" at first. When that album first came out, he was doing a promotional interview with Diane Sawyer on ABC. Diane (who also happens to be married to Mike Nichols) was a friend of Nancy's and knew what the song was about, so she prompted Steve to play it solo on his banjo. Steve spluttered as he started to introduce the song and was nearly overcome by tears. "I'm just gonna play it," he said, and he did so, very beautifully. The lead melody of the song is a gently rising figure that is intuitively elegiac, yet not remotely funereal. It sounds like a song that would play under the closing credits of a particularly fulfilling family movie that you're sorry to see come to an end.

I aggressively threw myself into work in the first few months of life without Nancy. My basic attitude was that if I was in a dressing room in Boston or Grand Rapids, straightening my tie before a show, it would feel kind of normal, as if I was just on the road as usual. Whereas at home in the Palisades, sleeping alone in that big bed . . . well, that would take some getting used to.

We were, as a couple, like a big 747 jet plane, powered by two engines. But now one engine is out. Nevertheless, the plane is still filled with passengers, and there's a lot of responsibility, a lot of lives still to influence. So the plane must continue to fly with one engine. It travels onward, but with a bit more effort and struggle, and with no time to flirt with the stewardess or get a coffee.

Steve Martin was one of the people who best understood my need to keep moving forward. For all our years of friendship, he and I had never performed together onstage, live. Yet in June of 2011 we were given an opportunity to do just that, headlining the TBS Just for Laughs comedy festival in Chicago. We billed our show as "Steve Martin and Martin Short in a Very Stupid Conversation." We're more polished now, but that first time out, we just sort of winged it. . . .

> **STEVE:** Marty, let me say that it's been a longtime dream of mine to perform here at the Just for Laughs comedy festival in Chicago. And tonight, I feel I am one step closer to that dream.
> **MARTY:** Steve, you'd tell me if you'd had a stroke, wouldn't you?
> **STEVE:** Not necessarily.
> **MARTY:** But Steve, you're right. It *is* a thrill to be here. And can you believe that we're playing to a sold-out house?
> **STEVE:** Well, Marty, I actually believe that it's *we* who have sold out.

Steve did some banjo tunes, I did some characters, and then the two of us interviewed each other about our respective careers.

> **STEVE:** What's the worst job you've ever had?
> **MARTY:** I once did a pilot in 1980.
> **STEVE:** I didn't ask you the worst *sex* you'd ever had.

I vacated the stage while Steve played banjo, and Steve pretended to nap in a cot onstage while I sang my ode to Osama bin Laden, "Bastard in the Sand," set to the tune of Elton John's "Candle in the Wind." I also did an interview with Steve as Jiminy Glick, telling him, "Your skin is so youthful. I'm not saying it's firm. But it's very youthful." To the crowd, Jiminy said, "There are very few people as pale as Steve who actually have a heartbeat. He looks like a coloring book that hasn't been colored in yet. He once got a sunburn from his Kindle reader. "

Steve and I so enjoyed the experience that we've continued to do this double act for a handful of dates every year, but with increasing amounts of preparation and set-list determination, because Steve, for some reason, cares about professionalism.

A big adjustment to life without Nan was learning how to go about having fun, enjoying oneself. How would it work? "Ticket for one, please." "A table? No, I'll just sit at the bar, thanks." Steve was always encouraging me to come back to his place in St. Barth's. I was understandably apprehensive, because it was a place I'd only ever been with Nan. But, like all fears in my new, widower's existence, this one had to be conquered. So I agreed to come join Steve and Anne for a January vacation.

In my mind, St. Barth's was a couples' paradise—and, therefore, a daunting place for me to go, for the first time, as a single man. But as it turned out, whatever trepidation I was feeling as I flew down was wholly preempted by Steve's anxiety about the paparazzi who were lurking everywhere. Princess Diana visited St. Barth's once, and the tabloid photographers never left. Now, obviously, in certain circumstances, when you're a celebrity, having your picture taken is part of the agreement. However, it's another thing entirely to walk out of the surf with seawater flowing out of your nostrils, your hair plastered flat onto your forehead, and your stomach protruding like you've just eaten Kim Jong-un, to discover a telephoto lens pointed right at you, cradled by some goofball who's been hiding in the bushes most of the day. Later on the pictures show up in some supermarket paper, and people looking at them say to themselves,

"Gee, I had no idea he was with child!" At no point in my life has my nickname ever been Ol' Washboard Abs. Even during athletic competitions in my youthful prime, when someone would call out, "Shirts and Skins," I would pray that the Shirts team would pick me. And to be sure, those celebrity weeklies are rarely looking for the money shot of someone's *good* side.

My coming to St. Barth's on this trip particularly concerned Steve, because, he explained, he had been down for a week before I'd arrived and found the island to be more paparazzi-infested than ever. So the thought of *two* well-known actors galumphing together in the water would attract still more attention than one galumphing by himself. But Steve, wily fellow that he is, had an idea.

Steve happens to have an enormous Twitter following, in the many millions. So, upon my arrival, he presented his scheme. First, the two of us would pose for some ridiculous pictures on a private beach, with Eric Fischl taking the photos. Then Steve would tweet out one of these pictures, thereby diminishing the value to the tabloids of an "exclusive" photograph of Steve Martin and Martin Short together on holiday. After that, Steve hoped, we would be left alone.

We went all in on the props. At a beach store, we got a plastic pail and shovel, along with a big green inflatable alligator. Then the three of us headed down to a private beach. Steve and I both wore black swim shirts. I styled myself as a sort of beach-blanket Ed Grimley, with my hair mussed up and my trunks hitched high. Eric snapped a few different pictures of Steve and me goofing around: some with me wearing the pail on my head and licking the back of the shovel, others with me clutching the pail in one hand and the alligator in the other. It was one of the photos from the latter setup, with Steve gently placing a guiding arm around me, that he tweeted out to his followers. His caption: "Never too busy to help others, I take time from my vacation to spend quality hours with St. Barth's village idiot."

Steve was pleased with how his plan was working out; indeed, the photo created a ripple in the Twitterverse, and whether by accident or design, we all felt a little less harassed in the days that followed. As we were leaving the beach the day of the shoot, though, I happened to notice what appeared to be a homeless man, fast asleep on the sand. *Hmm, that's strange. Could he be one of . . . nah, can't be.* And I didn't give the guy another thought.

Until, that is, a month or so later, when I was back in the States, en route by car service from Chicago's O'Hare Airport to South Bend, Indiana, to visit my youngest son, Henry, at Notre Dame. A bunch of magazines were tucked into the driver's seat back. I pulled out the *Star* and began flicking through it. And then I saw it: a page with the headline "Stars: Are They NORMAL or NOT?" Beneath it a photo showed just me—Steve cropped out entirely—with the pail on my head, licking the shovel like a deranged moron. The "napping" fellow I'd seen that day was indeed a paparazzo; he'd taken a bunch of shots of us from a different angle, with us none the wiser.

I slouched back in the car seat. This, I thought, will make my children so very proud.

In any event, I kept myself very busy and very scheduled in the aftermath of losing Nancy. I did a few episodes of the 2011–'12 season of *How I Met Your Mother* as Garrison Cootes, the righteous vegan boss of Jason Segel's character, Marshall Eriksen. For the CBC, I did a new hour-long television special entitled *I, Martin Short, Goes Home.*

To promote a DreamWorks animated movie for which I'd

voiced a character, *Madagascar 3: Europe's Most Wanted*, I went to Cannes one week in May 2012, promptly flew back to New York to do a little stint cohosting *Live with Kelly* with Kelly Ripa (in that historic interregnum between the Era of Philbin and the Era of Strahan), and, the very same day, made an appearance on the fourth hour of the *Today* show.

I was in an upbeat mood that week because the weekend before, my youngest, Henry, had graduated from Notre Dame. It had not been an easy road for Henry after his mom died, but he figured it out, worked hard, and got the job done. Lots of people came up to me at the graduation ceremony and said, "What a wonderful job you did raising Henry"—and while I appreciated the sentiment, I found myself replying, "Well, let's just be clear here. While I was filming a picture in Acapulco, Nancy was up at 5:20 a.m. taking him to hockey practice."

The day I did double duty on *Live with Kelly* and *Today*, I dashed straight from ABC, where the former was filmed, to NBC, where the fourth-hour hosts, Kathie Lee Gifford and Hoda Kotb, awaited me.

I know Kathie Lee a little, dating back to when she hosted the morning *Live* show with Regis Philbin, and I was a guest, and she'd also bravely subjected herself to the Jiminy treatment the first season I did *Primetime Glick*. So I bounded into *Today*'s studio on Rockefeller Plaza, wearing the same outfit and makeup I'd worn on *Live with Kelly*, got my mic clipped on, and commenced the *Madagascar 3* plugfest.

In the course of our chitchat, we started talking about Henry's recent college graduation and how wonderful an occasion it had been for my family. Thus prompted, Kathie Lee said, "You and Nancy have got one of the greatest marriages in show business. How many years now for you guys?"

That sounded odd: How many years *now*? I fumbled for a reply: "We, uh . . . married thirty-six years."

"But you're still, like, *in love*," Kathie Lee said. Okay, now I realized that she was actually unaware of Nancy's death. If we had been taping, I would have simply stopped the interview and told her that Nancy had died two years back. But we were live, and in the moment, I decided that it would embarrass Kathie Lee if I corrected her on the air. Let it pass, I thought. We'll move on.

"Madly in love, madly in love," I responded to her, truthfully. And that, I assumed, was the end of it. Only it wasn't.

"Why?" Kathie Lee asked.

I tried to wrap it up in a bow. "Cute! I'm cute."

"And you make each other laugh, right?"

Oh, dear, this is becoming a thing, I thought. Was it possible she thought we were taping a rerun?

We went to commercial right after that, and I gently told Kathie Lee that Nancy had died in August 2010. She was mortified, but I bore not an ounce of malice toward her. She does a zillion interviews a week, and she got confused.

In the course of rushing from one morning program to another, I'd neglected to shut off my cell phone, as real professionals do when appearing on live television. The phone started vibrating as soon as I exited through the door of the *Today* studio. It was Paul Shaffer. "Did I just hit my head?" he said, stifling his Paul laugh. "What was . . . I can't . . . What I just saw . . . It really couldn't have happened, could it?"

As soon as I hung up with Paul, the phone buzzed again. Steve Martin. He was cracking up with laughter. "Okay," he said, "I'm reading a transcript of this thing. I haven't seen it, but there's already a transcript online."

A transcript online? That was the first time I came to understand how social media can make things go crazily out of control. Suddenly, Kathie Lee's allegedly "cringeworthy" gaffe was all over Twitter, Facebook, and the blogosphere. The next day I had to do a junket for *Madagascar 3*, sitting for one five-minute interview after another, and every single interviewer was asking me about Kathie Lee. I had to tell the DreamWorks people to make them stop, because no one was asking any questions about the movie.

Besides, Kathie Lee wasn't wrong. Nan and I *did* have one of the greatest marriages in show business. And I *do* think of my late wife in the present tense, as a way of keeping her memory alive. I just usually do this internally, in the comfort of my own home . . . not out loud, on live national television.

There was a missing voice in the blitz of phone calls I received in the immediate aftermath of the Kathie Lee episode: Nora Ephron's. No one got on the phone faster after such episodes than Nora, and her take was always the cleverest and most perfectly distilled of all. Nora had been such a boon to me and the kids since Nancy's death. That first Thanksgiving, I assigned each kid to handle a different part of the meal preparation so that the dinner would remain a family affair. Henry was in charge of dessert, and it was Nora, on the phone from New York, who offered him step-by-step guidance on baking the perfect apple pie. I could hear her through the receiver telling him, "First of all, don't do anything your father tells you, and go to Gelson's and buy the Pillsbury pie crust, because no human being can do one better!" She phoned Henry ninety minutes later to remind him to take the pie out.

Steve too was used to hearing from Nora on a regular basis, and by the end of May 2012, he was getting concerned that she had neither called nor responded to his e-mails. "Have you heard from Nora?" he finally asked me.

"I just had dinner with her and Nick about ten days ago," I replied.

"Oh, good," Steve said. "But can you do me a favor? Can you look in your datebook and verify that it was ten days ago?"

I looked, and I was wrong. It had been more like four weeks since I'd dined with the Ephron-Pileggis.

Our whole circle of friends was worried. But I remembered that in 2006, when I was in New York doing *Fame Becomes Me*, she'd briefly been on the drug prednisone for some reason or other. She never really opened up about it, and I instinctively respected that, so we didn't ask questions. I had wondered back then if she had lupus, but before I knew it, Nora had roared back to health as if nothing had ever been wrong, writing two more plays and directing *Julie & Julia*. At that point I reassured myself that Nora would be okay, just like last time.

What I didn't know, and virtually none of her friends did, was that Nora had been diagnosed with a rare blood disorder back in 2006, and had been prescribed the prednisone to stabilize her condition. It had worked remarkably well, as I would later learn when her son Jacob Bernstein wrote about the full extent of her medical ordeals in the *New York Times Magazine*. But right around Memorial Day weekend 2012—again, I only learned this after the fact—the blood disorder developed into aggressive leukemia.

When Nora didn't show up at the annual Shakespeare in the Park fund-raiser at the Delacorte Theater in Central Park, held that year on June 18, the alarm bells started ringing in everyone's heads. Nora relished that night, the de facto beginning of summer for cultured NYC types, and always bought a table or two. She still had the tables, but she and Nick weren't at them. A week later

Jacob called to deliver the devastating news that his mom was gravely ill and wasn't going to last much longer. And oh, by the way, he said, Nora had left specific instructions for her memorial service in a file carefully marked EXIT on her Mac desktop. I, per Nora's instructions, was to be the first speaker. "Don't hesitate to be funny," Jacob said.

I was stunned. *Be funny? When one of my rocks of sanity is crumbling?*

Then I took a breath and realized that this was not the first time I had been in such a situation. Four years earlier, in the summer of 2008, my beloved Buddha of a manager, Bernie Brillstein, had passed away at the age of seventy-seven, and Lorne Michaels and Bernie's former business partner, Brad Grey, had deputized me to be master of ceremonies at *his* memorial, at UCLA's historic Royce Hall. As saddened as I was then, I rallied and came up with material that resonated with the comedian-heavy crowd:

> *A man who enjoyed the success of others. . . . A man who didn't have an enemy in the world. . . . A man who never said an unkind word about anyone. . . . It would be so much easier tonight if we were memorializing a man like that.*
>
> *Bernie Brillstein was an integral part of Hollywood and show business. Many of us use expressions today that Bernie created—expressions like "Go fuck yourself," and "How about you go fuck yourself?"*
>
> *This is such an ironic evening for me, because Bernie always used to say, "Kid, I'm going to get you a gig at Royce Hall if it kills me."*

And on and on it went. So, okay, I could handle doing Nora's memorial. But first I had to break Jacob's news to my kids, who adored Nora and would never forget how she had been there for them, so it felt like a replay of their mother's death. Telling them was hard, and as I expected, they all cried. Three days after Jacob's call, Nora was gone.

Nancy and Nora: two brilliant, tough, funny women, so simpatico in life and so fascinatingly private in their approaches to death. As Deb Divine said after Nora died, "I think it's getting more interesting on the other side."

I remember Nora sitting with us in our house in August 2010, hearing me go on about how, per Nancy's wishes, we weren't going to have a proper funeral.

"No funeral," Nora said, her hand to her chin. "Interesting idea!" And of course I now realize she'd been taking notes, figuring out her own plans.

On July 9, 2012, I fulfilled my late friend's request to be the opening act at her memorial service, which was held in Alice Tully Hall at Lincoln Center. The other speakers included Tom and Rita, Mike Nichols, Meryl Streep, Rosie O'Donnell, and Nora's two boys, Max and Jacob. I won't give you the whole speech (especially since Nora's sister Delia good-naturedly claimed authorship of a brilliant line I attributed to Nora, "Hazelnuts are what's wrong with Europe"), but here's how I kicked it off:

> *Oh, Nora. Darling, lovely Nora.*
>
> *How is it possible for me to put into words what we have been feeling these last long weeks?*
>
> *When Nora's son Jacob asked me to speak today, he said, "Don't be hesitant to impersonate my mother."*
>
> *And I thought to myself: I can't impersonate your mother,*

because right now I'm having the best pink cake from Amy's I've ever had in MY LIFE. DO YOU KNOW WHAT I MEAN?

For whenever I heard Nora's voice, I always just delighted in that subtle, original, hilarious delivery of hers.

And I always thought, You know, I have that!

But then I thought, Oh, yeah . . . she had content.

I loved to talk to Nora, and I always found myself calling my friends afterward to tell them something Nora had said. I remember last March, Nick and Nora came to an evening for the Roundabout Theatre, honoring Rob Marshall. And Rob's sister Kathleen heard that they were attending, and quickly sent Nora an e-mail asking her if she would go onstage and read a letter from Mayor Bloomberg.

Nora's e-mailed response was, "Oh, Kathleen . . . How could I ever say no to you—and yet I have."

SEPTEMBER OF MY YEARS—BUT AN UNUSUALLY *TEMPERATE* SEPTEMBER

My life has been defined by round numbers. I was born in 1950, was orphaned at the age of twenty (in the year 1970), and was widowed at the age of sixty (in the year 2010).

The forty years bracketed by those last two events constitute the better part of my adulthood. They were an extraordinary four decades, throwing more experiences at me than that unusual boy in the Whitton Road attic could ever have imagined: success, failure, friendship, first love, true love, marriage, fatherhood, fame, fortune, misfortune, euphoria, grief.

When I look back on my life—and, by the way, if I do say so myself, I have a pretty remarkable memory; or, as I said to someone the other day, "I remember where I was in the third month of my twenty-seventh year, just like that *Taxi* actress renowned for her 'super-memory,' Marilu . . . um . . . uh . . . what's her name?"—I see moments where it might have been understandable had I turned to drugs or ice cream.

But I never succumbed. My natural tendency, no matter what difficult period I'm going through or have been through, is to be happy. No doubt this is a trait coded in my DNA, a likely inheritance from my mother. I must also give credit to my blessed, sweet, lunatic siblings. They too have the happy gene, so, being the youngest, I've also been the beneficiary of trickle-down happiness. My sister, Nora, and my brothers Michael and Brian maintained their positivity after David and my parents passed, and they've remained beacons of support and love every moment since. To this day, when the four of us are together, we love nothing more than to drink rum and Cokes, play card games (Oh Hell being our favorite), and laughingly taunt each other, going way too far under the protective guise of "Only kidding!" Hanging with my brothers and sister is still one of my greatest joys.

Scott Wittman likes to joke that, of all the comedy people he knows, and he knows many, I am "the only one who's truly *laughing* on the inside." But my upbeat nature is also a function of resilience: a firm belief in what I told my son Henry that night before Nancy died—that tough experiences Teflon-coat you and strengthen you against further adversity. This lesson is, I suppose, a major reason I wrote this book: because along the way I've picked up the wisdom that bad things happen, and yet the sun still comes up the next day, and it's up to you to carry on living your life and keeping your setbacks in perspective. You also have to understand that on some level, these horrible and sad things happen to everyone; the mark of a man is not just how he survives it all but also what wisdom he's gained from the experience. My cheerfulness on TV talk shows isn't faked, but it is also far from the product of a life gone perfectly.

As I write this, I am sixty-four years old, with, I hope, many more years to live and lots more to do. And, by the way, no face work. I know you're thinking, "No kidding." But cosmetic surgery just doesn't work on a man. Were I to take the plunge, no one would ever say, "Whoa, who's that really hot thirty-eight-year-old dude?" They'd say, "Who's that sixty-four-year-old who's been in a fire?"

Being in one's sixties isn't the same as it was in my father's time. (And he only made it to sixty-one.) The actor David Niven was three years younger than me when he wrote one of the great Hollywood memoirs of all time, *The Moon's a Balloon*, in 1971, but it seemed the book of a man ruminating on a life that he was consciously winding down. I don't feel that I'm at that place yet, and thankfully there are nice people in show business who reassure me constantly that I am not deluding myself. Some of them aren't even on my payroll.

When you start your career, you worry about how you're going to pay the rent. But when that's covered, you feel an even greater pressure: How do you stay interested? For me, the answer has always lain in the theater. Live performance—in its potential for danger, fun, and anarchy—is what sustains me. So I do solo concerts all the time. These shows are alternately billed, as the mood fits, *An Evening with Martin Short*; *A Party with Marty*; *Sunny von Bülow Unplugged*; *If I'd Saved, I Wouldn't Be Here*; *Marty with a T*; *A Short Day's Journey into Night*; *Sunday in the Park with George Michael*; *Stroke Me, Lady Fame*; *No Lump Yet*; and *Marty Christ, Superstar*. "Solo," though, is something of a misnomer; I'm joined by my adept and funny pianist and musical director, Jeff Babko, who worked with me on my talk show and now plays keyboards in Jimmy Kimmel's band. Someday Jeff, Paul Shaffer, and Marc Shaiman will form a band that won't necessarily do great business but will be a reliable crowd-pleaser, especially with their opening number, "Mr. Sunshine Could Also Be a Prick."

Two years ago, at the age of sixty-two, I hosted the Christmas episode of *Saturday Night Live*. I opened with a musical number: a mildly raunchy version of the holiday song "It's the Most Wonderful Time of the Year." I hopped atop the piano (played by Paul Shaffer, returning to his roots and on temporary loan from CBS), then hopped off, and proceeded to jog through the hallways of the eighth floor of 30 Rock, a pretext for cameo appearances by Tom Hanks, Jimmy Fallon, Kristen Wiig, Samuel L. Jackson, and Tina Fey. I had an elaborate plan for that opening number in which, after hopping off the piano, I'd step into a harness and swoop over the audience. During some of my swoops, while I was suspended up high, the camera would cut away to some pretaped segments, mid-song. In one, Jiminy Glick was going to be interviewing Lorne Michaels, asking him the *tough* questions, such as, "Why don't we hear so much about John Belushi? Is it bad management?"

As the week went on, the whole routine got whittled down and simplified, with no harness or flying or cutaways. Lorne correctly reminded me that *SNL*, as its name implies, is *live*, and that to pretape half the monologue would run counter to the spirit and energy of the show. Besides, I got to have my special on-camera moment with Lorne after all: a misdirection joke in which I chanced upon him with Tina and held up a sprig of mistletoe, with the audience expecting that it would be Tina I'd kiss. In dress, I merely gave Lorne a gentle peck. But live, I totally surprised him, dipping him in my arms and planting a wet smacker right on his lips. Whether or not there was a hint of tongue involved shall remain entirely between Lorne and me.

That experience, of me submitting a ton of material beforehand, only some of which got used on the show, is not atypical. I've become known as a performer who obsessively overprepares, even for a talk-show appearance. The guest spots I do unfold loosely, but not without careful preparation—I always send ahead pages upon pages of material, their gist being, "What if the host asked me *this*? Might that be a rich, fruitful area where the two of us will find common ground and have a good TV moment?"

I've done more of these guest appearances with David Letterman than with any other host, for two reasons. The first is that he is, in my opinion, the smartest and funniest and hippest of them all. I shall miss seeing him on TV every night, now that he's easing into his well-deserved retirement. The second reason I've kept coming back to Dave's show is my long, unbroken friendship with his bandleader, Mr. Paul Shaffer. It never ceases to astound Paul and me that, forty-plus years later, we're basically carrying on our late-night goofing off from Avenue Road in Toronto, only on national television. We still feel like we're getting away with something, and every time I come to New York to do a *Late Show*, Paul and I celebrate after the taping by hitting the town. We customarily keep the limo that *Late Show* has provided (thanks, Dave!), visit three hot places that Paul has selected, grabbing a drink, having a meal, and usually closing down some bar or cabaret, where we take over the piano and alarm the unwitting patrons by putting on an improvised show.

The question I get asked the most these days—in private, not on TV—is: Will I ever remarry? Fix-ups are suggested, and JDate profiles are created on my behalf. (For the last time, I'm *not Jewish*!)

I appreciate the good intentions, and in no way do I dismiss the idea of companionship. But here's the issue: for me, it's very tricky to separate the idea of moving on from the act of forgetting, of closing the chapter on something. And at this point, I'm still very much married to Nancy. My life in our house in the Palisades these days is a bit like Roland Young's in the 1930s comedy *Topper*, in which he was blissfully haunted by the ghosts of two deceased friends, a fun-loving couple played by Cary Grant and Constance Bennett. In my case, it's Nancy with whom I happily converse, even while the rest of the world can't see her.

As I've already mentioned, I've become adept, having lost my brother and parents early, at keeping people alive who have passed. And it's more natural for me to do this with Nancy than with anyone else, because in our thirty-six years together we became so intimately familiar with the workings of each other's minds that I can convincingly play out the conversations we would be having today, about things that postdate Nancy's death—the continued adventures of our three kids, the arrival of HRH Prince George of Cambridge, the Chris Christie "Bridgegate" scandal, and such curiosities as twerking, Ted Cruz, streaming original series on Netflix, and the cronut.

Then there are the personal experiences that I want to share with Nan before anyone else hears about them—the little episodes that she, most of all, would get a kick out of. I was in Baltimore not too long ago doing one of my concerts, and I was staying in a nice suite in a luxury hotel. A private foyer separated the suite from the main hallway. I opened the door to retrieve my newspaper one morning to see that the paper was not right at my feet, where it should have been, but leaning against the inside of the other door, the one that opened onto the hallway. So I jogged up the private foyer to get the paper—only to hear the door to the actual suite slam shut behind me. Which would not have been such a big deal, except for the fact that I was naked. And by "naked," I mean without so much as a stitch or a timepiece.

I pathetically turned around and tried the door to my suite—but, as I'd already suspected would be the case, it was locked. Yes, I was living that nightmare that everyone fears their whole life, and/or believes is a ludicrous premise that only ever happens in sitcoms: *I was locked out, naked, in public!*

So what else could I do? I peeked out the other door, looking into the main hallway, and surveyed the scene. Not too far down the hall was a courtesy telephone resting on a little stand. Well, it was something. So I picked up the paper, held it over myself strategically—though I was grateful that it was the Sunday *New York Times*, it still didn't cover everything that needed covering—and set off in the direction of the phone. Just before I got to it, I noticed a housekeeper's cart by a room with a door open. *Oh, good.* Poking my head through the open door, I said, "Hello?" This prompted a guy in the next room to open his door, see a naked Martin Short standing before him, and then slam his door shut as fast as he possibly could.

Finally the maid came out of the room she was cleaning and saw me. "Oh, Mr. Short!" she said. "You have *made my day!*" She didn't let go of the moment quickly. She circled around me slowly, looking at me from behind, and went, "*Ohhhhhh.*"

Once I got over the embarrassment, I was let back into my suite, and put a robe on (which is now my strategy in hotels at all times, even when I'm fully clothed in a suit), I thought, Nan, how the hell did I let that happen? And I could hear her laughter—loving, but with a touch of "Serves you right"—in my ears.

I think this is healthy. I can't stand when the dead are talked about in hushed tones or banished from our thoughts. I go back to that line that my brother David spoke to me in that strange Technicolor dream: "I'll see you in a fleeting moment." Meaning, *I'm not far away.* After Nancy died, I read a 1910 sermon by the

Oxford theologian Henry Scott Holland that has evolved over time into a funeral prayer. It begins:

> Death is nothing at all.
> It does not count.
> I have only slipped away into the next room.
> Everything remains as it was.
> The old life that we lived so fondly together is
>   untouched, unchanged.
> Whatever we were to each other, that we are still.
> Call me by the old familiar name.
> Speak of me in the easy way which you always used.
> Put no sorrow in your tone. Laugh as we always
>   laughed at the little jokes that we enjoyed together.

Nancy has only slipped away into the next room. So some nights, when I'm really missing her, I'll grab a rum and Coke at twilight and sit on the couch on our front porch, or perhaps upstairs, on the balcony off of our bedroom, with the Pacific Ocean in view. I'll call out, "Hey, Nan!" Forming the words just feels good in the throat. Or I'll do this thing we did in the car, when I was driving. Nancy would say "Hand of a hand," a cue for me to place my right hand in her left. "Kiss the hand," I'd say in response, and she would lift my hand to her lips. I still offer my hand to Nancy—it's how I initiate our conversations.

These, our talks, go on internally, not out loud. You won't find me sitting out there chattering away, switching seats, schizophrenically playacting both parts. But we do talk, Nancy and I, and I can totally hear where she agrees with me and where she disagrees. I can sense the moments when she's had enough of Marty and wants to summon Ed. And then I can hear Ed say, for the thousandth time, "He's to be pitied, Miss Nancy, 'cause, like, he just won't let things go, I must say." And finally Ed will be dismissed, and Marty will come back.

"Hey, Nan."

"Hey, baby. Hand of a hand."

"You see, Nan, it's like I always told you: it's better to have loved a Short than never to have loved a tall."

"Who made that up?"

"What do you mean, 'Who made that up?' *I* did!"

"No, you didn't. I think your brother Michael did."

"What are you talking about? I've been saying that for years."

"Oh, I know you've been *saying* it. But who wrote it? I thought it was Michael."

"Well, you thought wrong."

"Gee, you're an arrogant little thing, aren't you?"

"I think I'm sweet."

"Tell me if this wouldn't piss you off."

"What, Nan, did FDR just say something?"

(*Laughter.*)

"It's an awfully pretty house, isn't it, Mart?"

(*As Ed Grimley.*) "It surely is, Miss Nancy."

"Go away, Ed!"

(*Still as Ed.*) "Yes, Miss Nancy."

"Mart?"

"Yeah?"

"Are the kids really okay?"

"Nan, they're fine."

"Why do you always say that?"

"'Cause they are. They're doing the best they can."

"Anything in my teeth?"

"Nan, can you believe that you've been gone for four years?"

"Has it been that long?"

"Absolutely."

"Well you'd know, with that *Rain Man* memory of yours."

(*Robotically, like Dustin Hoffman in* Rain Man.) ". . . married on a snowy Monday on December 22, 1980."

"Are you having a cocktail, baby?"

"I sure am."

"Is that your first?"

"It sure isn't. And it may not be my last. So judge not!"

"Hey, I don't judge."

"Yeah, right."

"Aren't you a happy boy!"

(*Pause as the cocktail glass is refilled.*)

"Nan?"

"Ya, Mart?"

"Where'd you go?"

No answer this time. And none expected. Because I've asked the unanswerable. But not to worry. There's still life to be lived, laughs to be had, children to cherish, dear friends to be gossiped about, and costars to be upstaged. As for the grander questions, their answers will surely reveal themselves. Someday. In a fleeting moment.

ACKNOWLEDGMENTS

To me, it's a little daunting to determine who to acknowledge and thank when you're writing about your entire life: "between the forceps and the stone," as Joni Mitchell once put it. Who do you exclude? The doctor who pulled you out seems pretty important. In my case, he later became a very successful plastic surgeon; what Leonardo was to canvas, Dr. Schleckman was to saggy neck skin. Of course, there are the myriad schoolteachers who guided and authors who inspired; too many to list. And I'm thankful for the family I was blessed to be born into—the spectacular Shorts—as well as the guidance, patience, and endless love of my three children, Katherine, Oliver, and Henry. For me, there's nothing more rewarding than getting a deep-tissue massage while glancing over and seeing one of your kids getting tutored in math.

More specific to this book—which I'm anxious to read—I can't thank enough my collaborator, David Kamp. His cleverness and craft kept the year or so that we worked together as fun, focused, and painless as a thing like this can be. When I get to work with a writer I admire, everything seems to fall into place. So I must also thank Dick Blasucci, Paul Flaherty, Michael Short, David Feldman, Jon Macks, and all the other brilliant writers with whom I've been lucky enough to collaborate over the years.

I've always enjoyed working by committee, and have always understood that life is just so much easier when you can get the honest opinions of people you trust. So I deeply thank my manager, Marc Gurvitz, as well as my agents, Stacy Mark and Mel Berger. And as far as the late Bernie Brillstein goes, not a day goes by in which I don't think of something he once said and burst out laughing.

At HarperCollins, bless you, David Hirshey, Kathy Schneider, Rachel Elinsky, Leah Wasielewski, Milan Bozic, and Sydney Pierce, and Emily Hirshey, for so seamlessly facilitating the journey of this memoir.

As far as the front and back covers of this book are concerned, photographer Sam Jones and his team of airbrushers are simply the best you can get—and again, thanks, Sam, for the bike.

To my beloved friends, there's simply no life without you guys. Thanks for the advice and the love and the billion dinners and laughs. Without you all . . . I'd look for new friends and get them.

Oh, dear, I'm sure I'm leaving people out. Again, it's a horrible sort of list to have to come up with. Can you imagine? All right. Enough. I'm at my cottage as I type. I think it's time for a swim.

—M.S., Snug Harbour, Summer 2014

ABOUT THE AUTHOR

MARTIN SHORT is an Emmy and Tony award–winning Canadian-born actor and comic, adored for his work on *SCTV* and *Saturday Night Live*, as well as such great comic movies as *¡Three Amigos!* and *Father of the Bride*, not to mention dozens of memorable talk show, primetime, and theatrical appearances, from *Damages* to his one-man Broadway hit *Martin Short: Fame Becomes Me*. He lives in Pacific Palisades, California.

DAVID KAMP is a longtime contributing editor for *Vanity Fair* and the author of *The United States of Arugula*, as well as several humor books. He lives in New York City.